'Banned in the USA'

Cinema and Society Series
General Editor: Jeffrey Richards

Published and forthcoming:

'BANNED IN THE USA'
British films in the United States and their censorship, 1933–1960

Anthony Slide

I.B.Tauris Publishers

LONDON · NEW YORK

Published in 1998 by I.B.Tauris & Co Ltd,
Victoria House, Bloomsbury Square, London WC1B 4DZ
175 Fifth Avenue, New York NY 10010

In the United States of America and in Canada distributed by
St Martin's Press, 175 Fifth Avenue, New York NY 10010

A full CIP record for this book is available from the British Library
A full CIP record for this book is available from the Library of Congress

ISBN 1 86064 254 3

Library of Congress catalog card number: available

Printed and bound in Great Britain by WBC Ltd, Bridgend

Contents

General Editor's Introduction

It is impossible to understand the nature and operation of the cinema in its heyday without a full appreciation of the work and influence of the censors. They provided the framework within which the cinema operated. They dictated the limits of what was permissible on the screen. Throughout the era of the cinema's pre-eminence as *the* popular medium of entertainment, there was a continual dialogue going on between the film-makers and the censors.

In recent years there have been a number of notable studies of the operation of film censorship in America, but until now there has been no systematic investigation of the attitude of the American censors to imported British films. Anthony Slide is the first scholar to have studied the files of the Production Code Administration as they relate to the release of British films. His book is a major addition to our knowledge and understanding of the censorship process.

His trawl of the files reveals the censors' overwhelming concern with moral issues, violence, bad language and decorum. His study is peppered with fascinating revelations. Among them are the problems experienced by films based on the plays of Ivor Novello – of all people – which were deemed 'immoral'; the censors' sensitivity about films involving the kidnapping of children, which derived from the sense of horror America experienced over the Lindbergh kidnapping case; and the American concern over the British preoccupation with toilets. Slide is at pains to dispel various myths about the censors, notably, that they insisted on twin beds in all film bedrooms. After his in-depth examination of the workings of the system he is left with an admiration for chief censor Joseph I. Breen and his staff, in particular for their understanding of the film-making process and their sympathy with and admiration for the British film industry.

Jeffrey Richards

Introduction

In March 1983, the files of the Production Code Administration were donated to the Margaret Herrick Library of the Academy of Motion Picture Arts and Sciences. For the first time, scholars and students had the opportunity to study the manner in which films released in the United States were subject to a unique form of self-censorship.

Since the files became available for research, a number of books have been published, analysing the approach of the Production Code Administration to individual films, and attempting to provide an overall view of film censorship in the United States from the 1930s through the 1960s. *Banned in the USA* is the first book to examine how the film output of one country, the United Kingdom, fared at the hands of America's guardians of morality. Its publication necessitated the reading of more than 1,000 files, most containing many items of correspondence and other paperwork. It was an exhilarating and exhausting project, but it would be foolish to claim that the end result is an exhaustive work. The inventory to the files is by title only, with no indication as to a film's country of origin, and titles are US release rather than original titles. It was, therefore, impossible to ensure that all British films released in the United States were included. Similarly, the files are working files, not archival study dossiers, and what they contain is what the staff of the Production Code Administration decided to include. There was never an obligation to keep the files up-to-date or to include all inter-office memoranda. Some files lack a copy of the

Certificate issued for a specific film, even though it is obvious that the work in question met the requirements of the Production Code. Some files contain nothing more than a review of the film from *Variety* or a British trade paper. An added disadvantage is that the files are from the Los Angeles headquarters of the Production Code, but most British films in the 1930s and 1940s were handled by the New York office. While an attempt was made to duplicate information in the files on both coasts, there are, of course, many missing files and much missing paperwork.

At the same time, these files provide considerable documentation unrelated to censorship but important to an overall study of British cinema. Often, the files make it possible to identify when a film first went into pre-production or began shooting; the dates of first, revised and final shooting scripts; casting changes; working titles; title changes; and other matters relative to production.

I can claim with pride that I have read more files of the Production Code Administration than any other user since the records were made public, a claim that the staff who had the onerous task of pulling and refiling all those files will be happy to endorse. In reading the files, my attitude towards the Production Code and its administrator, Joseph I. Breen, underwent a dramatic change. My initial feeling was that Breen and the Production Code Administration staff were puritanical reactionaries hindering and frustrating creative talent. However, the more files I read, the more I came to admire Breen and his associates. They had an impossible task, upholding a moral code which was often out of step with the times, but they did their work with dedication and with tremendous speed. Time and time again, I noted that a script could be received, read and analysed in a couple of hours. With remarkable equanimity and good feeling, Breen and his staff would work with British producers, taking on the unenviable task of making a script or even a finished film acceptable under the requirements of the Production Code.

There was a creativity among these men, the equal of that found among many British and American film-makers. Their understanding of the film-making process was extraordinary. They knew how much a simple fade-out could change the meaning of a scene, the implication that dialogue without accompanying visuals might have, how the casting of one actor over another could alter a characterization, or how the rearrangement of shots might remove a suggestion of impropriety.

Behind the scenes and subjected to ridicule rather than praise, Joseph I. Breen and his associates contributed as much to world cinema as did Hollywood's leading producers, directors and screenwriters. One might theorize that their involvement in a project could as much have helped as harmed it. The argument was always that art did not require blasphemy or profanity to make a point and that basic morality remained unchanged regardless of passing trends. It was a point of view that might not win over Noël Coward, when applied to *In Which We Serve*, but other British film-makers, including Michael Balcon, Michael Powell and Herbert Wilcox, came to acknowledge and grudgingly accept the precepts of the Production Code.

If the staff of the Production Code Administration were brilliant exemplars of the editorial art, producers both in Europe and the United States might not have fully understood at the time just how fortunate they were. Certainly, I am aware of how lucky I have been in the creation of this book to have the support and encouragement of Philippa Brewster's editorial hand at I.B.Tauris and similar and inspiring enthusiasm from Jeffrey Richards, editor of the Cinema and Society series. Every bit as diligent and hard-working as the staff of the Production Code Administration is the archival staff of the Margaret Herrick Library of the Academy of Motion Picture Arts and Sciences, and I extend special thanks to Scott Curtis, Barbara Hall, Doug Johnson, Howard Prouty and Faye Thompson.

Anthony Slide
Studio City, California
Berwick-upon-Tweed, Northumberland

1

The Production Code and Film Censorship in America: A Concise History

Unlike the United Kingdom, the USA has never embraced a nation-wide programme of film censorship. From the beginning, it was strictly a local issue. Chicago was the first community to enact film censorship, under the auspices of its police department, in November 1907. Pennsylvania created a film censorship board in 1911, and it was followed in 1913 by Kansas and Ohio. In an effort to discourage the censorship of films in New York City, the film industry helped finance the creation, in 1909, of the National Board of Censorship of Motion Pictures, which would review and evaluate films and which became, in 1916, the National Board of Review of Motion Pictures, Inc. Its seal of approval, 'Passed by the National Board of Review', was required to be affixed on films by most communities during the silent film era, but by the 1930s, the Board's approval had become relatively worthless. As of 1938, only Providence, Rhode Island, still required films to carry the Board's seal of approval, and then only for Sunday screenings. As early as 1921, the New York state legislature became dissatisfied with the National Board of Review and created the New York State Motion Picture Commission as a local censorship authority.

The threat of some form of national film censorship loomed large in the early 1920s as more and more voices were raised in protest against what was seen as a tide of immorality sweeping across the film industry and overflowing into the content of its productions. With the film community beset by a variety of scandals, thirty-seven states announced potential legislature relating to the censorship of motion pictures. Headline after headline depicted the industry in a negative light. In 1920, actress Olive Thomas committed suicide, with her death linked to drug addiction. In 1921, comedian Roscoe 'Fatty' Arbuckle was charged in the rape-murder of actress Virginia Rappe. A year later, William Desmond Taylor was murdered, and two stars, Mary Miles Minter and Mabel Normand, were revealed as having enjoyed sexual relationships with the director and were possibly implicated in his killing. In 1923, matinée idol Wallace Reid died as a result of heroin addiction.

As public outrage mounted, the leading Hollywood producers met in January 1922 to form the Motion Picture Producers and Distributors of America (MPPDA), a trade organization which would liaise with the public, present a unified front against the demands of organized labour, and defend the industry against state and federal censorship. To head the new organization, the producers named Will H. Hays (1879–1954), a curiously small and unprepossessing man whose most notable physical features were his large ears. Hays's credentials were impressive. He was a professional politician, understanding of the ways of Washington, DC, who had been chairman of the 1920 Republican National Committee and subsequently served as postmaster general in the administration of President Warren G. Harding.

In 1927, Hays established the Studio Relations Office as part of the MPPDA. Headed by Colonel Jason S. Joy, it was to serve as a self-censoring board for the industry, with Joy reading scripts and reporting potential problems to producers. With a published list of 'Don'ts' and 'Be Carefuls', the Office was evidence, at least on the surface, that Hollywood was concerned as to the moral content of its films. In reality, producers paid little if any attention to Colonel Joy's comments, and the many cuts routinely ordered in Hollywood films outside the USA – for example by the British Board of Film Censors – were indicative that American films did not meet community standards around the world.

It became obvious that if Hollywood was unwilling to take steps to control the content of its productions, outside action was necessary.

In the summer of 1929, Martin Quigley (1890–1964), an influential figure within the industry as publisher of the trade paper *Motion Picture Herald*, and, perhaps more importantly, a leading Catholic layman, conceived of a production code. He discussed his concept with Joseph I. Breen (1888–1965), a fellow Catholic, and the public relations officer for the 1926 Eucharist Congress. The two men realized that for the code to be implemented, it was necessary at first to bypass the Hollywood producers. Instead, they presented the idea to the Catholic hierarchy and to the executives in the film industry's corporate offices in New York, men with a financial rather than a creative interest in film-making.

In January 1930, Will H. Hays read the proposed code, and, a month later, it was approved and adopted by the major studios. In October 1930, Hays hired Joseph I. Breen as the public relations man charged with 'selling' the new code to the American public through community groups, parent–teacher associations, women's clubs and the like.

Colonel Jason S. Joy remained responsible for the enforcement of the code, but in September 1932 he resigned to become a story consultant for Fox, and was succeeded by James Wingate, the former chief censor for the State Education Department of New York. Wingate was faced with an impossible task. Once again, producers were simply ignoring the code. The Depression was at its height and the film industry faced economic disaster. In order to survive, it had to produce films that appealed to the public, films starring Mae West, films about gold-diggers and good-time girls, films that quite patently did not meet the requirements of the Production Code.

The years 1933 and 1934 were ones of crisis. Reformers were theatening to march on Washington, DC to demand federal censorship of motion pictures. In desperation, on 5 March 1933, Hays met with the MPPDA board and urged the adoption of realistic self-regulation. In the meantime, the Catholic Church and Martin Quigley determined the need for dramatic action. For many years, the Bank of America (founded as the Bank of Italy) had been the leading financial backer of the film industry, providing funding for the creation of Columbia Pictures, the Walt Disney Studios, Twentieth Century Pictures, and many independent production companies. The Catholic Church took its complaints directly to the bank's chairman, A. H. 'Doc' Giannini, who, along with his brother and the bank's founder, A. P. Giannini, was a devout Catholic. On 1 August 1933, Giannini attended an industry dinner and warned producers that they could not afford to alienate the Church and, by extension, the Bank of America.

Still the industry was slow to respond. The first positive step came in December 1933, when Hays appointed Joseph I. Breen as administrator of the Studio Relations Office, replacing James Wingate. The Catholic Church continued its attacks on the industry, and on 23 May 1934, Cardinal Dougherty of Philadelphia urged the city's 823,000 Catholics to boycott motion pictures, describing them as 'the greatest menace to faith and morals in America today'. Earlier, on 11 April 1934, the Episcopal Committee of the Catholic Church informed the Catholic bishops that it planned a 'legion of decency' and wanted all Catholics to pledge support for 'clean films'.

An agency of the Catholic Church in America, the National Legion of Decency was the closest the country ever came to having a national censorship board outside the control of the film industry. As an editorial in *America* (13 December 1941) pointed out: 'the Legion has no legal authority, and wishes none. Its appeal is to the decent citizens in every country, and this, it is confident, will not go unheeded.' The National Legion of Decency rated films into four categories:

Class A: Section I – Unobjectionable for General Patronage
Class A: Section II – Unobjectionable for Adults
Class B – Objectionable in Part
Class C – Condemned

Very few productions were, in reality, 'Condemned' by the National Legion of Decency, but in that number were four British titles: *The Girl from Maxim's*, *I Am a Camera*, *Living Dangerously* and *The Private Life of Henry VIII*. While condemning the last, the National Legion of Decency approved 120 Nazi films submitted during 1936 and 1937 and refused to condemn productions on the basis of their anti-Semitic content.

It was not until June 1934 that the film industry adopted a binding production code, at which time Will H. Hays renamed the Studio Relations Office the Production Code Administration (PCA). As the Administration's director, he appointed Joseph I. Breen.

It was an inspired choice in that Breen was a moralist, a staunch anti-Communist and an extreme anti-Semite. In letters never made public by their recipients, Breen would frequently denounce American-Jewish influence; in a typical letter to Martin Quigley, dated 1 May

1932, he referred to 'lousy Jews ... 95 percent of whom are Eastern Jews, the scum of the earth'. Breen was obviously a man who could uphold the values that most Americans espoused while despising the primarily Jewish leaders of the industry that he was to regulate.

The Production Code was a 'moral document', updated and expanded as the years progressed, and published annually in the trade yearbook, the *International Motion Picture Almanac*. It encompassed three general principles:

1. No picture shall be produced which will lower the moral standards of those who see it. Hence the sympathy of the audience shall never be thrown to the side of crime, wrongdoing, evil, or sin.
2. Correct standards of life, subject only to the requirements of drama and entertainment shall be presented.
3. Law, natural or human, shall not be ridiculed, nor shall sympathy be created for its violation.

The PCA maintained a list of words and phrases that must be omitted from all motion pictures, including God, Lord, Jesus, Christ (unless used reverently), fairy (in a vulgar sense), goose (in a vulgar sense), lousy, nance, nuts (except when meaning crazy), slut, tart and whore. Damn and hell were also on the banned list, but could be used 'in proper historical context', or 'for the presentation in proper literary context of a biblical or other religious quotation or a quotation from a literary work'. Thus, Rhett Butler's famous line from *Gone with the Wind* escaped excision by the PCA.

Words offensive to film-goers in other countries were banned: Chink, Dago, Frog, Greaser, Hun, Hunkie, Kike, Nigger, Spig, Wop and Yid. The PCA also took note of words that might have crude meaning outside the United States, and, for example, the following were listed as inappropriate for use in films intended to be screened in the United Kingdom: bum, bloody, sissy, gigolo, punk, sex appeal, sex life, shag and shyster.

All major studios were ordered to submit scripts and treatments directly to Breen, and appeals against Breen's judgement could be made only to the MPPDA's board in New York. A $25,000 fine was to be levied on all released films that violated the Code. The majority of theatres were owned by the major studios, members of the MPPDA, and it was agreed that theatres belonging to such members could not screen films that did not bear a Production Code seal. As a result, even independent and foreign producers that might not belong to the MPPDA were forced to obtain PCA approval or risk being unable to book their films into most theatres in the United States.

From humble headquarters in a run-down building at the corner of Hollywood Boulevard and Western Avenue, which also housed Central Casting, and later from above a drugstore on La Cienega Boulevard, Joseph I. Breen and his staff wielded phenomenal, not to say dictatorial, power. The staff were all college-educated and, according to one employee, Albert E. Van Schmus, the 'fundamental morality was Catholic morality'.[1] At the beginning of each week, scripts were arbitrarily handed out to staff members who would liaise with assigned representatives from each studio. All correspondence was signed by Breen, with a number at the letter's close indicating the employee handling the film.[2] All letters concluded with the standard phrase, 'As you know, our final judgment will be based on the finished picture.'

In addition, the PCA maintained offices in New York, out of which most foreign films were reviewed through the 1940s, and Certificates from which always began with a zero. An additional Code governing advertising and publication of still photographs was introduced in 1935. Before a Certificate was issued, producers also needed to register the title with the MPPDA's Title Registration Bureau, set up to ensure that more than one company did not release a film with the same title and that no objectionable word or phrase was used in a title. The lack of title registration or the registration of a title by another company might well delay US release. For example, London Films, Inc. could not obtain a Certificate for *The Tales of Hoffmann* because in August 1950 Cinopera and Columbia Pictures had registered the title; it took a year to persuade the companies to withdraw their registration and for the title to become clear for use by London Films.

Funding for the activities of the PCA came from fees charged to producers for the issuance of a Certificate. As of 1944, the fees were:

---

1. Barbara Hall *Oral History with Albert E. Van Schmus* (Beverly Hills, CA: Academy of Motion Picture Arts and Sciences, 1990/1992), p. 100.

2. There is no overall record of which numbers were assigned to which employees, although it is known that Geoffrey M. Shurlock's number was 2, Jack Vizzard's 14 and Albert E. Van Schmus' 17. For the sake of convenience and in that Breen did read and sign all correspondence, for the purposes of this book he is designated as the author of all letters on which his name appears.

Features:
    Class A – Negative cost over $200,000: $825
    Class B – Negative cost $100,000 to $200,000: $525
    Class C – Negative cost $25,000 to $100,000: $100
    Class D – Negative cost less than $25,000: $50
Features Reissued: $25
Short Subjects (less than 3,000 feet): $25

All films produced outside the United States were charged half the regular fee.

In 1945, Will H. Hays retired, and was succeeded by Eric Johnson, who renamed the MPPDA the Motion Picture Association of America (MPAA). Breen and Johnson did not enjoy a friendly relationship, and, in 1947, the latter tried to replace Breen with Stephen S. Jackson, a New York juvenile court judge. However, studio executives did not care for Jackson's style, and the coup failed.

The beginning of the end for the Production Code Administration came in 1952. In retrospect, *The Moon is Blue* is such an insignificant and minor production that it is impossible to understand how it could have created such a stir, let alone have sounded the death-knell for the PCA. But it was not so much the film as the intransigence of its producer/director Otto Preminger. The latter announced plans to film the stage comedy by F. Hugh Herbert, and routinely submitted the script to Breen. He objected to what he described as the 'blue language', together with the use of the word 'virgin' and the suggestion of seduction. After a lengthy battle with the PCA, the film was denied a Certificate. Somewhat hesitantly, United Artists (which was not at that time a member of the MPAA) released *The Moon is Blue*. The film met with widespread critical approval and, more importantly, was booked into theatres that previously would have refused to play a film without a PCA seal. What had happened was that thanks to the Consent Decree signed between the major studios and the US Justice Department, theatres that were once owned by the studios were now independently controlled and operated, no longer associated with the MPAA through the studio connection.

The success of *The Moon is Blue* at the box-office and the failure of either the PCA or the National Legion of Decency to prevent such popularity meant that for the first time independent producers might consider adult stories and themes without fear of internal censorship.

As the 1950s progressed, more and more films were to be released without a Code seal.

In 1954, Joseph I. Breen retired, receiving a honorary Oscar from the Academy of Motion Picture Arts and Sciences, 'for his conscientious, open-minded and dignified management of the Motion Picture Production Code'. Breen was succeeded in October 1954 by Geoffrey M. Shurlock, one of whose first acts was to deny a Certificate to Otto Preminger's drug-themed *The Man with the Golden Arm* (1955). The man who presided over the PCA in its final years was born in England (in Egremont, Cheshire) on 10 August 1894, the son of a captain in the merchant marine. The family moved to the USA in 1901, when the father retired, and Shurlock became an American citizen on 25 April 1930. He joined the MPPDA in 1932 as an assistant to James Wingate, and served as acting head of the PCA in 1941–42, while Breen took a leave of absence to serve as vice-president at RKO. Shurlock retired on 2 January 1968, replaced by Eugene G. Dougherty.

Joseph I. Breen was gone, but Martin Quigley, although retired as publisher of *Motion Picture Herald*, was still active. In a curious move, the producer and director of *Lolita*, James B. Harris and Stanley Kubrick, hired him to argue their cause before the Production Code Administration and the National Legion of Decency. On the surface, it seemed unlikely that either body would approve the film, but, surprisingly, in January 1962, *Lolita* was passed, with cuts, by the PCA. By a slim margin, the National Legion of Decency voted not to 'Condemn' the film but to grant it a 'Separate Classification'.

By the 1960s, the classifications of the National Legion of Decency had little relevance either to the audience or to Hollywood. Nobody paid any attention in 1964 when the Legion found only fifty-two of the 270 films that it classified acceptable for family viewing. On 8 December 1965, Archbishop John J. Krol of Philadelphia, chairman of the Episcopal Committee, announced the National Legion of Decency was to be renamed the National Catholic Office for Motion Pictures (NCOMP). As of 1 January 1971 it became the US Catholic Conference – Division for Film and Broadcasting, and, as of the present, it still issues film ratings, utilizing the old categories, but with 'B' and 'C' replaced by 'O' for 'morally offensive'.

Changes in society's view of morality resulted in a Supreme Court ruling in 1965, voiding a Maryland law that had created a film censorship board. The following year, the neighbouring state of Virginia abolished film censorship. At the PCA, Shurlock quietly issued a Certificate for *The Moon is Blue*. In the autumn of 1966, Jack Valenti, who had replaced Eric Johnson as president of the MPAA, introduced a new production code, with cautionary comments superseding rules. For the first time, the PCA might label films as 'Suggested for Mature Audiences'. Virtually worthless, the new production code was described by *Newsweek* as 'a glittering diadem of hypocrisy'.

In 1968, the PCA closed its doors, and the Production Code was replaced by a voluntary rating system, effective from 1 November:

G – General audiences for all ages

M – Suggested for adults and mature young people

R – Persons under sixteen restricted unless accompanied by a parent or adult

X – No one under sixteen admitted

A number of British films easily fell into the last category, including *The Devils*, *If...* (subsequently cut for 'R' rating), *The Killing of Sister George* and *Performance*.

With modifications, the rating system continues to the present. Unlike in the United Kingdom, it remains voluntary, with theatres or local communities under no obligation to honour its restrictions.

2

The Production Code and the British Film Industry

In order to ensure a substantial American release and playdates at theatres owned by members of the MPPDA, most British productions were routinely submitted to the Production Code Administration for approval. In the 1930s until the outbreak of the Second World War, at which time 20th Century-Fox took over release of the films, Gaumont British had its own US distribution arm, Gaumont British Picture Corp. of America, liaising with the PCA staff in New York. A close bond came to exist between the two entities, so much so that, in 1937, Joseph I. Breen and Gaumont British discussed the possibility of the PCA's having a permanent representative in the United Kingdom.[1] The Gaumont British productions were always submitted to the PCA not in script form but as feature films already released in the United Kingdom. However, from the 1940s onwards, the J. Arthur Rank Organization maintained offices in New York and at the studios of Universal-International, in which it had a financial interest, and its staff would submit scripts to the PCA for approval prior to production.

It would be easy, and gross foolishness, to misinterpret the relationship between the PCA and the British producers. Because British films

---

1. Discussed in a letter from Joseph I. Breen to Arthur A. Lee, vice-president and general manager of Gaumont British Picture Corp. of America, dated 23 September 1937.

were released in the USA in the 1930s and the 1940s cut by as much as 50 per cent, it is often assumed that such excisions were a response to censorship. In reality, most editing took place prior to the submission of the films to the PCA and was undertaken by American distributors, including Gaumont British Picture Corp. of America, in order to make the productions palatable for American audiences and, most importantly, of a suitable length to play the second half of a double bill.

In reverse, a British film might have a published running time equal to that in the United Kingdom despite cuts in dialogue required by the PCA. Rather than physically cut the film, and the dialogue, the American distributor would generally resort to what is today called 'blooping', the removal of a word or a group of words from the soundtrack of a print or negative through the placement of blooping tape over the offending item(s) on the track. Blooping tape was not in use in the 1930s, 1940s or 1950s, and, instead, distributors would utilize black India ink to erase the word(s) on the soundtrack. This was a particularly common occurrence when the PCA asked for deletion of words of profanity or blasphemy, such as hell, damn or God. As a result of the use of blooping tape or India ink, there is no cut in the action, but the soundtrack goes momentarily dead. Obviously, lip-readers in the audience had no problem in identifying the missing word(s).

One might labour under the illusion that Joseph I. Breen, as an Irish American, would be unsympathetic towards English producers. One would be very wrong. It is obvious that Breen and his associates had tremendous respect for the British film industry, and laboured long and hard to find solutions to problems that the contents of the productions might create. Of Morris Helprin, the US representative of London Films, Inc., Gordon S. White wrote to Breen, he 'is one of the nicest guys whom we have to deal with ... and we are glad to do everything we can to help him'.[2] Typical of the attitude of the PCA staff is a letter dated 27 November 1941, from Francis S. Harmon to the US distributor of *Love on the Dole*: 'I am sure you know of our continuing desire to render maximum service to British producers who are maintaining production in the British Isles under very great difficulties.'

There was a certain amount of hypocrisy evident in the behaviour of certain British producers. Sydney Box was on excellent terms with

---

2. Letter from Gordon S. White in the PCA's New York office to Joseph I. Breen, dated 10 November 1948.

Breen, even asking that he look at potential scripts while on vacation at London's Dorchester Hotel, but Box would take advantage of the intransigence of the PCA to publicize, quite unfairly and untruthfully, that his production of *The Bad Lord Byron* had been banned in the United States. Breen was an easy target for ridicule, as Frank Launder discovered with *Lady Godiva Rides Again*. The British press promoted some films – *Brewster's Millions*, *I Am a Camera* and *In Which We Serve* – as *causes célèbres*, and who could help being amused by the notion that Laurence Olivier had had to substitute 'dastard' for 'bastard' in order to release *Henry V* in the United States? Whatever British producers might be stating for public consumption, in private they were appreciative of Breen and his staff. For example, in regard to *Jamaica Inn*, Charles Laughton wrote to Francis S. Harmon: 'I have naturally in the past looked upon any form of censorship with a rather dark eye but in this case it certainly is a shining example of the dictum that Mr. [Erich] Pommer tells me you hold that censorship can be progressive.'[3]

Perhaps the close relationship between Breen and the British producers was based covertly on the reality that the majority were not Jewish. The notion that a major production and distribution company could be founded by a staunch Methodist such as J. Arthur Rank must have appealed to Breen's sense of propriety. The Rank staff, both in New York and Los Angeles, were keen to retain a good working relationship with the PCA, and, if they discovered that a Rank film had been improperly handled from a censorship viewpoint by an American distributor, Breen would be informed. Jock Lawrence at Rank's New York office stressed that his organization did not want to be associated with non-Seal films.[4] Breen established a close personal friendship with a number of British producers, and with Joseph Brooke Wilkinson, secretary to the British Board of Films Censors from 1913 to 1948, to whom Breen often turned privately for advice and to whom his letters would conclude, 'All my love … '[5]

Breen's closest friendship was with Herbert Wilcox, and Wilcox and his wife, Anna Neagle, would often socialize and correspond informally

---

3. Letter dated 18 October 1938.

4. Letter from Jock Lawrence to Joseph I. Breen, dated 10 November 1949. As indicative of the close personal relationship between Breen and the staff of the Rank Organization, it concludes, 'Love to Mary, from me and Mary.'

5. See, for example, the letter from Joseph I. Breen, dated 6 August 1937, regarding *The Citadel*.

with Breen and his wife, Mary. Breen described Wilcox as 'a warm, personal friend of mine',[6] and the producer would frequently seek out Breen's opinion on potential film projects. In 1947, when Wilcox pondered a screen adaptation of Hall Caine's novel *The Eternal City*, Breen strongly advised that he dismiss the story from any consideration in view of its indication that Pope Pius X had fathered an illegitimate child. In April 1954, Wilcox corresponded with Breen in regard to a film of the novel *The White Witch of Rosehall*, on which 'a certain star had set his heart'.[7] Again, Wilcox heeded Breen's advice – a film was out of the question because of the gross illicit sex and immoral relationship between whites and negroes – and noted, 'You have done a hell of a job over the years', jokingly acknowledging that he should have used 'heck' rather than 'hell'.

At the same time, Breen never permitted his friendship to interfere with his administration of the Production Code. Privately, Breen viewed *I Live in Grosvenor Square* with Wilcox, but he wrote, on 5 December 1945, to Gordon S. White at the PCA's New York office that the film should be examined carefully and that some dialogue might need changing.

As with all foreign productions in the 1930s and 1940s, with the exception of those financed or released by the Hollywood studios, British films were supposed to be submitted to the New York staff of the Production Code Administration, working out of 28 West 44th Street. As Breen pointed out in 1939: 'Specifically, I would say that scripts for foreign pictures should be read in New York. If, however, the company elects to have them sent here, we have no recourse but to agree.'[8]

In the early years, British producers had something of an advantage over their American counterparts in having the films reviewed by the New York office. The staff there were relatively inexperienced, and productions such as *The Private Life of Don Juan*, which would have been rejected outright by Breen in Los Angeles, were able to scrape through with a Production Code Seal and comparatively little cutting. However, by the late 1930s, the approaches of the New York and Los

---

6. Letter from Joseph I. Breen to Gordon S. White in the PCA's New York office, dated 5 December 1945.

7. Letter dated 27 April 1954.

8. Letter from Joseph I. Breen to Vincent G. Hart in the PCA's New York office, dated 13 April 1939.

Angeles offices were synchronized, and it mattered little which PCA member of staff on which coast handled a specific film. If anything, British producers were more anxious to have their films viewed by Breen in Los Angeles on the mistaken assumption that a personal friendship with him might in some way improve their chances of obtaining a Certificate with only minor cuts.

Certainly, there can be no question that British producers familiar with the workings of the British Board of Film Censors felt relatively comfortable with the censorship process of the Production Code Administration. Accidentally or by design, it was very much based on that of its British counterpart. Producers were encouraged to submit films in script form, and the staff would analyse the script, page by page, noting potential problems, unacceptable language, objectionable action and the like. The letters sent by the PCA to producers, after a reading of the scripts, are almost identical in form to those from the office of the British Board of Film Censors.

Some of the myths that have developed through the years in regard to the Production Code Administration appear, in reality, to have originated with the British Board of Film Censors. A long-standing joke told against the PCA is that it required married couples to occupy twin beds and that it was permissible to have a couple in bed only provided that the man kept one foot on the floor. The latter is pure fantasy. The issue of twin beds originated in 1938 with *The Mad Miss Manton*, when the British Board of Film Censors objected to a scene showing a couple in bed together. Because of this action by the British Board of Film Censors, Joseph I. Breen recommended to American producers that they avoid additional cost in having to film a variant scene for the British market by in future utilizing only twin beds in bedroom sequences. Certainly, there is no reference to the need for twin beds in the published Production Code.[9]

The Production Code does contain warnings and restrictions which would not be issues with the British Board of Film Censors, some of which might appear surprising. British producers were consistently warned to avoid advertising in their films. While there is no evidence that they were accepting money for paid advertising, a large number of products and services are prominently displayed in British films.

---

9. Discussed in Jack Vizzard, *See No Evil: Life Inside a Hollywood Censor*, Simon and Schuster, 1970, pp. 114–15.

Often, their removal was impossible because of the siting of a product in a particular scene, and where excision was possible with a cut in the dialogue, both contemporary and modern audiences might wonder if some hidden meaning was present. For years, Americans have queried why the phrase 'Cook's Tours' has been edited out of prints of Hitchcock's *The Lady Vanishes*, wondering if it has some obscene connotation.

A more serious issue in British films was the amount of drinking. The Production Code was quite specific on the subject, at least as far as the United States was concerned: 'The use of liquor in American life, when not required by the plot or for proper characterization, will not be shown.' While the PCA acknowledged that the stress of wartime bombing might result in excessive alcoholism in the United Kingdom, it was felt that far too many British productions emphasized visits to pubs and social drinking at an unacceptable level. Even a film such as *The Mudlark* came in for criticism because of John Brown's over-indulgence.

Juvenile delinquency, real or perceived, was also a problem in British films, and one which the PCA staff could not legislate against but merely disapprove. Breen and his associates worried that showing how to make 'ill-smelling gases' in *The Housemaster* might encourage children in the audience to imitate the experiment. While describing *Just William's Luck* as 'A sort of British "Our Gang" comedy',[10] the PCA was bothered by the amount of juvenile delinquency portrayed (not to mention the bad habit of William's father, who went to bed with a lighted cigarette in his mouth).

From a modern viewpoint, alcoholism comes under the heading of political incorrectness, and here British producers were considerably at fault. In regard to 'National Identity', the Production Code quite clearly states: 'The history, institutions, prominent people and citizenry of all nations shall be represented fairly.' Then, as now, xenophobia in the media was a prominent stain on the British character – as witness any issue of the *Daily Telegraph* or the *Daily Mail* – and British film producers have presented rampantly offensive national characterizations as a matter of routine. The French, uniformly described as 'frogs', are the most stereotyped of the various nationalities to be found in British films. Others pointed out by the PCA as described or presented in

---

10. Letter from Arthur H. DeBra to United Artists, dated 5 January 1949.

offensive fashion include the Chinese (*The Gang's All Here* and *Broken Blossoms*), Indians (*Bhowani Junction*), Mexicans (*Across the Bridge* and *The Secret Agent*), Romanians (*Adventures of Tartu*), and even the Swiss (*The Secret Agent*). A reading of the PCA files suggests that any non-white in a British film of the 1930s, 1940s and 1950s was automatically described as a 'nigger', a term unacceptable under the provisions of the Production Code since its inception. Even the use of 'blacks' in *Diamond City* was deemed offensive to African Americans by Breen, while his successor, Geoffrey M. Shurlock, was concerned with the insensitivity towards non-whites in *Island in the Sun*. Religious groups fared little better, with Muslims under attack in *The Golden Salamander*, and perhaps most egregiously the obscene Jewish characterization of Alec Guinness as Fagin in David Lean's *Oliver Twist*.

British producers crossed the boundaries of good taste in other areas. *The Angry Hills* depicted the abuse of women. *A Fish Called Wanda* was widely criticized in the United States for its inclusion of a comic character who stuttered. More than thirty years earlier, the PCA had rejected *The Galloping Major* because of a character with a stutter, informing the producer that it 'engenders great indignation among numbers of movie patrons in that it derives comedy from the affliction of others'.

On 27 December 1940, the board of directors of the MPPDA approved a resolution 'concerning brutality and possible gruesomeness, branding of people and animals, and apparent cruelty to children and animals'. As a result, both real and apparent cruelty to animals were disallowed under the Production Code. Despite being a nation of animal lovers, the British maintained a film industry for which apparent if not real cruelty to animals was a staple ingredient of many productions (one is again reminded of *A Fish Called Wanda*) and the PCA had frequently to tell British producers at the script submission to avoid the torture or suffering of animals on screen.

Toilet gags tend to be a curiously British delight, and scatological references are scattered throughout British productions from the 1930s onwards. All were rejected and deleted by the PCA, even those as innocent as Wendy's needing a coin to use the toilet in *Genevieve*. Deleted were references to toilets in *The Perfect Woman*, *The Ship That Died of Shame* and *Traitor Spy*, a sign reading 'Ladies Rest Room' in *Radio Follies of 1935*, and any physical suggestion of a toilet in the bathroom shared by Mr Perrin and Mr Traill in the film of the same name.

The English might simply be effete, as Noël Coward has suggested, but the English producer also had a healthy, or perhaps not so healthy, regard for gay humour and gay types, and 'sex perversion or any inference of it', was forbidden under the Production Code. As a result, it was impossible for Sid Field, the creator of the 'What a perform-ance!' or camp comedic style, to be seen on American screens in any film for which a Production Code Certificate had been acquired. His starring role in *London Town* meant that the Rank Organization's first major post-war production remained unreleased in the United States for seven years. The 'pansy joke' of Jack Buchanan's reacting to a husky soldier singing in a soprano voice in *When Knights Were Bold* was deleted, as was the innocuous comment of one man to another in *Crackerjack*, 'Oh, boy, if you could only cook'. Breen insisted that there be no 'pansy' inflection in the references to HMS *Peculiar* and HMS *Suggestive* in *Meet Me Tonight*. Because of the slang meaning of the word 'queer' in the United States, a reference to the Pope being 'rich and queer' in *Odd Man Out* had to be rewritten. The implied lesbianism in *Prison Without Bars* had to removed, while both *Oscar Wilde* and *The Trials of Oscar Wilde* were initially rejected by the PCA. The homosexuality in the last two films was explicit, but Joseph I. Breen and his associates were equally adept at identifying implied homosexuality. A character spraying himself with perfume in *Adventures of Tartu* was suspect, as was the characterization of 'Soho types' in the script for *Five Days*.

The Production Code contains five paragraphs relating to nudity:

1. The effect of nudity or semi-nudity upon the normal man or woman and much more upon the young and upon immature persons, has been honestly recognized by all lawmakers and moralists.
2. Hence the fact that the nude or semi-nude body may be beautiful does not make its use in the films moral. For, in addition to its beauty, the effect of the nude or semi-nude body on the normal individual must be taken into consideration.
3. Nudity or semi-nudity used simply to put a 'punch' into a picture comes under the head of immoral actions. It is immoral in its effect on the average audience.
4. Nudity can never be permitted as being necessary for the plot. Semi-nudity must not result in undue or indecent exposures.
5. Transparent or translucent materials and silhouette are frequently more suggestive than actual exposure.

The Code here is little more than a generalization, but Breen and his staff were very explicit in terms of what constituted semi-nudity. No flesh could be visible between the tops of a woman's stockings and her briefs or whatever other costume might cover the crotch area. No bikini could be worn on screen, and, presenting far more of a problem for European film-makers, the traditional costume worn in the performance of the can-can was forbidden. Not only did British producers frequently include can-cans in their films, but they would also often portray chorus girls in attire similar to that worn by can-can dancers. Prior to production of *The Red Shoes*, Michael Powell and Emeric Pressburger were warned that Breen could not approve the costumes of the can-can dancers if bare flesh was visible above their stockings. *She Shall Have Music* featured both chorus girls displaying bare legs above their stockings and an artistic dance number with an 'undue amount of nudity'. It was often a problem in that while important plot development was taking place in the foreground, improperly clad chorus girls were parading in the background. To cut would destroy a film's continuity, and sometimes – as with *The Frog* – Breen allowed technical violations of the Code by British producers to pass. *London Melody* showed flesh above the stocking top, and it was granted a Certificate, but only on the understanding that no precedent was set.

London Melody's leading lady, Anna Neagle, and another major British star of the 1930s, Merle Oberon, were both possessed of assets that caused Breen and his staff considerable concern – their breasts. Cleavage could not be shown. The gap between the breasts should be never visible, but securely covered by the bodice. As late as *Captain Horatio Hornblower* (1951) it was a problem with Virginia Mayo. One solution adopted by some distributors was to print the film sufficiently dark at the sequence where the cleavage was visible, thus obscuring the 'gap'.

Anna Neagle and Merle Oberon were not the only British stars of the 1930s whose films were a constant source of concern at the PCA. Jessie Matthews had a penchant for wandering around on screen in her 'scanties', while her directors were particularly partial to crotch shots of the lady. Miss Matthews's dialogue and her song lyrics were similarly suggestive. Jack Buchanan's films boasted risqué dialogue, female and male semi-nudity and even a miscegenation joke in *This'll Make You Whistle*, all of which had to go for the American market. The actor's 1935 vehicle, *Brewster's Millions*, was the first British film to be the subject of an appeal against the PCA by its distributor. The latter lost, but released the film uncut anyway and without a Certificate. In that the majority of the cuts required by the PCA had been made by the British Board of Film Censors, here is an unusual situation in which a British film is released in the United States in a version longer than that seen in its country of origin.

George Formby's films had difficulty in finding American audiences, as much because of their vulgarity as the insular quality of the comedy and the songs. Extensive cuts were required in both *Come on George* and *Let George Do It*, although the latter was eventually released without a Certificate. Hal Roach was obviously an admirer of Will Hay and, on a number of occasions, acquired US rights to his films with a view to releasing them in heavily cut versions. Given the problems with the PCA faced by *Boys Will Be Boys* and *Hey! Hey! USA*, it is very obvious that censorship cuts would outnumber cuts required to make the Hay films palatable for American audiences.

While the musicals of Ivor Novello might appeal to middle-class, middle-aged ladies, they found a far from sympathetic audience at the Production Code Administration. Both *The Dancing Years* (1950) and *King's Rhapsody* (1955) were judged immoral because of their storylines, with Geoffrey M. Shurlock having to point out to producer/director Herbert Wilcox that the London stage and British cinema were far more relaxed in their approach to the illicit sex and seduction of Ivor Novello's *The Dancing Years* than was the PCA.

The relaxed British approach to religion did not sit well with the heavy Catholic morality of the Production Code Administration. *Kind Hearts and Coronets* encountered innumerable problems with the PCA, with a major and ongoing one being the comic characterization of the Reverend Henry D'Ascoyne. The PCA demanded deletion of a Boy Scout masquerading as a clergyman in *The Gang Show*. Prior to production, the Rank Organization was advised that *Made in Heaven* could not be approved because of its comic characterization of the vicar. Geoffrey M. Shurlock pointed out to M-G-M that the remake of *The Barretts of Wimpole Street* would make a mockery of religion and prayer if it showed Elizabeth Barrett's father as 'a synthetically pious, Bible-spouting villain'. The storyline for *Jamaica Inn* had to be rewritten with one of the central characters of the Daphne du Maurier novel changed from a clergyman to a country squire. Michael Powell and Emeric Pressburger thought they had got around the problem of the sexually frustrated nuns of *Black Narcissus* with the invention of a unique order, neither Roman Catholic nor Protestant. The film-makers were hoist by their own petard when Joseph I. Breen insisted on writing a foreword for the film, explaining the status of the nuns to American audiences. Similarly, both *Major Barbara* and *The October Man* ran into problems with their depiction of the Salvation Army, and even the seance in *Night of the Demon* had to be presented in such a way as to avoid offence to any religious group. The Production Code was clear:

1. No film or episode shall throw ridicule on any religious faith.
2. Ministers of religion, or persons posing as such, shall not be portrayed as comic characters or as villains so as to cast disrespect on religion.
3. Ceremonies of any definite religion shall be carefully and respectfully handled.

The Production Code notwithstanding, Breen determined that the provision relating to ministers of religion did not apply to Dr Syn because the central character, played by George Arliss, was in reality a pirate masquerading as a minister.

It was the British historical character which presented the biggest problem to both British producers and the PCA. The reality of history was not subject to change, as producers and the PCA staff wrestled with the lives of *The Bad Lord Byron*, Mrs Fitzherbert in *Beau Brummell*, *Bonnie Prince Charlie*, the Prince Regent in *The First Gentleman*, Madame Dubarry in *I Give My Heart*, *Lady Hamilton* and *Nell Gwyn*. Faced with a costume drama depicting questionable morality, Joseph I. Breen's solution was to have the film's audience learn from history. British producers could make films on the lives of such famous mistresses of history as *Lady Hamilton* and *Nell Gwyn*, provided the opening and closing sequences of the films showed the women in jail, in abject poverty, paying the moral price for the lives they had led, or better still, all three. Curiously, the men in those lives – the individuals who had actually committed adultery – were not required to suffer. Just so long as they died before 'The End' title. Nowhere is the art and craft of the Production Code Administration more obvious than in its reworking, but not rewriting, of British history. Compensating moral values or a voice for morality were what Breen demanded of all films with questionable or suggestive storylines and characters. If British producers had problems in handling moral compensation, Breen and his staff were more than happy to write additional scenes and dialogue – and they never asked, or were considered, for screen credit. It might be fashionable to dismiss Breen's 'tinkering' with the scripts of such important films as *Lady Hamilton* and *Nell Gwyn*, but it is debatable whether the films suffered as a result of Breen's input, and it may well be that his contribution benefited these and other British historical productions. Certainly, he made producers and writers go back and rethink their work, and had, perhaps, more strength and power behind him than many a studio head could muster in dealing with his creative staff.

The framing story built around a film with an unacceptable storyline might be a convenience in a historical context, but the PCA was very much aware that such a device could be misused. When the distributor of *Ten Minute Alibi* suggested that his story of an unpunished murder could be made palatable through presentation of it as a dream, the PCA scoffed at the new ending as 'patently phony and so crudely a makeshift'. Joseph I. Breen and his staff might be moralists, but they were intelligent and practical ones, and they were not easily defrauded by a false storyline. They were more intelligent than many screenwriters, and, most certainly, the intellectual superiors of the minor American distributors responsible for the release of quite an incredible number of often unimportant British films of the 1930s.

'Compensating moral values' was Joseph I. Breen's favourite phrase. They were what made an unsavoury story acceptable under the requirements of the Production Code, and, happily for British producers, could often be injected by Breen and his staff into a script at the pre-production stage. In their simplest form, compensating moral values were presented through a voice for morality – as for example with *The Astonished Heart* – with a major supporting character condemning the immoral behaviour of the principal players. The crucial issue was that an immoral act, such as adultery, was acceptable on screen provided that it was not condoned. In *Love on the Dole*, the promiscuous nature of the storyline was legitimized with the addition of a voiceover indicating that the offending couple would marry and become respectable. Sex should never be presented as fun, and, if it was, there was always a price to pay.

For both the Catholic Church and the Production Code Administration, suicide was a mortal sin, one that could never be condoned on screen. It became a major problem for British producers who would often permit a villain, usually a sympathetic murderer, whose victim(s) deserved to die, to avoid standing trial through the simple expediency of suicide. The Production Code was rigid in that 'Suicide, as a solution of problems occurring in the development of screen drama, is to be discouraged unless absolutely necessary for the development of the plot, and never shall be justified, or used specifically to defeat the ends of justice.' Judicious rewriting and re-editing were necessary to make films such as *The Blind Goddess*, *Gentleman of Venture*, *The House of the Arrow*, *The Hypnotist* and *The Shop at Sly Corner* acceptable for American audiences. In the first, a central character was knocked down and killed by a bus rather than take his own life. In *The House of the Arrow*, the suicide of the leading lady was removed and the final scene recut in such a way as to suggest she had been arrested for her crimes. The suicide of the elderly antique dealer in *The Shop at Sly Corner* became a heart attack. In *The Ware Case*, the Clive Brook character no longer confesses to murder prior to his suicide, but instead appears to kill himself out of despondency over his wife's adultery.

The morality of the Production Code required not only that justice be done, but that justice be seen to be done. Subtle hints of justice were generally disliked by the PCA staff, and so, for example, in *Kind Hearts and Coronets*, it was not enough simply to imply that Louis's murders would not go unpunished. It needed to be underlined to the cinema audience that, through his memoirs, Louis had convicted himself.

Violence and brutality in British films were long a problem, dating from the 1930s through to the 1950s, when the Hammer horror productions were criticized for their gruesome quality. Shots of a stake through Lucy's breast were cut in Hammer's 1958 version of *Dracula*, and among cuts in *The Mummy* the following year were a man's tongue being cut out, and the sound effects accompanying arm and neck breaking. Drastic cuts were made in Hammer's *The Revenge of Frankenstein* at the script submission stage, including floating eyeballs in a tank, the heaving of a body into a tank and the dropping of the brain of a dwarf into fluid. The most offensive British film noted in the PCA files is *Cosh Boy*, released in the USA under the provocative title of *The Slasher*. After viewing the film on 8 December 1952, the PCA complained, 'There were no decent people in this saga of unrelented evil', and asked the distributor to withdraw the production from the certification process. Time and again, the PCA warned British producers about violence, noting, for example, a 'blood bath' flavour to the first draft script of *The Master of Ballantrae*, and pleading, in regard to *The Bandit of Zhobe*, 'please keep the slaughter to a reasonable minimum'.[11]

A seemingly innocuous film, such as the Jessie Matthews vehicle, *Gangway*, over-emphasized a gun fight between rival gangs, while Joseph I. Breen complained that Alfred Hitchcock's *The Man Who Knew Too Much* contained 'slaughter the like of which had not been seen since *Scarface*'.[12] The film has the dubious distinction of being banned in Chicago. The ongoing problem was that British film-makers insisted on showing machine guns (which the PCA classified as illegal weapons) in the hands of criminals and often used against the police. Further, British films depicted too many scenes of police officers dying, or at least being shot, at the hands of criminals, disapproved of under the Production Code, unless absolutely necessary to the plot.

The whole issue of crime on screen was a complex one in that while the Production Code remained silent on a number of issues, the PCA staff had informal agreements with law enforcement agencies as to what could and could not be shown. The specifics of a criminal act were unacceptable, together with the manner in which fingerprints might be lifted by police officers. *Dial M for Murder* (1954) was a breakthrough film in one respect, in that it was the first production in which the wiping of fingerprints – crucial to the plot – was depicted.

On a minor level, the PCA also had an agreement with fire officers that cries of 'fire' should never be heard in films for fear of creating a false panic in theatres. *Blanche Fury*, *Happy Ever After* and *The History of Mr Polly* were some of the British films from which the offending word was ordered removed. Arson was similarly unacceptable, resulting in the cutting of a scene of the title character with a lighted torch, setting fire to furniture, in *Sweeney Todd, The Demon Barber of Fleet Street*. On the whole, British film producers complied with the requirements of the Production Code Administration with little complaint. There were, of course, disagreements, but they were generally confined to correspondence. Initially, Michael Balcon balked at the PCA's response to the first script for *Saraband for Dead Lovers*, but within days Balcon was back in touch with the PCA, assuring it that a compromise was possible. Similarly, Terence Rattigan was disturbed when the PCA

---

11. Letter from Geoffrey M. Shurlock to B. B. Kahane at Columbia Pictures, dated 21 April 1958.

12. Letter from Joseph I. Breen to Will Hays, dated 26 January 1935.

reported that an early script for *The Prince and the Showgirl* contained two basic elements in violation of the Production Code. Six months later, the changes required by the PCA had been made, and a year after Rattigan's original expression of concern, he was being thanked by the PCA for his handling of the script changes. While there was a fair amount of grousing to Breen, there were surprisingly few formal complaints registered against the PCA in regard to British films, and those that were made were generally by the Americans, with the majority from the American releasing organization United Artists. Indeed, when the American distributor of *Oliver Twist*, Eagle-Lion Films, Inc., threatened a formal complaint, the Rank Organization stepped in, distancing itself from the distributor's action and claiming that only the producer had the right to file such a complaint.

Up until the Second World War, the PCA's involvement with British films was strictly through the American distributor, which, many times, happened to be Gaumont British Picture Corp. of America. The PCA conducted almost no correspondence directly with British production companies, and there is no evidence that scripts of British films were submitted to the PCA in advance of production, with the exception of titles from M-G-M British and Gabriel Pascal. Films were viewed by the PCA staff at the request of American distributors who made the appropriate cuts. Expressions of blasphemy and profanity were routinely 'blooped'. Subtle cutting could often modify a storyline, making it conform with the Production Code. Alternatively, a printed title or, more likely, a newspaper headline had the desired effect. These were all changes and cuts that could be made in the United States without reference to the British producer and without the necessity of shooting additional footage in the United Kingdom.

There was a drastic change in the 1940s, initiated by the J. Arthur Rank Organization, with British producers submitting early drafts of scripts prior to shooting, and often making changes in such scripts at the request of the PCA. It is very obvious that the British producers regarded the American market as financially too important to lose, and heeded the demands of the Production Code Administration. What British viewers saw on screen was often what the PCA determined they should see and it might well be argued that American standards of morality were, to a certain extent, forced on British audiences. At the same time, it is obvious that the requirements of the Production Code were often in synch with the thinking of the British Board of

Film Censors. What the PCA was demanding was identical to what its British counterpart asked of producers, although the latter was far less concerned with what is now identified as political correctness and adopted a far more healthy attitude towards matters sexual.

Once the basic storyline was acceptable to the Production Code Administration, filming could go ahead. Producers were generally unconcerned at the use of words such as 'hell' or 'damn' that could not be heard on American screens. Thanks to the 'blooping' process, prints could easily be made to conform to the wishes of the PCA. British film-makers would also record 'wild lines', with actors re-recording portions of speeches for the American market; these lines were dubbed in place of extant lines. Audiences were, and generally still are, unaware that actors on screen are not always speaking the same words as those heard on the soundtrack.

Watching a British film from the 1940s or 1950s, it is often obvious that a spoken line of dialogue or a piece of action unacceptable to the PCA is always preceded and followed by an editorial cut. Some extant shooting scripts for British films are clearly marked as to what material needs to be removed for an American version, and directors in the United Kingdom must have been aware of these strictures while shooting. Thus producers could remove the offending material for an American release without the excision being apparent. It would be naughty to point out that this makes a mockery of the 'auteur' theory, except perhaps that it transfers the authorial process from the director to Joseph I. Breen.

There are relatively few examples of distinct American versions being made of British films. However, evidence that Michael Balcon filmed an American version of *The Blue Lamp* would imply that the producer made American versions of other films, in that *The Blue Lamp* is much too insular in content to warrant such unique treatment. Gabriel Pascal did record a new soundtrack for portions of *Major Barbara*. With *Pygmalion*, Pascal made both a British and an American version. The latter not only contains variant dialogue, but also utilizes different camera angles and, most extraordinary, a different musical score. Here is quite clearly a film of which a more 'commercial' version was made for the United States market, with the requirements of the Production Code playing only a small part in the producer's decision. Another example is *The Third Man*, with the American version containing an opening speech not by director Carol Reed but by Joseph Cotten.

The power of Joseph I. Breen over British producers was quite substantial. When the J. Arthur Rank Organization decided to make an anthology film based on stories of W. Somerset Maugham – it was eventually titled *Quartet* – an assortment was submitted to the PCA, and the final film created from those which the PCA identified as having minimal problems under the Production Code.

At the same time, the relationship between the British producers and Breen was often relatively informal. When Renown Pictures produced *No Orchids for Miss Blandish*, it was the wife of the company's president, George Minter, who contacted Breen from New York's Plaza Hotel and who was told that Breen had read English newspaper clippings about the film and advised it would not receive formal PCA approval.

Senior executives within the British film industry appear to have fared somewhat better in their dealings with the PCA than did the rank and file studio personnel. Stella Jonckheere, the literary editor at Ealing Studios, made the mistake of arguing that illicit sex could be shown in *Dance Hall* because it was 'reasonable behaviour in modern times'.[13] She was quickly corrected in her belief, with the PCA pointing out that fornication was not reasonable at any time.

In the 1930s and 1940s, the opinions and demands of the Production Code Administration held sway, but by the mid-1950s, the climate had so changed within the American film industry that fewer and fewer British producers bothered to submit scripts to the PCA. The only constant attention paid to the PCA was by the major Hollywood studios, producing or financing films in the United Kingdom. More often than not, an American distributor would submit a film for approval, but upon hearing the PCA's requirements for conformity would withdraw its application, releasing the film without a Certificate. The situation became intolerable for the PCA, which relied on the certification process to fund its activities, but could not charge for a Certificate when none was issued even if its staff had gone through all the bureaucratic motions. Even the Rank Organization, the PCA's most loyal support in the 1940s and early 1950s, would often submit scripts for approval and then sell the US rights for a film to a distributor uninterested in a Code Seal of Approval. When the Rank Organization

---

13. Quoted in letter from Joseph I. Breen to Jock Lawrence of the Rank Organization, dated 5 December 1949.

decided to follow in the footsteps of Gaumont British and create its own American distribution arm, Rank Film Distributors of America, Inc., few of its releases were submitted to the PCA for approval.

The 1950s marked the end of an era in the censorship of British films in the United States. The collaboration between the PCA and British film-makers was at an end. It had perhaps been a one-sided relationship, but, as Joseph I. Breen was always quick to point out, it had never been a dictatorial one. As he once wrote to the Rank Organization: 'It is not so much a question of what *we* want ... We do not want *you* to do anything.'[14]

---

14. Letter to Jock Lawrence, dated 29 June 1949.

3

THE FILMS

Across the Bridge (1957)

On 17 April 1951 a script was submitted by Kenneth Bates of the New York office of the J. Arthur Rank Organization, Inc., and nine days later, Joseph I. Breen responded that while the story, adapted from a novel by Graham Greene, was basically acceptable, it contained elements that were not. The script followed the fortunes of an international financier who flees to Mexico and assumes another man's identity, only to discover that the man is a thief wanted by the police. The Production Code required that 'the history, institutions, prominent people and citizenry of all nations shall be represented fairly', but this script showed the Mexican police in an unfavourable light. Further, it depicted brutal third-degree methods of interrogation. Among other problems were deliberate cruelty towards a dog and presentation of Delilah as a prostitute. No Certificate was ever issued, and the film, uncut, was released by Rank Film Distributors of America, Inc. in January 1958.

The Adventures of Tartu (1943)

As early as 3 July 1941, a script was submitted by M-G-M, and, four days later, the PCA responded that the basic story met the requirements of the Production Code. The script recounted the adventures of a British secret agent who, posing as a Romanian, is parachuted into occupied Czechoslovakia to destroy a Nazi poison gas factory. Twenty-one pages of script with problems were noted, including negative references to Romanians, sexual suggestiveness, drinking scenes and unacceptable brutality. In particular, the PCA objected to the presentation of Lieutenant Vogel as 'abnormal sexually'. In this regard, the PCA commented that scenes of men spraying themselves with perfume were generally objectionable and it recommended they be omitted. Certificate No. 9245 was issued on 20 May 1943 for a film now titled *Sabotage Agent*. However, the film was released uncut as *Tartu* by M-G-M in August 1943.

The African Queen (1952)

A temporary script for *The African Queen* was first submitted by Warner Bros on 12 April 1947. The story, set in Africa during the First World War, centred on the relationship between a profane Canadian skipper and a correct British missionary's sister. Four days later, Joseph I. Breen replied that the basic story complied with the requirements of the Production Code. He requested that the producers secure proper technical advice from the Protestant Motion Picture Council as to the treatment of the story's religious elements; he required elimination of profanity and any hint of intimacy between Rose and Allnut. Breen also noted that Negroes resented the appellation 'black' and suggested a line by Allnut be changed to 'native fellers'.

John Huston's script was submitted to the PCA on 26 March 1951, and on 2 April Joseph I. Breen reported that the director's basic story was not acceptable in view of the immoral relationship between Rose and Allnut, beginning on page 108 and continuing to the film's conclusion. He also insisted that there be no lampooning of the devotion of Rose's missionary brother, that effeminacy in one of the male characters be eliminated and that the natives be properly dressed. Tentative Certificate No. 15611 was issued on 22 October 1951, and confirmed on 7 March 1952. With a running time identical to that in the UK, *The African Queen* was released by United Artists, opening at the Capitol Theatre, New York, 20 February 1952.

Against the Wind (1948)

A treatment dated 18 November 1946 for this story of a Catholic priest working with the resistance in 1943 Belgium was submitted to the PCA

by A. Reginald Allen at the Universal studios office of the J. Arthur
Rank Organization, Inc., on 17 February 1947. On 25 February, Joseph
I. Breen wrote to say that the story was 'unacceptable' because of the
characterization of Father Jacques, shown in a number of 'extra-
curricular activities' and engaged in a number of 'quite definitely
unpriestly things'. Breen urged the producer to contact a responsible
Catholic authority, and, taking up his advice, associate producer Sid
Cole did meet, on 21 March 1947, with the Very Reverend Monsignor
Collingwood at the office of the Archbishop of Westminster. The
Monsignor reviewed a draft script dated 28 February 1947, and a number
of changes and deletions were made and forwarded to Breen.

On 2 April 1947, Breen confirmed that the Monsignor's suggested
changes would eliminate his previous objections; he also noted a
number of minor problems, including profanity, suggestive dialogue
and unacceptable use of the word 'nigger'. A revised final shooting
script, dated 13 June 1947, was read by Breen, and on 27 June, he
listed some further minor changes that were necessary. Two years later,
on 23 June 1949, Breen wrote to his son at Eagle-Lion Films, Inc.,
that he had viewed the film, and that it still contained some undeleted
phrases mentioned in his earlier letter. After the necessary changes,
Certificate No. 12580 was issued on 17 August 1949. Cut to 88 minutes,
Against the Wind was released by Eagle-Lion, opening at the Little
Carnegie Theatre, New York, 6 July 1949. Pennsylvania required the
elimination of a scene showing Picquart taking a suicide tablet. Ohio
required the same elimination, together with a sequence showing the
filling of an explosive brick and the line 'Blast the RAF'.

Another Shore (1948)

In this romantic comedy from Ealing Studios, a day-dreaming Dubliner
seeks the means to finance a trip to the South Seas.

On 13 April 1948, a second draft shooting script was submitted by
A. Reginald Allen at the Universal studios office of the J. Arthur Rank
Organization, Inc. Three days later, Joseph I. Breen advised that the
basic story was acceptable under the provisions of the Production
Code, but called Allen's attention to a number of details, including
excessive drinking, profanity, references to trafficking in white slavery
and dope, and the business of three toilet rolls. Tentative Certificate
No. 15129 was assigned.

On 27 February 1951, Breen angrily wrote to the Rank Organization that the film was circulating with only a tentative Certificate of approval. On 2 March 1951, Kenneth Bates at Rank's New York office explained that the film was one of a group sold to Pentagon Pictures, Inc., which did not wish a Code Seal. Rank had asked Pentagon to delete the Certificate No. from all prints, and on 5 March 1951, Breen cancelled the tentative Certificate. Cut to 77 minutes, *Another Shore* was released by Pentagon on 10 February 1951.

The Astonished Heart (1950)

Based on a play by Noël Coward, this romantic drama involves a married psychiatrist, Christian Faber, who falls in love and has an affair with Leonora Vail. The experience ultimately leads him to despair and suicide. What was identified as the final shooting script for the film adaptation was submitted to Joseph I. Breen on 2 February 1949 by Kenneth Bates of the New York office of the J. Arthur Rank Organization, Inc. Breen's reply on 1 March 1949 was to Jock Lawrence of that office, stating that the 'story of adultery without sufficient compensating moral values' could not be approved. Breen was disturbed that Faber's wife Barbara condoned her husband's relationship with another woman, and that Leonora was free to go on from one affair to the next. He suggested that Faber's assistant Tim become the film's voice for morality.

A month later, on 13 April 1949, Lawrence met in Hollywood with Geoffrey M. Shurlock and Jack Vizzard, and the following day Breen sent him a six-page list of agreed changes to the script. That same day, Lawrence also sent Vizzard eight pages of revised script, and on 20 April 1949 Breen replied that the changes for the most part would seem to contain what was requisite for bringing Coward's story within the requirements of the Production Code, but he still suggested specific dialogue changes.

The film's associate producer, Vivian Cox, mailed a further six revised pages to Rank's New York office on 17 May 1949, but warned Lawrence that Noël Coward was reluctant to make all these changes. On 1 June 1949, Lawrence sent Breen a revised script, which he felt met 'all the philosophic requirements'. Two days later, Breen responded, suggesting that some problems could be resolved with the deletion of the indication that Faber's wife suggests he go off with Leonora. Breen also pointed out to Lawrence that he was aware the film was already in production.

Meanwhile, the production team in London was becoming extremely nervous and, on 13 June 1949, Lawrence was forced to telephone Breen that he had been informed that to make the film acceptable to the PCA would 'ruin the story'. On 23 June he reported that Noël Coward had returned to the UK from his home in Jamaica, and that he was reworking the script and would now play the leading role, replacing Michael Redgrave. Producer Sydney Box urged Lawrence, on 28 June 1949, to let Breen know that he had given up three days of his holiday in Cornwall to go over the script. Breen was not impressed. On 29 June 1949, he wrote to Lawrence:

> Please have in mind that our sole purpose is to be helpful ... While it is most commendable for you to assure us that you are 'diligently trying our best to live up to what you want,' please note that it is not so much a question of what *we* want. The question is, whether or not in our judgment, the finished picture is acceptable under the provisions of the Production Code. We do not *want* you to do anything.

On 1 July 1949, Vivian Cox reported to Lawrence that both Tim and Susan had become the 'voice for morality' in the script, and that Coward had written a new scene, bringing in the characters of Ernest and Alice to add their own condemnation. On 13 July 1949, Breen confirmed to Lawrence that the '"voice for morality" which we have discussed so many times, is now probably sufficiently strong', and on 20 July 1949, he issued a tentative Seal No. 13669.

In January 1950, Universal brought over director Anthony Darnborough to edit the film for a US release. He made a number of explicit changes and additions. The line, 'You're very dishevelled. Your eyes are shining and your brooch is undone. It's all highly suspicious', was changed to, 'You're very dishevelled and your brooch is undone. It's all quite inexcusable.' A nightmare scene with Christian Faber as both doctor and patient was added. New dialogue was recorded between Barbara Faber (Christian's wife) and Susan Birch, in which the latter philosophized on the immorality of the contemplated action. A scene in a car between Christian Faber and Tim, in which the latter neither approved nor disapproved of Christian's actions, was deleted. Finally, a voice quoting from the Bible, 'The Lord shall smite thee with madness and blindness and astonishment of heart', was added.

Joseph I. Breen viewed the new rendition on 10 January 1950, and it was the version released by Universal-International, opening at the Park Avenue Theatre, New York, on 14 February 1950. In Ohio, the entire scene between Christian and Leonora in a car in the woods was removed.

Autumn Crocus (1934)

When C. L. Anthony's play about an unhappy holiday romance between an English schoolteacher and a Tyrolean innkeeper opened on Broadway in November 1931, it was seen by a member of the Studio Relations Office staff who noted 'No Code complications' in his file. Subsequently, Certificate No. 0174 was issued on 23 October 1934, subject to certain deletions. Lines such as 'She makes me feel like a chorus girl week-ending in Brighton' were to be removed, together with references to Audrey and Alaric travelling together as man and wife, and the latter's asking the vicar to read a book titled *A Remedy for Sex*. Released by Captain Harold Auten, the film opened at the Little Carnegie Theatre, New York, on 24 October 1934, cut to 72 minutes.

The Bad Lord Byron (1949)

After reading a draft script of *The Bad Lord Byron*, dated 16 October 1947, Joseph I. Breen wrote on 11 November 1947 to A. Reginald Allen at the Universal studio offices of the J. Arthur Rank Organization, Inc. He noted the story was unacceptable from the standpoint of the Production Code, with its suggestion of an adulterous and incestuous affair between Byron and his half-sister Augusta Leigh, and the adulterous relationship between Byron and the Countess Guiccioli, condoned by the latter's husband and brother. Further, Breen pointed out that religious and other circles were objecting in principle to films whose central characters had loose morals, regardless of whether or not they had the approval of the PCA.

A revised script was submitted on 19 January 1948 and, eight days later, Breen responded with the same complaints. Revised pages were submitted on 6 and 17 February with the same result. In May 1948, producer Sydney Box announced in the UK that his film had been banned in the United States. The PCA responded that this was not true – the film had never been viewed for approval or disapproval. It was not until 1951 that *The Bad Lord Byron* was released in the USA on a states rights basis, with no Certificate, but with the approval of the censorship boards of Maryland, New York and Pennsylvania.

Bank Holiday (1938)

Tells the stories of a cross-section of holiday-makers in a south coast resort during the August Bank Holiday weekend, one of the plots centring on an unmarried couple planning a 'dirty weekend'.

Tentative Certificate No. 01847 was issued on 10 November 1937, but when the film was viewed by the PCA on 22 February 1938, it was found to be in violation of the Code. The film argued that providing a couple loved each other, a sexual relationship was proper and accept- able; there was considerable dialogue in regard to such a relationship and no compensating moral values. In an internal memorandum, dated 23 February 1938, Joseph I. Breen praised the film as 'a very very good picture', but noted that the story could hardly be re-edited.

At the request of producer Gaumont British, the film was reviewed on 27 February 1938, and it was agreed that Hollywood producer Larry Darmour would find an efficient cutter and have him go reel by reel through the film, removing all objectionable scenes. The film was viewed for a third time on 24 March 1938, and to Breen's 'sheer amazement' the cutter had so transformed the story as to make it acceptable under the Code. He had deleted 1,450 feet of film, added new printed commentary and gathered in 'wild lines' on the soundtrack. The Certificate, initially issued by the New York office, was confirmed on 11 April 1938, despite the New York office never having seen the production. That same day, Martin Quigley wrote to Breen, con- gratulating everyone involved and praising 'the prophylactic process' used to clean up the film. On 25 April 1938, the title was changed to *3 on a Week-End*, and, as such, the film was released by Gaumont British Picture Corp. of America. Cut to 72 minutes, it opened at the Continental Theatre, New York, on 3 June 1938.

Beau Brummell (1954)

After researching the life of Mrs Fitzherbert, Joseph I. Breen wrote to Dore Schary at M-G-M on 9 July 1953 to say that while the basic story of a film then titled *The Life and Times of Beau Brummell* seemed to meet the provisions of the Production Code, there was unacceptable treatment of adultery between Mrs Fitzherbert and the Prince of Wales. It was 'a complete justification and glorification of this immoral relationship, and one for which the sympathy of the audience is elicited'. Aside from that basic difficulty, there were a number of other problems: throughout was an unacceptable use of the word 'damme'; the steward of Brooks' Club was suggestive of 'a sex pervert'; the suggestion of a sex affair between Beau Brummell and Patricia was unacceptable; the woman in a doorway soliciting Brummell was indicative of prostitution and should be eliminated.

On 9 July 1953, Breen reported to Schary that he had read a new script, dated 15 June 1953, and it offered fewer problems: the expression 'damme' still had to be removed; a line which suggested justification of the immoral relationship between Mrs Fitzherbert and the Prince had to be deleted; the use of animals needed to be coordinated with the American Humane Association; the vulgar sequence of the Prince examining a male dog and discovering it female was not in good taste; and the expression 'a leper is loose in the streets' needed elimination. Certificate No. 16960 was issued on 13 July 1954, on the understanding that the 'ejaculation' used throughout was now definitely 'demme' and not 'damme'. With an identical running time to that in the UK, *Beau Brummell* was released by M-G-M October 1954.

Bhowani Junction (1956)

The script, derived from John Masters' novel, charts the loves of an Anglo-Indian girl at the time of the campaign for Indian independence.

At the request of Robert Vogel at M-G-M, on 8 April 1954, Shurlock and his colleague Hodenfield performed a rush job in reading the script. While most queries were minor, they noted a major Code problem arising from the fact that the lead, Victoria, lives during part of the story as the mistress of the British Colonel. At this point, M-G-M advised the PCA that it would probably not release the film in India as the material might be considered 'explosive'. A conference took place between the PCA and M-G-M on 12 July 1954, and it was agreed that the script be rewritten to avoid the issue of the live-in arrangements between Victoria and the Colonel. When filming started in January 1955, the script was still not completed. Only the first fifty pages could be submitted to the PCA, and these still contained the illicit sexual relationship, together with many minor problems. A revised script, dated 12 February 1955, resolved the one issue, but as revised script pages continued to be submitted through April 1955, a new problem developed with unacceptable emphasis on Victoria in her underwear and almost nude. Geoffrey M. Shurlock wrote to M-G-M on 22 March 1955 to say that she should not be seen in 'girdle, bra and panties'. As late as December 1955, the PCA read six pages of retakes, despite Certificate No. 17728 being issued on 28 November 1955. With a running time of 110 minutes, the film was released by M-G-M in May 1956.

Black Limelight (1938)

Black Limelight was viewed by Vincent G. Hart in April 1939, and found in violation of the Production Code in that a married man has an illicit relationship with a young girl, resulting in her pregnancy. Further, the man's wife condones the adultery, and the murder of the girl is shown in detail. On 17 April 1939, Budd Rogers of Alliance Films Corporation withdrew his application for Code approval, but the PCA was concerned that the film would receive wide distribution because of its star, Raymond Massey, and spent time with Rogers working to re-edit the production. On 12 May 1939, the PCA viewed a revised version but still found problems relative to adultery in the dialogue. Six days later, Certificate No. 02544 was issued for a new cut version containing no suggestion of the adulterous relationship between the married man (Charrington) and the girl (Lily James). The suggestion that Lily's bungalow was provided by Charrington was eliminated, together with talk of the girl's pregnancy and lines by the police indicating that Charrington was responsible for her condition. A speech by Charrington's wife condoning his adultery was re-edited to one of condemnation. At most, the film now contained only a suggestion of adultery, but it was still heavily cut in Pennsylvania. With a running time of 63 minutes, *Black Limelight* was released by Alliance Films Corporation and opened at the Globe Theatre, New York, 25 August 1939.

Black Narcissus (1947)

After reading the screenplay about the impact of the East upon an order of Anglican nuns in a Himalayan convent, Joseph I. Breen wrote to William Burnside at Eagle-Lion Films, Inc., on 26 April 1945:

> While the story is not quite clear and concise, to us it has about it a flavor of sex sin in connection with certain of the nuns, which, in our judgment, is not good. We are apprehensive that any motion picture in which there would be even the slightest implication of sex link or sex longings or desires on the part of women consecrated to religion, would give great offense to religious-minded folk in this country and might well call forth very vigorous and, possibly, violent protest from them. If there is any thought to tell the story in this way, we strongly advise against pursuing the undertaking any further.

On 28 March 1946, Michael Powell and Emeric Pressburger sent Breen a 'near-to-final' script, pointing out that after research they had come up with an Anglo-Catholic order of nuns, affiliated neither with the Roman Catholic nor the Protestant Church. The use of this order would permit the projected storyline without giving offence to any religious group. Breen replied on 17 April 1946 that he had read the screenplay and the basic story seemed to meet the requirements of the Production Code. He drew attention to some lines that were sex-suggestive and to other minor matters.

On 25 May 1946, Powell and Pressburger sent a friendly letter to Breen, who replied 'very cordially' on 4 June:

> I do hope that the picture will come through with flying colors. Confidentially the type of pictures which we have been witnessing in recent weeks are, for the most part, pretty ordinary stuff, with the element of *dullness* the pre-dominant feature of most of these films. The market is right, I think, for a half-dozen off-the-beaten-path type of picture, and I hope that *Black Narcissus* will come through as one of these.

After viewing a print of the film, Breen cabled Powell and Pressburger on 5 June 1947: 'Whole staff agrees your film *Black Narcissus* is superb.' He then went on to suggest a foreword explaining that the nuns in the film were Anglo-Catholic and not Roman Catholic, and provided the film-makers with the necessary copy. Certificate No. 11874 was issued on 13 June 1947 and, the next day, Powell and Pressburger confirmed that the foreword would be included. Despite the foreword, *Black Narcissus* was condemned by the National Legion of Decency. Minor eliminations of dialogue were required in Pennsylvania, and Massachusetts required deletion of a scene showing the character of Dean in shorts talking to the nuns, and a scene showing Ruth with her legs exposed.

With a running time identical to that in the UK, *Black Narcissus* was released by Universal-International. It opened at New York's Fulton Theatre on 13 August 1947.

The Black Rose (1950)

On 3 May 1947, Joseph I. Breen wrote to Jason S. Joy at 20th Century-Fox to say that he had read a script about the adventures of a thirteenth-century English nobleman in the China of Kublai Khan, dated 26 April 1947, 'with considerable pleasure', and the material was basically acceptable under the provisions of the Production Code. He asked that proper technical advice be sought in connection with religious scenes and those involving animals. There were eighteen script pages with problems, including the need to amend the statement 'by holy rood', references to 'taking' women, the need to change the name of 'The House of Beautiful Flowers', undue exposure of Walter in a sunken tub, and a horse being shown falling backwards on a bridge. Certificate No. 14095 was issued on 31 May 1950. With a running time of 120 minutes, the film was released by 20th Century-Fox and opened at New York's Roxy Theatre on 1 September 1950.

The Blue Lagoon (1949)

On 19 February 1946, Joseph I. Breen advised A. Reginald Allen at the Universal studios office of the J. Arthur Rank Organization, Inc., that the synopsis of the H. de Vere Stacpoole novel – a synopsis written in 1916! – had been read, and that the book would make an acceptable screenplay under the provisions of the Production Code. It was the story of two children shipwrecked on a tropical island who grow up, mate and produce a child of their own. He did point out that Emmeline could not be a blood relative of Dick, that the 'mating' should be of mature persons over the age of consent, that there should be no detail of lovemaking or childbirth, and that the suicide of the parents would need entirely to be removed. On 7 January 1948, Breen wrote that the screenplay, dated 23 October 1947, had been read, and that it met the requirements of the Production Code. He asked for avoidance of the suggestion of nudity or undue exposure, deletion of two references to 'biology', noted sex-suggestiveness in scenes between the two leads, required there be no showing of the bed, pointedly suggesting immediate consummation of the marriage, and that 'make a baby' be changed to 'have a baby'. Certificate No. 12940 was issued on 19 April 1949. Cut to 97 minutes, the film was released by Universal-International in July 1949.

The Blue Lamp (1950)

The first British 'police procedural' thriller details the life and death of an ordinary London policeman, and the growing threat from juvenile delinquents, represented by Tom, Spud and Diana.

A draft shooting script, dated 8 April 1949, was submitted to the PCA by Kenneth Bates of the New York office of the J. Arthur Rank Organization, Inc. On 9 May 1949 Joseph I. Breen noted that the basic story met the provisions of the Production Code but found unacceptable the unmistakable suggestion of a sex affair between Diana (Peggy Evans) and Tom (Dirk Bogarde); he asked for the elimination of all sequences concerned with the relationship between the couple, together with the expressions 'tart,' 'For God's sake' and 'bastard', and the use of a blackjack (truncheon). Breen subsquently read a revised script, dated 27 May 1949, but found the same problem in the relationship between Diana and Tom. On 9 January 1950, Sir Michael Balcon cabled details of an American version that he was making, with a scene in Tom's flat amended to lose the inference that he was living with Diana. Further, Balcon would change 'little cow' to 'little fool', 'stupid cow' to 'stupid fool', and 'bastard' to 'rat'. The revised version was viewed by the PCA on 19 May 1950 and, two days later, Certificate No. 13840 was issued. With a running time identical to that in the UK *The Blue Lamp* was released by Eagle-Lion Films, Inc., in June 1950. The local censorship board in Massachusetts required deletion of some dialogue in reel 4 and the problematical 'bastard', which had crept back into reel 10.

Bonjour Tristesse (1958)

On 31 March 1955, Geoffrey M. Shurlock wrote to M-G-M to say that a synopsis of the Françoise Sagan novel had been read and, as a story of gross immorality without any compensating moral values, it was unacceptable under the provisions of the Production Code. It detailed the philandering exploits of a French playboy as observed by his seventeen-year-old daughter, who is growing up to imitate him. As studios pondered whether to acquire screen rights to the novel, similar letters were also sent to 20th Century-Fox and David O. Selznick. The latter planned to end his film version with a display of penitence on the part of father and daughter, thus injecting a proper voice for morality. On 13 June 1956, Shurlock wrote to Otto Preminger at Carlyle Productions, Inc., that a script had been read and the basic story met the requirements of the Production Code. He noted the need for moral recognition of Cecile's immoral action in seducing Cyril and urged that there be no emphasis on the bed in Cyril's room, and that consideration be given to rewriting Elsa's line, 'I refuse to be treated like a wife'. A second script, dated 28 June 1957, was read, and it contained only minor problems. Certificate No. 18721 was issued on 3 December 1957. With a running time of 93 minutes, the film was released by Columbia Pictures in February 1958.

Bonnie Prince Charlie (1948)

The initial approach to the PCA regarding *Bonnie Prince Charlie* came from Jason S. Joy at 20th Century-Fox. On 11 May 1948 he submitted a script for the film, which he noted was being produced by London Film Productions, Inc., for release by his studio. Six days later, Stephen S. Jackson responded, complaining that the script contained duplicate pages and many missing scenes. Further, he could not approve the sex affairs between Prince Charles and Clementina and between Charles and Flora. He also noted that the film appeared already to have been shot. Gordon S. White, director of the Advertising Code Administration confirmed to Jackson on 20 May 1948 that his supposition was correct, and that he had already approved some 400 still photographs from the production.

There was no further correspondence from 20th Century-Fox and, after a gap of three years, Code Certificate No. 13175 was issued to

Lopert Films Distributing Corporation on 30 January 1951. The Certificate was subsequently withdrawn in April 1952 because Lopert failed to pay the PCA's fee of $575.00. Prior to that action, *Bonnie Prince Charlie* was eventually released in the USA in January 1952 by Snader Productions, with a running time of 101 minutes.

Boys Will Be Boys (1935)

The Will Hay comedy was viewed on 13 August 1935 by James Wingate and F. W. Allport of the PCA staff. The former opined: 'This story is played in an environment of rowdyism and crime, including crooked gambling with cards for money, pickpocketing and rowdy and crooked football. There is no spokesman for morality nor is there any contributing element for good throughout the picture.' 'In my opinion,' wrote Allport, 'the picture is either acceptable under the Code, possibly with one or two minor deletions of some pickpocket scenes, or is unacceptable as a whole, on the ground that it tends to lower moral standards.' PCA staffer Vincent G. Hart viewed *Boys Will Be Boys* on 20 August 1935 and wrote: 'No mantle of farce can cover the fact that crime is shown in detail with emphasis on the criminal tendencies of youthful students. The main character conspires with his father, a convict, to rob.' An appeal was made to Joseph I. Breen as to what to do and, on 3 September 1935, he wrote: 'our recommendation is that you settle the matter yourselves.'

Gaumont British Picture Corp. of America made appropriate cuts and Certificate No. 0657 was issued on 17 September 1935. After making the cuts, Gaumont British pondered whether to bother releasing the film in the USA, but after a test preview decided to go ahead.

Brewster's Millions (1935)

In this classic farce, a penniless young man has to spend £500,000 in a fixed period in order to inherit £6 million.

On 21 February 1935, Joseph I. Breen wrote to Harry D. Buckley at United Artists Corp. to say that he had reviewed the print of *Brewster's Millions*, and the basic plot and treatment were acceptable from the point of view of the Production Code. However, he listed eight elements in the film to which he had a grave objection:

- The shot of Freddie coming out of the bathroom with a newspaper in his hand (toilet humour).
- The line by Brewster: 'Straight through and first to your left.'
- The shot of a girl's posterior, followed by Brewster's line: 'You ought to be in pictures.'
- The line by Brewster to the dance director: 'One hundred of those who might be either' ('use of any material based on perversion or perverts, or suggestive of those subjects, is absolutely taboo').
- The line: 'Do you mind telling me just how do you bribe the captain?'
- The shot of water dripping off the grindstone, and Brewster's reaction to it.
- The shot of the dragon hopping around the post, followed by a dog running and sniffing this post.
- All material which dealt with the posterior of the dragon.

On 27 February 1935, Vincent G. Hart reported to Breen that all the cuts had been made with the exception of the line, 'Just how do you bribe the captain', and Certificate No. 655 was issued.

It appeared that an amicable conclusion had been reached, and Breen was satisfied that all vulgarity had been removed from the scenes in which star Jack Buchanan was disguised as the rear-end of a dragon. But, without warning, Harry D. Buckley at United Artists advised Will Hays that his company intended to appeal the cuts directly to the board of directors of the MPPDA. Screenings were arranged at the UA projection room in New York on 14 March 1935, and at the Roosevelt Hotel in Hollywood on 19 March 1935, attended by senior studio executives, including Sol Lesser and Hal Roach. They were all supportive of Breen, and even comedy producer Roach found the gags relating to the dragon's posterior to be in bad taste. On 26 March 1936, Will Hays wrote to United Artists that the board had considered and rejected the appeal.

United Artists refused to accept the decision, and released the film uncut and without a Certificate. Because some of the cuts – Freddie leaving the bathroom and the grindstone – had been required by the British Board of Film Censors, *Brewster's Millions* became one of the few British films to be released in the United States with a running time longer than that in the UK It opened at New York's Rivoli Theatre on 6 April 1935, and was also screened in Kansas, Massachusetts, New York and Ohio without censorship cuts; only Pennsylvania required minor cuts in dialogue.

The Bridge on the River Kwai (1957)

On 12 October 1956, Geoffrey M. Shurlock wrote to Columbia Pictures saying that the material was basically acceptable under the requirements of the Production Code. He directed the producer's attention to the following items: the girl on the calendar should not be nude; 'damned' and 'hell' should be eliminated; the nose picking must be eliminated; the women and men should not strip themselves naked when removing leeches; the women should not bathe in the nude; the last surviving Japanese should not be killed in an unduly brutal manner; discretion was advised when Barnet almost loses all his clothes; avoid anything unduly bold when the girl aids Shears to overcome his severe cold; and the killing of Joyce and Warden should not be excessively brutal. It would appear that this was not the script utilized in the film, and on 27 November 1956, without comment, the final script was approved. Tentative Certificate No. 18737 was issued on 13 August 1957, and confirmed 16 October 1957. With a running time identical to that in the UK, *The Bridge on the River Kwai* was released by Columbia, and opened at the Palace Theatre, New York, on 18 December 1957.

Brief Encounter (1945)

Prior to its production, William Burnside of Eagle-Lion Films, Inc., submitted the script of *Brief Encounter* to Joseph I. Breen on 6 February 1945. Breen responded on 9 February suggesting only minor changes, including changing 'Thank God' to 'Thank heaven' and deleting the phrase 'get me into trouble', and adding:

> In shooting this picture, please take care to keep down to the minimum any scenes of physical contact, kissing or embracings between your two leads – this in view of the fact that they are both married people. The four or five scenes of such embraces now present could be approved if you feel them necessary – though possibly you could omit one or two of these. In any case, please make certain that, in shooting the picture, no more scenes of this kind are injected.

On 4 October 1945, George Archibald, general manager of *Brief Encounter*'s producer, Independent Producers Ltd, confirmed to Eagle-Lion that the minor changes had been made and that no further scenes of physical contact had been added. Certificate No. 11819 was issued on 19 August 1946, subject to the deletion of a shot showing a man raising his hand to slap a woman on her posterior.

In the meantime, Universal had formed Prestige Pictures, Inc. to market films to art houses in the USA, and *Brief Encounter* became its first release on 24 August 1946. The running time was one minute shorter than the UK release length of 86 minutes.

Broken Blossoms (1936)

For reasons which remain unclear, the film industry suddenly became interested in D. W. Griffith's 1919 production of *Broken Blossoms* and its source, Thomas Burke's short story, 'The Chink and the Child', in the mid-1930s. In December 1934, M-G-M asked Breen's opinion of the short story, and he replied to Louis B. Mayer, on 21 December, that the story could be made into an attractive film, provided there was no implication of miscegenation and no physical contact between the Chinaman and the girl. On 11 May 1936, Merian C. Cooper of Pioneer Pictures, Inc., submitted the story to Breen. He, in turn, asked Martin Quigley's advice, and then replied to Cooper, on 14 May, that the story was 'hardly acceptable'. In the meantime, Breen learned for the first time (from Quigley) that a British production was in the works, based on Griffith's original film.

That film was viewed on 12 August 1936 by James Wingate and his associates in the New York office. They found it 'basically satisfactory', but demanded the removal of shots of a girl doing a 'muscle dance' in reels 1 and 2; deletions throughout of the derogatory term 'Chink' ('Chinky' was OK as a term of endearment); and the deletion of the shot of a boxer slapping a woman's backside. In view of plans to cut the film anyway for its US release, Wingate suggested the elimination of many shots depicting the brutality of the father towards the girl.

It was not until April 1937 that Nathan Cy Braunstein of Imperial Distributing Corporation stated that the deletions had been made and, on 23 April, Certificate No. 01337 was issued. Cut by between four and eight minutes, *Broken Blossoms* had already opened at the Belmont Theatre, New York, on 13 January 1937. It appears obvious that the distributor chose to ignore the PCA's required cuts in that Massachusetts, Ohio and Pennsylvania all demanded deletions, including the word 'Chink', scenes of violence against the girl and against the Chinese by a mob. *Broken Blossoms* was later reissued in the US under the title of *Limehouse Murder*.

Broken Journey (1948)

A plane crashes in the Alps and the assorted group of survivors copes with their plight.

On 14 April 1947, Joseph I. Breen wrote to A. Reginald Allen at the Universal studios office of the J. Arthur Rank Organization, Inc., that the story, then titled *Rescue*, seemed to meet the requirements of the Production Code, with one major exception. John deliberately commits suicide and that suicide is glorified. He also noted nineteen pages of script with problems, virtually all relating to profanity. On 14 September 1948, Breen viewed the film with his son at Eagle-Lion Studios, Inc., and found the problems were now limited to two uses of 'damn' and one 'silly bastards'. An argument over the latter ensued with A. Reginald Allen. Allen insisted that the line was actually 'silly baskets', but, on 13 October 1938, Breen insisted that the line in reel 5 sounded like 'silly bastards' and would have to be deleted. Certificate No. 12424 was issued on 1 April 1949, and the film, uncut, was released by Eagle-Lion in June 1949.

The Broken Melody (1934)

This is a romantic drama about a composer who is sent to Devil's Island and escapes.

On 2 April 1935, Douglas Mackinnon of the PCA went to the projection booth at the Pantages Theatre in Hollywood and examined the main title of *The Broken Melody*. He found that Code Seal No. 0217 had been spliced therein. It was removed, and an investigation revealed that the number had actually been issued to an RKO short, *Dumbbell Letters #7*. Olympic Pictures Corporation of New York, distributor of *The Broken Melody*, pointed out it had not submitted the film for PCA approval, and it knew nothing of the matter, suggesting that the Code Seal had been spliced in by a sub-distributor, Independent Film Distributing Corporation, Inc., in Los Angeles. The latter denied responsibility, as did RKO Theatres, which had screened the film in a number of its houses. A $25,000 fine could be levied on any MPPDA member who implied PCA approval when none had been obtained, and so the organization was quite aggressive in trying to track down the culprit. The matter was resolved in May 1935 when Olympic agreed to make minor cuts to the film and submit it for PCA approval. Certificate No. 916 was issued on 29 May 1935. Running for 68 minutes, *The Broken Melody* was first released in the USA on 30 October 1934.

The Brothers (1947)

Sydney Box approached Joseph I. Breen while he was in London in July 1946, and asked him to read a draft script, possibly written by Box, based on a novel by L. A. G. Strong and concerning Scottish clan rivalry. From the Dorchester Hotel, on 23 July 1946, Breen wrote to Box that the story was 'definitely and specifically in violation of the Production Code', because of a plot involving unpunished murder and illicit sexual relationships without compensating moral values. However, as a favour and against PCA regulations, Breen issued a provisional Certificate No. 12383 to the film in April 1947.

Breen subsequently viewed the film twice but was at a loss to suggest any possible way to handle the production's unacceptable treatment of murder. On 6 December 1947, A. Reginald Allen at the J. Arthur Rank Organization's offices at Universal sent Breen a script with a revised ending. On 12 December, Breen approved the new ending, in which the character of John (played by Duncan Macrae) does not drown Mary (Patricia Roc) on a fishing trip. He also asked for the elimination of the nude bathing scene with Mary in reel 4, together with the close-up of a clenched hand and the preceding kissing scene, both of which suggested a sexual situation.

Subject to Breen's changes, a formal Certificate No. 12383 was issued on 26 February 1948, and *The Brothers*, released by Prestige Pictures, opened at the Sutton Theatre, New York, on 4 May 1948, cut to 90 minutes.

Caesar and Cleopatra (1946)

Producer Gabriel Pascal and Joseph I. Breen were obviously great friends. On 9 August 1944, Pascal sent a shooting script 'dedicated to you' to Breen, concluding his accompanying letter: 'I hope you are well, also your sweet wife and the children. Please give them my love.' Breen responded on 14 September: 'We have read it with interest and enthusiasm, and feel sure that you have another hit in the making. To produce such an outstanding picture under the present difficulties in Britain will indeed be a triumph. And I don't need to add that I have no doubt that you will succeed fully.' After calling Pascal's attention to the need to clothe his female players adequately, 'which we feel certain you will handle with your usual excellent taste', Breen concluded: 'The above are merely details, which I am sure you would have taken care of anyway.' Certificate No. 11427 was issued on 11 June 1946 to United Artists, which released *Caesar and Cleopatra* on 16 August 1946, cut to 126 minutes.

The Camp on Blood Island (1958)

With its lurid title and setting in both male and female Japanese prisoner-of-war camps, *The Camp on Blood Island* might be assumed to have faced major hurdles in receiving a Production Code Seal, but such is not the case. On 20 August 1957, Geoffrey M. Shurlock approved the basic story, submitted in script form by Lippert Pictures, Inc. The number of words to be deleted was considerable, including 'bastards,' 'For God's sake', 'you friggin' Jap bastard,' 'whore', ('we suggested substituting the word "tramp"'), 'damn,' and 'yellow bastards'. Certificate No. 18729 was issued on 7 May 1958, subject to deletion of a nude bathing scene and several uses of 'bastard'. The film was cut to 81 minutes.

Captain Horatio Hornblower RN (1951)

On 28 September 1949, Joseph I. Breen wrote to Warner Bros that the script, dated 20 September 1949, had been read, and the basic story was acceptable under the provisions of the Production Code. Among the problems were profanity throughout, the need to avoid gruesomeness in the shots of men tied to stakes, that there be nothing offensive in the suggested nudity, no suggestion of a mercy killing, no lustful or open-mouth kissing, and that nose-thumbing and the expression, 'by the short hairs', be deleted. On 3 January 1950 the final script, dated 10 December 1949, was read. There was still need for the greatest possible caution in regard to scenes of violence, the need to delete blasphemy and the lines in which Lady Barbara offers herself to Hornblower, and the necessity to avoid anything offensive in the tattoo of a lady on Carter's forearm. Changed script pages were submitted on 20 January 1950. Certificate No. 14682 was issued on 9 August 1950, on the understanding that the expression, 'Madre de Dios', and an extreme breast shot of Virginia Mayo during a backgammon game were deleted. Uncut, the film was released by Warner Bros.

Carry On Nurse (1959)

The film was viewed by the PCA staff on 2 March 1960, at which time it was noted that, in order to issue a Certificate, it would be necessary to cut:

- The nurse massaging the boxer's back and bottom, her pulling the trunks off the same patient, and her comment: 'Imagine all that fuss, over such a little thing.'
- A similar gag with another patient, and the line: 'And to think I called you a baby.'
- The pre-surgical routine, involving the shaving of the same patient.
- A suppository gag involving the same patient.
- The gag of a visitor to the hospital referring to 'sliced nuts'.

The protracted business of a patient having to urinate. The tag joke involving rectal temperature-taking and insertion of a daffodil.

All in all, it was felt it would be better if the distributor withdrew his request for certification, although Geoffrey M. Shurlock admitted privately to a colleague on 30 August 1960 that 'confidentially this is a very funny picture'. Eventually, the PCA reconsidered, and Certificate No. 19857 was issued on 10 February 1961. Uncut, *Carry On Nurse* was released by Governor Films, Inc., in March 1960.

Christopher Columbus (1949)

A final script was submitted on 26 May 1948 by A. Reginald Allen at the Universal studios office of the J. Arthur Rank Organization, Inc. On 2 June 1948, Stephen S. Jackson confirmed that the basic story seemed to meet the requirements of the Production Code. He assumed that proper technical advice would be obtained in regard to the Spanish and religious aspects of the story, and, as result of his assumption, Father George Long of St Francis Church, Notting Hill Gate, was hired as a technical adviser. On 29 September 1948, Joseph I. Breen wrote to Allen that he had read script pages for an additional scene, indicating Columbus was the father of Beatrice's illegitimate child, and asked that the dialogue be rewritten so that both took cognizance of the fact that they were guilty of sin and expressed contrition. This was done, and on 20 October 1949 tentative Certificate No. 13229 was issued. Uncut, the film was released by Universal-International in October 1949. After the release, both the PCA and the distributor realized that the Certificate had never been confirmed and the film in its final form never approved by the PCA.

The Citadel (1938)

Plans to film A. J. Cronin's novel, indicting the British medical profession, took place during a period when there was considerable controversy in and outside of the industry as to the desirability of exposing medical quackery on screen. In February 1938, the American Medical Association pledged its support for a film denouncing quack doctors to be produced by Warner Bros. As a result, Will Hays's personal osteopath, Dr George W. Riley, expressed his concern that the film industry might intend to libel members of his and other semi-medical professions.

As early as 5 August 1937, Joseph I. Breen sent a confidential cable from his home address to the Hon. J. Brooke Wilkinson of the British Board of Film Censors, asking what his reaction might be to a screen-play based on A. J. Cronin's novel. Wilkinson replied the following day that he did not consider the novel an attack on the medical profession in general, but did feel that presentation of the faults of undesirables might shake confidence in the entire system. That same day, Breen passed this information on to D. A. Doran at Columbia Pictures, which was, apparently, considering acquisition of the novel.

Columbia did not proceed with its screen adapation, and the film was subsequently produced by M-G-M British. That version was viewed on 14 September 1938 by Breen and three other members of his staff, one of whom, Charles R. Metzger, produced a detailed five-page summary of the production. That same day, Breen took the unusual step of writing two letters to Louis B. Mayer at M-G-M. In the first, he told the studio head that the film in its present form was un-acceptable under the provisions of the Code; he objected to the shot of the birth of the child, the shot of the woman 'unduly exposed' lying under an ultra-violet ray lamp, and to the expressions 'By God!' and 'Good Lord!' In the second letter, Breen told Mayer that he was concerned with the general tone of the story in that it might be taken as a serious reflection on the medical profession as a whole. Further, Breen felt there was a problem in the discussion dealing with the issue of vivisection. He was passing copies of the correspondence on to Will Hays.

On 12 October 1938, Al Block at M-G-M responded to Breen's first letter. The scene of childbirth in reel 2 had been deleted; expressions 'By God!' and 'Good Lord!' had been cut by the sound department; and, in reel 8, the shot of the woman lying under the radium lamp had been cut to the absolute minimum.

In response to Breen's other comments, M-G-M prepared a foreword to the film: 'This motion picture is a story of individual character-izations and is in no way intended as a reflection on the great medical profession which has done so much towards beating back those forces of nature that retard the physical progress of the human race.'

Breen wrote to Hays on 15 October 1938, 'I don't like this foreword' but, noting that it was prepared under the personal supervision of M-G-M's chairman, Nicholas Schenck, there was nothing that he could do about it. Certificate No. 4591 was issued that same day.

With a running time of 110 minutes, equal to that of the British length, *The Citadel* was released by M-G-M on 4 November 1938. It opened the previous day at New York's Capitol Theatre.

The Constant Nymph (1933)

The MPPDA placed Margaret Kennedy's novel about the tangled romantic life of a free-living and impoverished composer on the 'banned list' of stories 'unfit for picturization' in 1923. However, the 1928 silent version opened at the Little Carnegie Theatre, New York, on 9 June 1929, and, five days later, it was approved by the Studio Relations office. (Only Pennsylvania had a problem with the film, requiring the title, 'I suppose she's your mistress' in reel 8 be replaced by 'I suppose she's your sweetheart'.) The 1933 version was viewed by the PCA's New York staff on 20 February 1934, and approved subject to elimination of 'damn' and 'damn nonsense'. Certificate No. 0598 was issued on 12 August 1935, and the film opened at the Roxy Theatre, New York, on 6 April 1934. Again, the only local censorship problem was in Pennsylvania, where dialogue deleletions were required in reels 1, 2, 6, and 8.

Contraband (1940)

This wartime thriller shows how a Danish merchant captain and a glamorous British agent round up a Nazi spy ring.

A print of *Contraband* was viewed by the PCA staff on 17 May 1940 and that same day F. S. Harmon wrote to Selznick International Pictures, Inc., advising of its conformity to the Code subject to deletion of a few uses of 'damn', 'Hell' and 'Good Lord'. Harmon also advised that the foreword stating the film was made with the cooperation of the British Admiralty, the British Ministry of Economic Warfare and the British Ministry of Information should appear on all prints in order that American viewers might have this in mind. In June 1940, producer-to-be Val Lewton indicated he was making further cuts to the film, which, in August 1940, was retitled *Blackout*. A problem arose the following month in that *Blackout* was already registered with the Title Registration Bureau by producers Sam Goldwyn and Edward Small (both of whom apparently had a financial interest in the production). Small's registration had lapsed, but because of the Goldwyn claim, the film was now to be a presentation of Samuel Goldwyn, Inc. It was that company which confirmed on 30 September 1940 that it had made the various required deletions and also advised the PCA that it had removed a dance sequence in which 'colored' and 'white' performers were shown together. Certificate No. 6507 was issued on 3 October 1940, and, cut to 80 minutes, *Blackout* was released by United Artists in November 1940. The local censorship board in Pennsylvania required elimination of a shot of Grimm being hit over the head with the butt of a revolver.

Crackerjack (1938)

Tentative Certificate No. 02184 was issued on 1 July 1938. The film was viewed by the PCA on 29 August 1938, and rejected as the glorification of a clever jewel thief who is neither apprehended nor punished. After a re-viewing on 1 September 1938, Francis S. Harmon and Vincent G. Hart came up with a list of major deletions that would make the film acceptable under the Code. To be removed completely was the sequence in which the thief visits a children's hospital and is portrayed sympathetically. A cut in the ending could imply that the thief was captured boarding the aeroplane. Other objectionable aspects were listed, including profanity, a reference to Lucky cigarettes, the song of the four gangsters, and the well-known 'pansy' gag line, 'Oh, boy, if you could only cook.' An extra scene was shot in the UK showing a Scotland Yard detective covering the thief with a gun and telling him he was under arrest. The new version was viewed by the PCA on 23 September 1938, and the Certificate confirmed that day. Cut to 72 minutes, and retitled *The Man with 100 Faces*, the film was released by Gaumont British Picture Corp. of America, and opened at the Rialto Theatre, New York, on 31 October 1938. It was the uncut version that played in New York, but Gaumont British claimed it was a mistake and that all subsequent prints were re-edited.

Crime over London (1936)

In this crime thriller, a group of Chicago gangsters plot to rob a London department store.

Tentative Code Certificate No. 02142 was issued for *Crime over London* on 15 June 1938. A month later, on 19 July, Vincent G. Hart and James Wingate got around to viewing the film, and the former wrote to Mack Littman of Criterion Film Productions, Ltd, that it could not be approved in its present form. Subsequently, C. E. Schwengeler at Gaumont British made a number of cuts, and while these improved the situation regarding the US release of *Crime over London*, F. S. Harmon, on 26 July 1938, demanded many more: all details of the jewel robbery to be removed; the scene of a man massaging a girl's legs at the beach to be eliminated; casual drinking to be substantially reduced; the shot of the gangsters' weapons on a table to be eliminated; the scene of the gangster and his moll enjoying themselves 'amid rich surroundings of the merchant prince' to be removed; the expression 'stick 'em up' to be eliminated from the soundtrack; the scene of the gangsters stuffing $80,000 into their briefcases to be materially shortened; drastic cuts to be made in the final reel involving the violent conflict between the gangsters and Scotland Yard men; and all shootings by the gangsters to be eliminated. With these cuts made, the Code certification was confirmed.

Released by United Artists, *Crime over London* opened at New York's

Rialto Theatre on 27 July 1938. On 12 August, Mack Littman wrote, complaining of the poor audience reaction to the film and requesting permission to reinsert the shot of the gangster leader, Joker Finnegan (played by Basil Sydney), squinting down the barrel of his gun, and a scene of Finnegan being shot by the girl (Margot Grahame) and her subsequently handing over the gun to the detectives. F. S. Harmon approved the reinsertions on 15 August 1938, subject to the addition of an instruction by the chief of detectives, 'Take her away', after the shooting of Finnegan – thus assuring audiences that the girl would be punished for the killing.

Dance Hall (1950)

With its basic storyline of factory women out for a good time, *Dance Hall* was not a likely contender for Production Code approval. The original script was not even considered satisfactory by the film's producer for examination by the PCA, but on 13 September 1949 a revised script (dated 12 August 1949) was submitted to the PCA by Kenneth Bates of the New York office of the J. Arthur Rank Organization, Inc. On 20 September 1949, Joseph Breen wrote to Bates to give him the not unexpected news that the 'basic story seems unacceptable under the provisions of the Production Code'. Breen noted the distinct indication of a sexual relationship between Eve (Natasha Parry) and Alec (Bonar Colleano): 'This sex affair as presently written is not treated with the proper compensating moral values nor the requisite "voice for morality" which is demanded by the Code for this type of sin.' Further, Breen demanded the greatest possible care in the selection and photography of the women's costumes, that the breasts be fully covered at all times and that Carole (Diana Dors) should, at the minimum, wear a slip and not a brassiere and pants.

On 28 November 1949, Jock Lawrence of Rank's New York office submitted a second revised script, together with an impassioned letter from Stella Jonckheere, literary editor at Ealing Studios, arguing that the affair between Eve and Alec be retained and enclosing new dialogue that would be shot for a US version. Breen was not impressed. On 5 December 1949, he responded:

> In her accompanying letter, which was addressed to you, the Literary Editor makes a strong appeal for the preservation of the

sex relationship between Alec and Eve, as contained in the earlier version of this story. We are frank to say, in reply to her argument, that we have little sympathy for her line of reasoning when she appeals that an illicit sex affair should be acceptable on the grounds that it is 'a straightforward representation of reasonable behavior in modern times.' We are not inclined to lend a solicitous ear to Editor Jonckheere's plea that fornication is 'reasonable' – in modern times or any other times – and we say this fortified by the knowledge that countless millions of people throughout the world would not entertain her criteria of reasonableness, either. Neither are we deeply impressed by her contention that the story itself is a sufficient 'voice for morality.' It seems to us that the only lesson the story teaches is that one must be more careful about having sex affairs before marriage lest one's husband get wind of it.

Breen continued: the 'Story would be definitely and completely unacceptable under the provisions of the Production Code.' He ordered the elimination of 'Cripes!' and 'Damn', and Alec's line, 'It's not etchings with me. I just say "Come up and see my kippers," and they come running.' Finally, he insisted that the PCA could not approve 'passionate, prolonged, lustful or open-mouth kissing'.

Two months later, on 8 February 1950, Kenneth Bates sent yet another revised script to Breen, who responded, on 20 February, that the 'basic story now seems acceptable', but was still concerned with offensive dance movements and 'offensive sex detail'. At that point, correspondence ceased. No PCA certificate was issued for the film. West Coast rights were subsequently acquired by Cinema Distributors, which opened the film at the California Theatre, San Diego on 10 December 1952. The running time was cut to 67 minutes and the production retitled *Dance Hall Girls*, perhaps to avoid confusion with the 1941 20th Century-Fox release, *Dance Hall*, or, more likely, to suggest the presence of 'offensive sex detail'.

The Dancing Years (1950)

Despite being typical Ivor Novello fare and receiving a 'U' certificate from the British Board of Film Censors, *The Dancing Years* created considerable controversy within the PCA and the industry. After a viewing of the film, submitted by Monogram Pictures Corporation, Joseph I. Breen responded on 2 November 1950 that it was clearly a violation of the Production Code inasmuch as it was a story of illicit sex and bastardy for which there was no indication of any compensating moral values. He suggested the elimination of a number of scenes. Monogram's Scott R. Dunlap angrily rejected Breen's opinion, suggesting that only his staff could find certain points objectionable under the Code. Dunlap withdrew the film from consideration, and released it through Monogram's subsidiary, Stratford Pictures Corp. It received limited screenings, opening at three Los Angeles theatres in November 1950.

On 7 January 1952, Sir Henry L. French, director-general of the British Film Producers Association, wrote a two-page letter to Breen, asking that the film be given exceptional consideration as it was 'pure romance' presented in 'a light-hearted, non-realistic spirit'. Breen was out of the office, undergoing surgery, but he asked Geoffrey M. Shurlock to arrange a rescreening of the film – only to discover that Monogram had no print available. Eventually, on 7 August 1952, the film was reviewed, and the next day Breen wrote to French that he could not accede to his plea for special consideration: 'Our Code is based on morals, not sentiment.' He did point out that by cutting a sequence in reels 5 and 6, the suggestion that the prince and Maria were sharing an apartment could be removed.

Monogram confirmed the cut on 18 September 1952 and, the next day, Certificate No. 14266 was issued. However, by this time, interest in the film had waned, and there was no new release of it.

The Deep Blue Sea (1955)

When first produced on Broadway, *The Deep Blue Sea* interested a number of Hollywood producers. Hal Wallis was the first to approach the PCA with a copy of the playscript, and, on 11 November 1952, Joseph I. Breen wrote to him to say that the basic story was in violation of the Production Code. It was a treatment of adultery with no adequate compensating moral values, and, further, the character of Hester was presented as a nymphomaniac. On 7 January 1953, a similar letter was sent to Jason S. Joy at 20th Century-Fox. However, when producer Anthony Veiller came up with a film treatment, he was told by Breen (who addressed him as 'Dear Tony') on 11 July 1954 that the story was now reasonably in conformity with the Production Code. Certificate No. 17709 was issued on 5 October 1955. Britain's first film in CinemaScope and DeLuxe colour, *The Deep Blue Sea* was released, uncut, by 20th Century-Fox in November 1955. It was classified 'B' by the National Legion of Decency as tending 'to create sympathy for immoral actions'.

Dial M for Murder (1954)

The importance of this film to Warner Bros is evidenced by the number of times that revised script pages were submitted to the PCA for approval. On 25 June 1953, Joseph I. Breen wrote to the company to inform them that the estimating script, dated 8 June 1953, had been read and the basic story conformed with the Production Code. He asked for deletion of profanity, two references to drugs, and the business involving the wiping of fingerprints. On 30 June, he wrote again to Warner Bros that he had read the changed script pages, dated 25 June, and that these were acceptable, except for one 'hell'. As a major breakthrough for Warner Bros, on 1 July 1953, the PCA agreed that henceforth the wiping of fingerprints in stories where such action was valid and essential to the telling of the stories would be permitted.

The scripts kept coming. On 22 July 1953, Breen reported on a revised estimating script, dated 17 July. On 4 August, he read the final script (dated 30 July). He reported on changed script pages on 24 August, 1 September and 15 September 1953. Eventually, on 24 November 1953 Certificate No. 16708 was issued. With a running time identical to that in the UK, *Dial M for Murder* was released by Warner Bros on 29 May 1954.

Diamond City (1949)

This period adventure film centres on rivalries among the diamond miners in South Africa in the 1870s and the imposition of law and order on their settlement.

On 27 October 1948, Joseph I. Breen wrote to A. Reginald Allen at the Universal studios office of the J. Arthur Rank Organization, Inc., saying that he had read a script titled *Diggers' Republic*, dated 11 October 1948, and that the basic story met the provisions of the Production Code. In a three-page letter, he raised a number of issues, most notably serious concern with the portrayal of Salvation Army personnel. Other problems included use of the term 'nigger' and open-mouth kissing; he wrote, 'the reference to Negroes as "blacks" will undoubtedly be very poorly received by Negroes in America. We suggest that some other word less offensive to the sensibilities of the Negro race be used.' On 2 November 1948, Breen reported on revised script pages, asking for elimination of 'by God' and the portrayal of men standing around the vaccination station joking and kidding about women as they undressed to be vaccinated. On 11 January 1949, he read a script dated 21 December 1948 and still had a problem with the vaccination station and other minor elements. Eventually, on 21 November 1949, revised script pages were approved. The final film was never submitted for approval, and no Certificate was issued. Released by Realart, *Diamond City* opened at the Hillstreet and Pantages Theatres, Los Angeles, on 2 February 1952.

The Dictator (1935)

This historical drama depicts the love affair between the unhappily married Queen of Denmark and the country's Prime Minister during the eighteenth century.

As *Farewell to Love*, the film was first viewed by the PCA in Los Angeles on 6 April 1935, and the following day Joseph I. Breen wrote to producer Larry Darmour with a list of deletions: the entire close shot of the Queen on her bed; the dialogue at the council table in regard to an heir to the throne; the scene in the tavern with a woman on the King's lap; the doctor kissing the girl; the Queen Mother's dialogue in the council chamber; over-exposure of the Queen's breasts: the Queen's visit to Struensee's room; the King's discussion of his wife's adultery; and 'damn' throughout. The film was reviewed by the New York staff on 9 May 1935, all deletions had been made, and Certificate No. 760 was issued that day. Retitled *Loves of a Dictator*, and cut to 83 minutes, the film was released by Gaumont British Picture Corp. of America, opening at the Roxy Theatre, New York on 31 May 1935.

Dr Syn (1937)

The George Arliss vehicle about the vicar of Dymchurch who leads a band of smugglers received tentative Certificate No. 01622 on 14 May

1937. For some reason, Gaumont British did not wish the PCA's New York office to have jurisdiction over the film, and on 9 September 1937 its US representative, Arthur A. Lee, visited Joseph I. Breen in Hollywood and invited him to view the film 'off the record' that same day. Breen did, and, the following day, he wrote to Francis S. Harmon in New York, suggesting that the Code provision forbidding the depiction of ministers of religion in comedy situations or as villains did not apply here because George Arliss was a pirate only masquerading as a minister. Further, it was not necessary to punish the Arliss character for his criminal activities because what he did was shown to be wrong. Finally, noted Breen, 'The thing that saves the story, under the Code, is that it is set back 135 to 150 years ago, and that it is pretty fantastic – it is not convincing or believable.' On 23 September 1937, Harmon wrote to Arthur Lee, paraphrasing Breen's remarks, and confirming the Certificate. *Dr Syn* was released by Gaumont British Picture Corp. of America in September 1937, uncut.

The Drum (1938)

This imperial epic features the suppression of a native revolt on the North-West frontier of India.

Under the title *Mutiny in the Mountains*, the film was viewed by the PCA on 12 May 1938, and, the following day, Francis S. Harmon wrote to United Artists that it conformed to the Production Code, except for one 'Good God', two burps by natives at a palace dinner, and the last part of the line, 'Dances where men lose some of their dignity and the women some of their chastity'. The last cut was not insisted upon because of a technical difficulty in dealing with it and the assurance that 'chastity' was used here in the sense of 'modesty' rather than 'virginity'. Certificate No. 01655 was issued on 1 June 1938. Retitled *Drums*, the film was released by United Artists, opening at Grauman's Chinese Theatre, Hollywood, on 23 August 1938, cut to 99 minutes.

The Edge of the World (1937)

Michael Powell's highly praised drama about life and love on the remote Scottish island of Hirta.

A print of *The Edge of the World* was viewed by the PCA staff on 14 June 1938, and, the following day, F. S. Harmon wrote to E. L. Lopert of Pax Films, Inc., that the main difficulty with the film was an illicit affair between the two leads, resulting in the birth of an illegitimate child. He suggested a manner in which this objectionable element might be taken care of:

> You have a sequence in the picture in which the girl is shown casting a miniature boat into the sea with a letter to the boy secreted in this boat and a sheep bladder attached that will keep it afloat until picked up by a passing fishing vessel. You then show a change in the wind which causes this article to be blown back to the shore of the island where the girl's father picks it up on the beach. He is shown opening the letter but the contents of the letter are not revealed. He is next shown confronting his daughter with the letter and asking her, 'Is this true?,' to which she replies in the affirmative. Then after a passage of time, she is shown with the baby and a good deal of footage is devoted to the christening. The gayety accompanying the christening creates the impression that everybody on the island is happy over the birth of this child. We suggest, therefore, an insert of the letter itself with a pertinent passage flashed on the screen reading somewhat as follows: 'My dear husband: Just think. We've been married now six months and you have been away from me for four. How happy I am that we went ahead and were married secretly before you left. I have great news for you. Our baby should be here ...

Happily, Pax paid no attention to Harmon's idea, and, cut to 74 minutes, *The Edge of the World* opened without Production Code approval at the 55th Street Playhouse, New York, on 11 September 1938. Massachusetts required deletion of 'damn' in reels 4 and 7, and removal of the scene in reel 6 beginning 'Is this true?' and ending 'Poor wee lassie'.

The End of the Affair (1955)

A synopsis of Graham Greene's novel about the crisis of conscience provoked by an adulterous love affair in wartime London was submitted by Jason S. Joy at 20th Century-Fox on 6 February 1952, with a note that Darryl F. Zanuck was of the opinion that the full value of the story could not be retained under the Production Code. Four PCA staffers read the synopsis and were in agreement with Zanuck that there was no treatment that could be made of the story – concerned as it was with lust and adultery – that would be acceptable under the Code. A script was submitted by producer David Lewis and, on 2 December 1952, he had a conference with the PCA, at which time he was advised it was unacceptable. A revised script was submitted by Lewis on 6 April 1954, and it was still 'troublesome'. On 28 May 1954, Lewis and director Edward Dmytryk met with Jack Vizzard, and revisions and eliminations were agreed upon. A further script was submitted on 1 June, with revisions some five days later. Certificate No. 17156 was issued on 20 October 1954, and the film was released by Columbia Pictures in May 1955, uncut.

Escape (1948)

This drama, based on the John Galsworthy play, details the escape from prison and plight of a man who accidentally kills a policeman.

A first draft continuity, dated 9 May 1947, was submitted on 13 May 1947 by Jason S. Joy at 20th Century-Fox. On 19 May, Joseph I. Breen responded that the story was unacceptable under the provisions of the Production Code in that it condoned and justified a certain type of lawlessness: when the central character escapes from jail, all the characters he encounters are sympathetic to his plight. The script was subsequently rewritten with the characters now urging the escapee to give himself up. Many other changes were also made at Breen's request; notably, the character of the girl in the opening sequence was rewritten to avoid the suggestion that she was a prostitute. On 9 July 1947, Jason S. Joy delivered the final script of the film to begin production in the UK within the next week and, two days later, it was approved by Breen. Certificate No. 12985 was issued on 26 April 1948. Released by 20th Century-Fox and with a running time identical to that in the UK, *Escape* opened at New York's Globe Theatre on 15 August 1948.

Escape Me Never (1935)

United Artists first approached the PCA in August 1933 in regard to a screen version of Margaret Kennedy's play about the romance of a composer and a young unmarried mother. Vincent G. Hart read the play and film treatment. He suggested that, for the US version, Gemma's child be legitimate, echoing a 13 August 1934 comment by Joseph I. Breen: 'I see no value in injecting this sordid element in the picture.' The other major problem was Gemma and Sebastian living together without being married, which, Breen wrote to Hart on 16 August, was the 'sort of carnal loose sex-relationship which, in our estimation, constitutes a violation of the Code'.

On 1 October 1934, Hart wrote to UA to say that he had read the first part of the working script and noted that Gemma's baby was now legitimate. He asked for the deletion of profanity throughout and of any line which inferred a sex relationship prior to marriage between Gemma and Sebastian. On 17 October 1934, Hart wrote again to UA that he had read the latter part of the script, noting more problems with profanity and the word 'skunk'. *Escape Me Never* was screened by the PCA on 2 May 1935 and Certificate No. 852 issued that day. Cut by two minutes, the film was released by United Artists, and opened at Radio City Music Hall, New York, on 23 May 1935.

Esther Waters (1948)

A copy of George Moore's novel was delivered to Joseph I. Breen on 6 September 1946. On 3 October 1946, he responded to A. Reginald Allen at the Universal Studios offices of the J. Arthur Rank Organization, Inc. Breen noted the basic story contained some major elements in violation of the Code, but he believed that an acceptable screenplay could be devised if:

- The details of Esther's seduction by William Latch, culminating in the birth of an illegitimate child, were not included.
- Peggy's adultery was omitted.
- There was no suggestion of collusion in the sin of adultery by Esther and William Latch.
- That when Esther and William Latch meet after seven years, he is free to marry her.
- The sexual immoral relationship between Sarah and Evans was eliminated.
- All compensating moral values for Esther and William Latch's sin, present in the novel, be retained.
- An occupation other than wet-nurse be devised for Esther.

On 22 September 1947, A. Reginald Allen submitted the first draft shooting script and, four days later, Breen expressed appreciation of the careful manner in which his suggestions had been followed. He called attention to some details, including unacceptable use of the term 'slut'; that there should be a definite implication that the police will apprehend Mrs Spires and her husband; and that care should be taken that kisses be not unduly passionate or open-mouthed. A final draft shooting script was submitted on 27 October 1947. Three days later, Breen still noted some problems.

It was not until 28 July 1949 that Certificate No. 12151 was issued. As *Sin of Esther Waters*, the film was released by Eagle-Lion Films, Inc., 1951.

The Fallen Idol (1948)

On 11 May 1948, Jason S. Joy at 20th Century-Fox submitted a script for a film titled *The Lost Illusion*, which the studio was to release in the United States. Joseph I. Breen responded on 18 May 1948 that the basic story was completely unacceptable in that adultery was not only not treated with proper compensating moral values but also condoned. He rejected the concept that the adulterous relationship between the two leading character culminated happily in the death of the wife, and, further, considered it an unacceptable element that the entire affair was played out in front of a child. Retitled *The Fallen Idol*, and with a tentative Certificate No. 13174, the film was viewed by the PCA staff in October 1948, and the unanimous decision was that the basic story was unacceptable. On 2 November 1948, Breen concurred, pointing out that the only way the film could be approved was with the removal of the scene between the prostitute, the police officers and the child, and the rewriting of the bedroom scene to imply that Julie (played by Michèle Morgan) was breaking up the affair. This information was passed on to London Films, Inc. by Gordon S. White of the New York office on 9 November

Five months later, in March 1949, it was learned that the film had been sold outright to David O. Selznick. In July 1948, the PCA discovered that the film had been submitted for approval by the New York and Boston censorship boards, and warned the Selznick organization that it would take steps to make it known that the film had not been approved by the PCA. No paperwork exists to indicate what happened next, but on 16 September 1949, Certificate No. 13174 was confirmed. *The Fallen Idol* went into distribution in November 1949 through the Selznick Releasing Organization, and, with a running time identical to that in the UK, it opened on 4 November 1949 at the

Sutton Theatre, New York. In April 1950, the film was re-released by
Eagle-Lion Classics, Inc.

Fanny by Gaslight (1944)

This Gainsborough melodrama featured the tribulations of an innocent
though illegitimate heroine (Phylis Calvert) pursued by a lecherous cad
(James Mason) but loved by a dashing gentleman (Stewart Granger).

The film was first viewed by the PCA staff on 20 September 1944.
The following day, Carl E. Milliken wrote to Eagle-Lion Films, Inc.,
saying that it was not in conformity with the Production Code. He
noted that the main character, Fanny, is illegitimate, and while
illegitimacy in itself was not sufficient to warrant Code refusal, it should
be avoided and not continually referred to, as here. He also found
problems with 'The Shades' being a brothel, with Fanny and Harry
posing as man and wife in Paris and occupying the same bedroom,
and with profanity throughout. In April 1945, the film was re-viewed
by the Los Angeles staff, and Joseph I. Breen suggested changing the
brothel to a gambling establishment, deletion of the scene in reel 8 in
which Fanny seeks a job in a pub, showing the holiday in Paris as
chaperoned, and deleting the hotel room sequence in reel 10. On 18
October 1945, Breen viewed a re-edited print, which he approved,
with praise for the work of the editorial staff at Universal. The
following day, Certificate No. 11272 was issued.

Aside from the content of the film, *Fanny by Gaslight* also had a
problem with its title. 'Fanny' was on the list of objectionable words,
as slang for bottom, and the title was rejected by the MPAA's Title
Registration Bureau in September 1945. On the argument that it was
also the title of the novel on which the film was based, it was approved
for use on 2 October 1945. However, because of a potential humorous
response to the title by theatre audiences in the USA, the film was
retitled *Man of Evil* on 17 December 1947. As such, it was released by
United Artists – the third distributor to be involved – in February
1948, cut to 90 minutes.

First a Girl (1935)

A plot involving a woman disgusing herself as a man who is a female
impersonator on stage did not of itself present any problems for the

Production Code Administration. When Arthur Lee of the New York office of Gaumont British Pictures Corp. presented the film for approval, a number of deletions were requested by Vincent G. Hart on 3 December 1935: the sales girls shaking their posteriors; Jessie Matthews admiring an acrobat's rear end; the manager trying to undress Matthews in her dressing room; girls drinking; a nude girl in a bathtub; and French officers entering and leaving Matthews's dressing room, with the line 'He's a man'. Certificate No. 0793 was issued on 6 December 1935, and *First a Girl*, cut to 78 minutes, opened at the Four Star Theatre, Los Angeles, on 31 December 1935, and at the Roxy, New York, on 3 January 1936.

The First Gentleman (1948)

After viewing a revised version of the film on 9 February 1948, Stephen S. Jackson of the PCA held a series of conferences with Joseph Friedman of Columbia Pictures in March and April of that year. Dealing with the profligacy and immorality of the Prince Regent, *The First Gentleman* gave the PCA considerable concern, met in large part by the condemnation of his behaviour in the storyline by his daughter and his mother, and a powerful scene of denunciation by his wife. The characterization of the Bishop of Salisbury was approved only because of an assurance by Columbia that the stage play by Norman Ginsbury, from which the film was adapted, had run for a considerable time in London without adverse comment, and the production's passing without cuts by the British Board of Film Censors was tantamount to official acceptance of this portrayal. A final problem of over-exposure of women's breasts in costuming was overcome after Columbia agreed to work on the negative, darkening the breasts as much as possible. Certificate No. 13419 was issued on 23 September 1948. Cut to 95 minutes and retitled *The Affairs of a Rogue*, the film was released by Columbia in February 1949.

Five Days (1954)

This British 'B' production features a bankrupt businessman who blackmails a friend into murdering him, so that his wife can claim the insurance.

On 8 February 1954, Joseph I. Breen wrote to Lippert Pictures, Inc.

that the script had been read and the basic story met the requirements of the Production Code. There were minor problems. The script referred to 'Soho types', and while Breen was not entirely clear as to what was meant by this term, he asked it be made certain they were not in any way suggestive of homosexuals, specifically prohibited by the Code. Certificate No. 16940 was issued on 14 July 1954, subject to deletion of a scene of two homosexuals in the bar and a scene of the barmaid with her breasts unduly exposed. Cut by two minutes and retitled *Paid to Kill*, the film was released by Lippert in the summer of 1954.

The Flanagan Boy (1953)

In this drama a ruthless woman persuades her boxer lover to help murder her husband and then poisons the lover when he confesses to the murder.

On 31 January 1950, producer Peter Proud of Mask Films Limited submitted a shooting script for the film, scheduled to start filming on 14 March. On 9 February 1950, Breen replied that the story was unacceptable from the standpoint of the Production Code. The major difficulty was over a sympathetic lead, Johnny, who, as a murderer, deliberately thwarts justice by committing suicide; and his friend, Sharkey, who perverts justice by planting a poison envelope on Lorna, hence causing her arrest for murder. Breen noted that scenes of adultery were far too graphically presented, and went on to list thirty-six pages of script with problems, ranging from profanity to Lorna's stretching her bathing costume. Two years later, on 8 January 1952, the PCA staff held a meeting with Anthony Hinds (producer) and Richard Landau (screenwriter) from Lippert Pictures, Inc., and the same problems were discussed. A shooting script dated 30 July 1952 was submitted to the PCA, and, on 28 August Joseph I. Breen wrote that the basic story now seemed to meet the requirements of the Production Code. He listed important details in need of alteration, including a toilet gag, love-making lying down, avoidance of grue-someness in the drowning of Giuseppe, and non-presentation of the 'precious autograph hunter' as a 'sex pervert gag'. On 16 April 1953, Certificate No. 16250 was issued for the film, retitled *The Bad Blonde*, subject to deletion of all 'bumps' by the female dancer and later imitations of the same by men. As *Bad Blonde*, and with a running time identical to that in the UK, the film was released by Lippert Pictures, Inc., in April 1953. It was heavily censored in Ohio and Maryland.

Forbidden Cargo (1954)

Late in 1954, *Forbidden Cargo* was acquired for US distribution by Republic Pictures, Inc., which submitted it to the PCA. On 4 November 1954, Geoffrey M. Shurlock advised that the basic story dealing with illegal drug trafficking was in violation of the Production Code. Subsequently, he met with Republic to discuss the matter and the possibility of substituting another prop in lieu of drugs. Such a reworking was impractical, and Republic returned the rights to the Rank Organization. On 23 May 1955, Gordon Films, Inc. informed the PCA that it had acquired the US rights. The PCA again viewed the film and again confirmed that a Certificate could not be issued because of the subject matter. US theatrical rights were next acquired by Mack Weinberger, who threatened to consult his nephew, a counsel for the American Civil Liberties Union, with a view to bringing a suit against the PCA. Nothing came of Weinberger's posturing. Eventually, the film was approved by the New York censorship authority in April 1956, and on 3 May of the same year, without a Certificate, the film was released by Fine Arts Films, Inc.

The Four Feathers (1939)

Tentative Certificate No. 02357 was issued on 3 March 1939. The film was viewed by the PCA on 2 May 1939, and Vincent G. Hart noted two minor problems: a young soldier being branded on the forehead, and shots of vultures feeding off the body of a dead horse. The latter was possibly gruesome, and, as to the former, the Code required the branding of people or animals to be 'treated within the careful limits of good taste'. It was agreed that the branding here met that qualification, and United Artists promised to reduce to a minimum the vulture shots. The Certificate was confirmed on 3 May 1939 and, cut to 115 minutes, the film was released by United Artists, opening at the Capitol Theatre, New York, on 3 August 1939.

French without Tears (1939)

Terence Rattigan's play about a group of Englishmen studying French and their romantic adventures was acquired for the screen in 1937 by Paramount Pictures as a vehicle for Marlene Dietrich. It went into production in the UK without Dietrich early in 1939. On 17 May 1939, Joseph I. Breen confirmed that the basic story met the requirements of the Production Code, but called attention to sixteen pages of script with objectionable items, ranging from the characterization of Chi-Chi as a prostitute to the expression 'frog' ('offensive to the French'). Certificate No. 5510 was issued on November 30, 1939, with the understanding that a pat on a woman's posterior be deleted, together with the line, 'I don't suppose Chi-Chi could either.' *French without Tears* was released by Paramount Pictures, opening at the Rivoli Theatre, New York on 1 May 1940, cut to 67 minutes.

The Frog (1937)

This Edgar Wallace thriller concerns Scotland Yard's attempts to smash a notorious criminal gang.

At some point in 1937, Joseph I. Breen took an unofficial look at the film, and noted difficulty with certain costumes in the nightclub sequence, in which the girls were shown exposing their garters above the knee. It was not possible to cut all these shots without ruining both the continuity and the music score, and, on 14 January 1938, Breen advised that while there was a technical violation of the costume regulations, these shots were not 'terribly offensive' and they might be passed in this instance. Tentative Certificate No. 02146 was issued on 15 June 1938, and confirmed on 25 November 1938, subject to deletion of a shot of the bank robber shooting a teller and the first shot of the dancing chorus. Cut to 60 minutes, *The Frog* was set for release by Gaumont British Picture Corp. of America, but distribution was taken over by 20th Century-Fox in the autumn of 1939.

The Gang's all Here (1939)

A comedy thriller featuring Jack Buchanan and Googie Withers as a husband and wife team of detectives hunting down a gang of jewel thieves.

For a film titled *Amateur Gangster*, the PCA issued Certificate No.
03354 to Fine Arts Film & Studio Corp. on 31 March 1942, subject to
the following deletions: reference to 'Bromo Seltzer' as constituting an
advertising plug; Younce's calling the Chinese laundryman 'a rice-eating
shirt destroyer'; the reference by John Forrest to gangster Alberni, 'I
notice you use a Maxim silencer' (the showing of silencers on guns in
the hands of criminals was discouraged under the Code); much of the
scene with Younce and Alice in the closet with the latter in her négligée;
and the line by Alice in bed, 'I suppose it's my fault that we haven't
any children', and John's reply thereto. Eventually, cut to 69 minutes
and retitled *The Amazing Mr. Forrest*, the film was released by PRC, on
29 March 1944.

Gangway (1937)

Jessie Matthews is cast in this musical as a newspaper reporter on an
transatlantic ocean liner in pursuit of a gang of jewel thieves.

Tentative Certificate No. 01623 was issued on 14 May 1937. The
film was viewed by the PCA staff on 17 August 1937, at which time
it was asked that 400 feet of film involving gunplay between rival
gangs be removed. Initially, Gaumont British baulked, but then agreed
to the cuts. An appeal was threatened, but, in the end, the company
removed 191 feet of gunplay from reels 7 and 8, and 13 feet of the
Trocadero gunplay sequence in reel 9. On 25 August 1937, the PCA
advised Gaumont British that in view of the cuts and the fact that the
film was already being screened in New York, it was deemed that right
of appeal had been waived. Released by Gaumont British Picture Corp.
of America, *Gangway* opened at New York's Roxy Theatre on 20 August
1937. Based on the reported running time at that presentation, it would
appear the film played in New York without cuts.

Gay Love (1934)

This musical comedy starring impressionist Florence Desmond and
singer Sophie Tucker deals with a music hall actress who falls for her
sister's titled fiancé.

The film was viewed by the PCA staff on 6 April 1936, and on the
same day Vincent G. Hart wrote to Olympic Pictures Corp. to say that
thematically it was in conformity with the provisions of the Production

Code. He asked that all profanity be deleted, along with the opening shot of Lord Eaton lying horizontally over Marie Hopkins. He expressed concern over the first three songs by Sophie Tucker, the characterization of Mae West by Florence Desmond, and her line as Garbo: 'If Christina wasn't all a queen should be, don't blame it on me, blame it on the four-post bed.' In August 1936, Hart reviewed reels 1, 7 and 8, and noted compliance with the majority of his recommendations. He did ask for deletions from the lyrics of 'Embarrassment' and 'Hotcha Joe'. On 30 September 1936, a new distributor, Chelsea Pictures Corporation, advised that all deletions had been made, and Certificate No. 01273 was issued on 1 October. It was subsequently discovered that none of the cuts had been made and, after viewing the film on 30 November 1936, the PCA asked Chelsea not to exhibit any prints with a Certificate of Approval. All cuts asked for by the PCA were required by local censorship boards, and New York eliminated an entire song, 'Extraordinary Man'. The film's running time in the USA was 65 minutes.

Genevieve (1953)

On 27 August 1952, Joseph I. Breen wrote to Kenneth Bates in the New York office of the J. Arthur Rank Organization, Inc., to say that the script, dated 22 July 1952, had been read. The basic story about two couples on the London–Brighton vintage car rally was acceptable, but it contained a major problem in the obvious indication that it was Ambrose's habit to take girls with him each year to Brighton for the purposes of illicit sex affairs. Nineteen pages with problems were listed, including a dog-wetting gag, Wendy's line, 'Make love to me', Wendy's impatience to get to a toilet, and the line, 'We were supposed to be saving to have a child', which might be interpreted as an offensive reference to birth control. The film was viewed on 26 August 1953, and the following changes agreed upon:

> Reel 3-A: The dialogue between Wendy and Ambrose would be trimmed to change the characterization of the latter as a lecher, and Allen's line, 'Let's not pretend we don't know why', would be deleted. Reel 4-B: The return of Wendy to the car for a coin would be deleted as 'toilet humor', as would the sex suggestive dialogue between Rosalind and Wendy regarding their husbands' interest in old cars and the 'other thing'.

In September, Rank agreed to the changes, and Certificate No. 16715 was issued on 17 September 1953. With a running time basically the same as that in the UK, the film was released by Universal-International in February 1954.

Geordie (1955)

Former actor George K. Arthur and his company Go Pictures, Inc. purchased the US rights to *Geordie* (a comedy featuring the adventures and misadventures of a Scottish Olympic hammer-thrower in Australia) for $30,000. Initially, he imported only one print, and informally asked Gordon S. White in the New York office of the MPAA to take a look at the film and give his opinion as to its American potential. White viewed the film on 9 March 1956, and liked it and Arthur, whom he described as 'a nice little fellow'. Because only one print was available and Arthur was unhappy about shipping it to Los Angeles, the PCA agreed that White should handle the certification process in New York. Certificate No. 05928 – probably the last Certificate to come out of New York – was issued on 15 March 1956. Cut by five minutes and retitled *Wee Geordie*, the film opened at the Fine Arts Theatre, Los Angeles, 16 January 1957.

The Girl from Maxim's (1933)

This is Alexander Korda's film version of a Feydeau farce about the romantic entanglements of a respected doctor in Paris in 1904.

In September 1936, the PCA advised the American distributor, J. H. Hoffberg Co., Inc., that the film would need re-editing, particularly the lengthy scenes of the can-can. On 10 December 1936, Hoffberg advised the PCA that it would withdraw its application for a Certificate of Approval due to uncertainty as to the future of the film in the USA. Subsequently, it cut *The Girl from Maxim's* down to 58 minutes and opened it at New York's World Theatre, on 17 September 1936 to uniformly bad reviews. Hoffberg would revive the film every few years. In 1941, it tried a reissue, and the local censorship board in Ohio required substantial deletions in reels 3 and 4, including an entire song, 'The Morning after the Night Before'. On 10 September 1942, the film was reviewed by the National Legion of Decency and placed in the 'Condemned' category, designated as 'Immoral in theme and treatment. Vice is portrayed attractively; virtue ridiculed. No moral compensation.'

Give Us This Day (1949)

This grim drama features an unemployed bricklayer seeking to provide for his family during the Depression and ending up entombed in concrete when a job he takes goes wrong.

The script for this controversial film, in which 'blacklisted' talent was involved, was submitted to the PCA by attorney Edward Mosk, who advised that principal photography would commence on 1 April 1949. On 22 March 1949, Joseph I. Breen advised that the basic story seemed to meet the requirements of the Production Code. He called attention to problems on seventeen pages of script, including over-emphasis on the labour pains of Annunziata; Geremio pulling out his eyebrows in close-up; a derogatory reference to the President of the United States; and the suggestion of an adulterous relationship between Geremio and Stella. Producer Rod E. Geiger replied on 5 May 1949 that the changes basically had been made, and Certificate No. 13967 was issued on 12 July 1950.

Meanwhile in New York, the Title Registration Bureau refused approval of the film under the name of the novel on which it was based, *Christ in Concrete*. The producer argued that there was nothing irreverent in the title, but Breen disagreed. On 30 November 1949, he wrote to Margaret Ann Young at the Bureau that the title *Christ in Concrete* was offensive:

> The statement of the producer – to the effect that 'there is no irreverent use of the title as a parallel to the contents of the picture' is not, in our judgment, true. On the contrary, we feel that such a title has a very definite parallel to the story, or, at least, that part of it which shows the leading character being buried in concrete, on a Good Friday, at three o'clock in the afternoon. This motion picture, despite the fact that it is acceptable under the provisions of the Production Code, is likely to provoke serious public controversy because of the nature of the story – and be-cause, too, of the reputation of some of those who are concerned with its production. It is an attack – or an exposé – of our present social conditions in this country, in which the emphasis is pretty much placed on the *wrongs* of our system.

Breen and the Bureau prevailed, and the film was released as *Give Us This Day* by Eagle-Lion Films, Inc., in January 1950. With a running time identical to that in the UK, the film opened at New York's Rialto Theatre on 20 December 1949. The local censorship board in Maryland required shortening of the scene of Geremio being buried alive.

The Glass Mountain (1949)

In this film a composer torn between his wife and his love for an Italian partisan girl who saved him during the war.

The Glass Mountain was viewed by the PCA staff on 10 December 1949 and found unacceptable because of an adulterous relationship treated without adequate compensating moral values. On 18 January 1950, Joseph I. Breen wrote to Eagle-Lion Films, Inc., suggesting two cuts which would eliminate the element of 'glorification and justification' of the adulterous affair: the scene on the mountain top between Richard and Alida, and the scene after the opera, where Richard learns of his wife's accident. James G. Minter at Renown Pictures Corporation Limited replied on 8 February 1950, with surprise and deep hurt at Breen's assertion that the film glorified adultery, and asked for reconsideration. A similar letter came from Renown's US representative, Richard Gordon, to whom Breen wrote on 23 February 1950 that what Renown had to say had little bearing on the problem at hand. However, after consideration and reviewing of the film, Breen eventually agreed that no adulterous relationship was actually depicted and was, in fact, rejected by Richard. On 11 April 1950, Certificate No. 14534 was issued. Cut to 90 minutes, the film was released by Eagle-Lion in November 1950.

Gone to Earth (1950)

On 14 June 1939, Joseph I. Breen wrote to David O. Selznick saying that the script had been read and the basic story met the provisions of the Production Code. It was the story of a gypsy girl torn between the love of a kindly clergyman and the desire of a cruel squire. He asked that there be no profanity, that Hazel should be wearing at least a slip while undressing, and that Edward's lines in regard to the fact that someone else had taken his wife's virginity should be softened. On 23 June 1949, a revised script was read, and it was noted that an

unacceptable element, in the form of a rape scene, had been introduced. A new script was read on 8 September 1949, and a number of
issues were brought up: there should be no intimate exposure of Hazel's
body when her dress is torn; no open-mouth kissing; the action at
Hunter's Spinney where Hazel meets Reddin was unacceptable and
both must be upright and not lying on the ground; and the symbolism
of the flowers falling from Hazel's hand and the second scene of
them bruised and trampled was unacceptable. When the film was
viewed on 2 October 1950, it was discovered that the moral values
found in the script were missing, Jennifer Jones's breasts were exposed
in a long scene in which she wore a low-cut red gown, and two scenes
of her making love to Reddin were unacceptable details of adultery.
The film's rejection was reported to David O. Selznick on 12 October
1950, and, seven days later, to London Film Productions.

On 22 November 1950, Geoffrey M. Shurlock met with David
O. Selznick. The producer read two additional scenes that he planned
to shoot in Hollywood, adding a voice for morality. He had cut 'bad
breast shots' and wrestling on the bed, and would 'double-expose' a
piece of furniture over the shot of rumpled bedclothes. Certificate
No. 15053 was issued on 20 December 1951. Cut to 82 minutes and
retitled *The Wild Heart*, the film was released by RKO in July 1952.

The Good Companions (1933)

As a Fox release, *The Good Companions* was viewed by the PCA staff on
1 July 1933, at which time various expressions of profanity were noted.
In September 1933, Vincent G. Hart discussed the problem with Fox,
and was told it would be impossible to make the cuts as they would
ruin the film, and, further, there were sixty-five prints in distribution,
each of which would need individually to be corrected. After discussion
with Will Hays, it was decided not to pursue the matter even though
it might be difficult to justify an inconsistent position. On the film's
reissue by Fox, Certificate No. 1650-R was issued on 15 October 1935.

Good Time Girl (1948)

Good Time Girl was described by the PCA as the story of a fifteen-
year-old girl who engages in one adulterous and two illicit sex affairs.
On 19 March 1947, Joseph I. Breen wrote to A. Reginald Allen at the

Universal studios office of the J. Arthur Rank Organization, Inc., to say that an incomplete script had been read, and that the material presented innumerable problems that precluded the possibility of developing a film that could be approved. In particular, Breen noted elements of sexual perversion, prostitution, perjury, excessive drinking, drunkenness and brutality. A 'radically different' version of the script was submitted, but it was similarly rejected on 21 November 1947. Breen viewed the film itself on 6 July 1948, and the next day wrote to Allen confirming its unacceptability.

On 10 November 1949, Jock Lawrence in Rank's New York office wrote privately to Breen that the film had been purchased by Edward Kingsley of Oxford Films and would be released by Eagle-Lion without a Certificate. Subsequently, it was acquired by Oliver Ungar of Distinguished Films, Inc. The film was reviewed on 7 December 1949, and Ungar advised that, with judicious cutting of 1,000 feet, it could be brought into conformity with the Production Code. This was done, but the title was rejected by the Title Registration Bureau, and Breen refused to issue a Certificate. After much arguing, the Bureau finally registered *Good Time Girl* on 17 January 1950, 'with much reluctance', and Certificate No. 14336 was issued on 2 February 1950. Cut to 81 minutes, *Good Time Girl* was released by Film Classics, Inc., on 11 May 1950. It was the subject of heavy censorship in Pennsylvania. At one point, the film was to have been retitled *Good Time Gal*, but this does not appear to have happened.

Green for Danger (1946)

On 19 March 1946, Joseph I. Breen wrote to A. Reginald Allen at the Beverly Hills office of the J. Arthur Rank Organization, Inc., that a script had been read. From the standpoint of the Production Code, it contained one unacceptable element in that the murderess, Esther, escaped justice by committing suicide. If such a plot device was to be retained, it would be necessary to characterize the woman as insane. Certificate No. 12129 was issued on 7 May 1947, and the film released, uncut, by Eagle-Lion Films, Inc., in July 1947. The company's advertising featured a hypodermic needle, and the MPAA expressed concern that this might suggest the story was concerned with drugs. The issue was resolved with the addition of the words, 'Weapon or Clue?'

The Heart of the Matter (1953)

Graham Greene's novel first came to the attention of the PCA when producer David O. Selznick asked for a report on its screen potential on 20 August 1948. Jack A. Vizzard read the book and felt that the major problems were the relationship between Scobie and his mistress, the visit to a Negro whorehouse by Wilson, and the climactic suicide of Scobie. On 28 August 1948, Vizzard had an angry telephone conversation with Selznick, in which the latter dismissed the Production Code as responsible for the downfall of the American film. He followed up the call with a letter to Joseph I. Breen, attacking Vizzard as 'impertinent'. Breen supported his staff, dismissed Selznick's complaints and, on 31 August 1948, refused to release a copy of the PCA report on the novel to him. The next year, on 15 January 1949, Milton Sperling at United States Pictures, Inc., submitted a synopsis for consideration, and followed it up with a meeting between him, the PCA staff and director Raoul Walsh.

Nothing came of American interest in a screen adaptation, and, as Selznick had predicted, the film was picked up for British production. On 26 February 1952, Zoltan Korda submitted a script, and on 5 March, Breen reported that a film could be made from the novel if Scobie was made the object of pity for his suicide. He listed thirty-three pages of script with problems, including profanity, use of the word 'nigger', and Yusef's being a drug addict. On 20 November 1952, he wrote to London Film Productions, Inc., that the basic story in the shooting script was acceptable under the provisions of the Production Code, but there were still many problems. Tentative Certificate No. 16413 was issued on 2 March 1953 but it was never confirmed. Cut by five minutes, the film was released by Associated Artists, Inc., on 18 November 1954; it opened in Los Angeles, at the El Rey Theatre on 20 May 1955.

Henry V (1944)

Certificate No. 10900 was issued on 5 June 1945, on the understanding that several uses of the word 'bastard' be deleted from all prints. Reports in the British trade press indicate that Laurence Olivier chose to dub in 'dastard' for 'bastard' throughout the film in order to comply with the PCA's demand. Cut to 133 minutes, the film was released by

United Artists, opening at the City Center Theatre, New York, on 17 June 1946.

Hey! Hey! USA (1938)

The comedic style of Will Hay was never particularly popular with the PCA. On 11 November 1938, F. S. Harmon informed Arthur A. Lee of the Gaumont British Picture Corp. of America that a Code Seal could not be issued for *Hey! Hey! USA*. Harmon pointed out that the film dealt with the kidnapping of a child for ransom, a sensitive issue in the United States. PCA's Vincent Hart and Gaumont British's C. E. Schwengeler studied the possibility of re-editing the film, changing the theme from kidnapping to a gangster feud. The boy, the son of a wealthy businessman, would agree to go along with the gang in order to identify the phony professor, and an extortion note would be substituted for the ransom note. The re-editing would necessitate the shooting of a number of newspaper inserts and considerable changes in the dialogue and action, and, as Harmon wrote to Lee, 'Whether or not the necessary changes can be made at this stage is primarily for you and your colleagues to determine.' Apparently, Gaumont British did go along with the proposed re-editing of the film, and Certificate No. 02147 was issued on 20 February 1939, subject to the deletion of a scene showing the boy smoking a cigarette and a shot of a man with a machine gun.

It would seem that *Hey! Hey! USA* was to be released in America under the title of *Chicago Ben* (Hay plays a character called Benjamin Twist), but Gaumont British ceased its US operations around this time. 20th Century-Fox was to take over distribution of the Gaumont British releases, but neither *Hey! Hey! USA* nor *Chicago Ben* are titles on the studio's release schedules.

High Treason (1951)

On 31 January 1951, Joseph I. Breen wrote to Kenneth Bates at the New York office of the J. Arthur Rank Organization, Inc., saying that a script titled *I Spy Strangers* had been read and the basic story met the requirements of the Production Code. It featured the success of Scotland Yard in foiling a gang of communist saboteurs. He asked that the US version omit all showing of machine guns in the hands of saboteurs, a cosh, and a revolver fitted with a silencer; and in the final gun battle that no scenes show police officers dying at the hands of criminals. Producer Paul Soskin argued that the characters in the film were not gangsters or criminals, but revolutionaries and fanatics, and surely that nullified the PCA's required cuts. Surprisingly, on 10 April 1951, Breen agreed, asking only that the slaughter of the police officers be kept to a minimum. Certificate No. 15268 was issued in April 1951 for the film now titled *Secret Plan X23*. Later that month, the title was changed to *Sabotage*. In May, it was changed to *High Treason* and, under that title, Pacemaker Pictures, Inc., released the film in June 1952, cut by three minutes.

The History of Mr Polly (1949)

H. G. Wells's story about a henpecked shopkeeper who flees to the countryside in search of a new life.

On 17 May 1948, Stephen S. Jackson wrote to A. Reginald Allen at the Universal studios office of the J. Arthur Rank Organization, Inc., to inform him that the script, dated 17 April 1948, had been read, and the basic story met the requirements of the Production Code. He noted two unacceptable sequences, the most serious being the setting of a house on fire using kerosene, and the other a burlesqued marriage ceremony. Jackson found problems on fourteen other script pages, including a nude dummy, a cry of fire, belches, profanity and the suggestion that Polly and the mistress of the inn were living together at the film's conclusion. The film was viewed on 10 October 1949, and issuance of a Certificate delayed because the cry of 'fire' remained in the print. The cutter was unable to remove it, and the producer was asked to re-record dialogue in the scenes involved. In May 1950, the PCA pointed out that the film was being screened by Eagle-Lion with the cry of 'fire' therein. The problem remained as of January 1951, and no Certificate was issued. After the initial Eagle-Lion screenings, the film was released, uncut, by International Film Corp. and opened at the Art Theatre, New York, on 24 October 1951.

The House of the Arrow (1940)

A. E. W. Mason's classic detective story in which Inspector Hanaud investigates the murder of a French widow.

The House of the Arrow was first submitted for PCA approval in March 1932 by Fine Arts Film and Studio Corporation. It was resubmitted, under the title of Castle of Crimes, in May 1944 by PRC Productions, Inc. It was viewed on 22 May and, the following day, Carl E. Milliken wrote to PRC's Sam Kastenbaum, noting the film's basic unacceptability in that the central character, Betty Harlowe (Diana Churchill), who has killed three individuals, commits suicide prior to police capture, thus escaping punishment. He suggested the scene be cut to give the impression that she is arrested; he also required deletion of the close-up of a hypodermic needle. This was done, and, on 20 November 1944, the PCA viewed a new version of the last reel, and assigned tentative Certificate No. 03909 to the film. The Certificate was confirmed on 21 November. Cut to 58 minutes, Castle of Crimes opened at the New York Theatre, New York, on 28 March 1945. Milliken had warned that local censorship boards might delete direct mention of the poison used in the killings (curare), and, sure enough, this happened in Ohio.

The House on the Square (1951)

This remake of Berkeley Square (1933) features an American in present-day London transported back to the eighteenth century and there finding romance.

On 6 November 1950, Joseph I. Breen wrote to Jason S. Joy at 20th Century-Fox saying that the script, Beyond Time and Space, had been read, and that the basic story met the provisions of the Production Code. He listed fifteen pages of script with problems, including a belch, the fight between Mendoza and Jackson being too brutal and Tom's fondling of the maid, and expressed concern that there be no exploitation of the pitiful state of the lunatics. He also suggested that the exorcism sequence be checked with a competent technical adviser; as a result, the studio consulted Monsignor Devlin, who found nothing objectionable. Certificate No. 15114 was issued on 4 June 1951, and, as I'll Never Forget You, the film was released, uncut, by 20th Century-Fox in December 1951.

The Housemaster (1938)

This comedy drama centres on the bid of a public school headmaster to dismiss a much-loved housemaster.

On 29 November 1937, Francis S. Harmon wrote to Budd Rogers at Alliance Films Corporation that the script, dated 1 November 1937, had been read, and that the material was in basic conformity with the Production Code. In the PCA's opinion, the references to liquor and the showing of liquor must be materially reduced, limiting it to the necessities of the plot and of proper characterization. He went on to list seventeen pages with problems, including profanity, drinking, suggestive female attire and the line 'I doped her', and stressed the importance of not showing how the students in the chemical lab made 'ill-smelling gases', for fear that children in the audience might be tempted to imitate them. Tentative Certificate No. 02521 was issued on 24 April 1939, and confirmed on 20 July. Released by Alliance, by that time the film had already opened – on 9 April 1939 – at New York's Little Carnegie Theatre.

Hungry Hill (1947)

A Daphne du Maurier story detailing fifty years of a feud between two families in nineteenth-century Ireland.

On 10 October 1945, Joseph I. Breen wrote to William Burnside at Eagle-Lion Films, Inc., that the script, dated 30 August 1945, had been read, and that it contained various sequences which could not be approved under the Production Code: Fanny Rosa swimming in the nude; an illicit sex affair between Johnny and Fanny Rosa; Johnny picking up a prostitute; and Johnny seducing Kate. In response, producer F. Del Giudice sent a second draft script on 1 December 1945, which took into account all the issues raised. On 20 December, Breen agreed that the script was now basically acceptable under the provisions of the Production Code, but still found minor faults. In particular, he stressed that there should be no visual suggestion that Fanny Rosa was swimming in the nude, and that the seduction of Katy was OK provided changes in the dialogue were made to strengthen moral values. On 25 March 1946, Breen wrote to A. Reginald Allen at the Universal studios office of the J. Arthur Rank Organization, Inc., that a revised script, dated 14 February 1946, had been read, and he was happy to note the changes and improvements. There were still minor problems, in particular the lack of a definite condemnation of Johnny's seduction of Kate. Eventually, on 28 January 1947, Certificate No. 12159 was issued. Cut to 92 minutes, *Hungry Hill* was released by Prestige Pictures (a subsidiary of Universal-International), and opened at the Esquire Theatre, Los Angeles, on 28 May 1948.

I Am a Camera (1955)

I Am a Camera opened in the United Kingdom with an 'X' certificate and in the United States without the Production Code Seal of approval, despite the often heavy-handed efforts of the film's American distributor to persuade the PCA to change its mind. The film is based on John Van Druten's play, which is, in turn, based on Christopher Isherwood's *Berlin Stories*, and as early as May 1953 a copy of the play was submitted to Joseph Breen. Noting 'very definite Code violations', Breen suggested revisions and these were forwarded to John Van Druten who was at the time living in Palm Springs. The playwright was not sympathetic to the suggested changes. He had commented to Cecil Smith in the *Los Angeles Times* (3 April 1955): 'The movies you know have always purified my characters until I could hardly recognize them. They tell me they haven't done that with *Camera*. Sally Bowles is a bad girl in the play and she's a bad girl in the movies.'

In the United States, the film was to be the first release of a new company, Distributors Corporation of America, formed by a group of exhibitors to encourage a greater output of product than the existing production companies could provide. The president of the new company, Fred J. Schwartz, was obviously worried about his initial presentation, and he tried, unsuccessfully, to schedule a hearing before the Motion Picture Association of America in August 1955 in order to explain why *I Am a Camera* was entitled to a Code Seal, disputing a letter of 25 July 1955 from Geoffrey M. Shurlock which stated 'the film deals with gross sexual promiscuity on the part of the leading lady, without the proper compensating moral values required by the Code'.

Without a Code Seal, *I Am a Camera* previewed at the Egyptian Theatre in Hollywood on 21 July 1955, and subsequently opened in Cleveland, Cincinnati and New York. On 1 September it was passed, without cuts, by the censorship boards in Chicago and Detroit.

On 25 August 1955, the production was condemned by the National Legion of Decency: 'This film in basic story, characterization, dialogue and costuming offends Christian and traditional standards of morality and decency and must, therefore, be judged as wholly unsuitable on moral grounds for all persons, youth and adult.' Catholic priests urged their congregations to boycott the film, and, after one such attack in the Queens borough of New York by the Reverend John S. Boyland of St Joan of Arc Church, *I Am a Camera* was pulled in January 1956 by the management of the Earle Theatre in Jackson Heights, Queens. In response to Boyland's denunciation of the film for 'corrupting the morals of the community', Fred J. Schwartz commented: 'Depicting a Godless society [pre-Hitler Berlin] cannot adversely affect the morals of our society.' (Presumably by Schwartz's definition, Hitler's Berlin was a godly community.)

The lack of a Code Seal denied *I Am a Camera* access to many theatres, and Schwartz regarded the PCA's action as little more than 'economic censorship'. In November 1955, he hired counsel Morris Ernst, arranged a screening at the Museum of Modern Art for community leaders, and had International Research Associates, Inc., prepare a questionnaire testing audience reaction to the film in comparison with other features approved by the PCA. Schwartz wanted desperately to make this a test case against the Code, but the problem was a lack of favourable critical reaction to *I Am a Camera*. Writing in the *New York Times* (14 August 1955), Bosley Crowther felt the film a problem for screen moralists. '*The Moon Is Blue* was defensible on moral grounds while *I Am a Camera* is not,' wrote Crowther. He criticized the producers for dropping the 'implications and significance' of the film's Berlin setting and for turning the story into 'a slapsticky bedroom farce'.

It was the abortion sequence that was the major stumbling block. 'It is hard to see how such material logically can be approved under the existing rules and intent of the Code,' wrote Bosley Crowther. On 20 February 1956, Fred J. Schwartz wrote to Geoffrey M. Shurlock agreeing to a prologue or epilogue in which 'a specific voice for morality' (Laurence Harvey) would be heard, condemning the heroine's promiscuity, but there would be no changes in regard to the abortion. Changes to the Code in December 1956 persuaded Schwartz again to approach Shurlock. The amended Code stated:

> The subject of abortion shall be discouraged, shall never be more than suggested, and when referred to shall be condemned. It must never be treated lightly or made the subject of comedy. Abortion shall never be shown explicitly or by inference, and a story must

not indicate that an abortion has been performed. The word 'abortion' shall not be used.

Shurlock responded to Shwartz on 31 December 1956: '*I Am a Camera* fails to meet all the above requirements. The subject is treated lightly and it is not condemned.'

It was very obvious that Schwartz and Distributors Corporation of America were fighting a battle that could not be won. No further entreaties were made to the PCA, and the distributor had to be content with a gross of $500,000 in the film's first six months of release rather than the estimated one million dollars it would have grossed with the Code Seal of approval.

I Give My Heart (1935)

I Give My Heart was viewed by the PCA on 7 April 1938, and the following day Francis S. Harmon wrote to J. H. Hoffberg Co., Inc., to say that the film did not conform to the provisions of the Production Code in that the illicit sexual relationship of Madame DuBarry was presented attractively and without sufficient compensating moral values. On 18 April, Harmon again wrote to Hoffberg that the difficulty with the film was a thematic one, and it would be hard to suggest cuts that might be made. As a result, the film was released uncut, without a Certificate, as *Loves of Mme DuBarry*, opening at the Squire Theatre, New York, on 1 April 1938. The state censorship board in New York did, however, require deletion of certain lines.

In Which We Serve (1942)

In Which We Serve proved to be one of the most controversial British films in the history of the Production Code. At first there was little to indicate any potential problem. The film – Noël Coward's story about the crew of HMS *Torrin* – was submitted for screening by United Artists on 15 October 1942, and the following day Carl E. Milliken wrote that it was basically in conformity with the Production Code. However, it would be necessary to delete expressions of profanity, such as 'hell' and 'God' and the descriptive words 'bastard' and 'lousy' from reels 3 to 12 inclusive. Tentative Certificate No. 03537 was issued on 27 November 1942.

That same month, United Artists, presumably at the urging of Noël Coward, appealed the cuts to the Board of Directors of the MPPDA, arguing that: 'To even suggest elimination is to suggest mutilation of a great patriotic document.' The use of the words 'lousy' and 'bastard' were legitimate in describing the enemy, and both had been used in speeches by New York Mayor Fiorello LaGuardia, reported in the 26 October and 23 November 1942 issues of the *New York Times*. What was profane in the use of 'hell' asked United Artists, when it accurately described what was happening to the innocents of Europe? 'For God's sake' was almost a prayer, and when a soldier wondered where his lost brother was, commenting, 'God knows where he is now', who else but God would know?

The Production Code Administration responded: 'The function of the Production Code is not to be patriotic, it is to be moral.' It stated: 'Surely the truest patriotism, the truest honesty, the truest dignity and the truest and most effective authenticity, are those elements on the screen which express themselves without indulging profanity and vulgarity.' It asked could the Sermon on the Mount have been strengthened if Christ called everybody 'a son-of-a-bitch'.

The MPPDA Board of Directors declined to approve the film without cuts, but did agree to allow the following lines to remain:

- For God's sake
- God knows where he is now
- all hell breaking loose
- the doctor hasn't ordered a damned thing

Ten expressions of profanity were to be deleted, and this decision was reported to United Artists on 1 December 1942. Three days later, the corporation replied that the ruling included four new deletions of profanity that had not previously been noted. It would make the other cuts but not these. On 9 December, Breen wrote that he would allow a Certificate to be issued without the corporation's making the four new deletions, agreeing that it was best 'to get this behind us'. Certificate No. 03537 was issued on 16 December. Released by United Artists, *In Which We Serve* opened at the Capitol Theatre, New York, on 23 December 1942. Because the film was not cut, but rather the offending words were 'blooped' on the soundtrack, the running time was identical to that in the UK. Further, any lip-readers in the audience could identify the words spoken but not heard.

The battle between United Artists and the PCA was widely covered in the press. An editorial in the 12 December 1942 issue of the *New York Herald Tribune* attacked the PCA, asking: 'Just what sort of people we have become, conducting a struggle in which our warriors cry "Shucks" and "Fiddlesticks"?' In the House of Commons, Information Minister Brendan Bracken described the Hays Office as 'old maiden aunt-like', although he declined to identify specifically the offensive words to his fellow MPs. Gossip columnist Hedda Hopper in her 10 December 1932 column attacked Bracken and applauded the Hays Office and 'Slugger Breen'. Similarly, the National Legion of Decency endored the PCA.

The PCA heard from many ordinary American soldiers. In an ironically censored letter dated 12 December 1942, Lieutenant O. D. Edwards with Company K 175th Infantry wrote to Breen that 'among men we curse and swear at Japs and Nazis. But not in front of children and women.' In a letter dated 11 January 1943, and widely circulated among the staff, Lieutenant Robert W. Nicholson wanted to know, 'What do *you* call the bastards?'

Island in the Sun (1957)

On 13 May 1955, Geoffrey M. Shurlock wrote to Columbia Pictures to say that the synopsis of the novel *The Sugar Barons*, featuring a series of interracial love affairs on a Caribbean island, had been read. It was in violation of the Production Code in that Maxwell takes his own life indirectly by causing the mob to kill him. There was also the issue of whether the novel constituted an unfair portrayal of the Negro race and whether it could unreasonably inflame the Negro people. On 18 June 1956, Shurlock had a meeting with Frank McCarthy of 20th Century-Fox. It was agreed that Jocelyn's affair with Euan would be treated with compensating moral values, and the affair between Mavis and Archer would not be portrayed as a sex affair. In support of the script, 20th Century-Fox submitted a letter from Truman Gibson, a Negro attorney and special assistant on Negro affairs during the Second World War. Certificate No. 18381 was issued on 3 June 1957. With a running time of 123 minutes, the film was released by 20th Century-Fox in June 1957.

It Always Rains on Sundays (1947)

Ealing Studios's East End drama followed the fortunes of a variety of characters over a weekend. A central theme is the escape of Tommy Swann from prison and his hiding out with a now married former girlfriend whose love is rekindled.

On 9 December 1946, Joseph I. Breen wrote to A. Reginald Allen at the Universal studios office of the J. Arthur Rank Organization, Inc., informing him that the script, dated 22 November 1946, had been read and in its present form was a violation of the requirements of the Production Code, as a story of adultery without proper compensating moral values. It would be necessary to remove the scene of adultery between Rose and Tommy and the suggestion of an adulterous relationship between Violet and Morry. Breen noted twenty-seven pages with problems, including Dicey picking his nose throughout, Vi standing in her underwear, George taking a bath, the emphasis on Vi wiggling her hips, the suggestion that Tommy strips in front of Rose, and Tommy kicking Collins in the stomach. An undated letter from producer Michael Balcon to Allen indicates he had altered the construction of the film to avoid suggestions of adultery, had acted upon all Breen's points, and sought an OK for Tommy to strip to the waist. On 15 February 1947, Breen wrote to Allen that the shooting script, dated 23 January 1947, had been read and the changes took care of various difficulties. There were still ten pages of script with problems; he asked assurance that 'camiknickers' were the same as a slip, deletion of the words 'tarting' and 'fanny' and was still worried about George's bath and Tommy's stripping. Certificate No. 12176 was issued on 20 June 1939, but Breen noted the following month that the final film had never actually been viewed by the PCA. Cut to 88 minutes, the film was in fact on release from Eagle-Lion Films, Inc., in March 1949. Local censorship boards in Ohio and Pennsylvania required elimination of the view of Rose preparing to commit suicide. Tommy's stripping was still giving problems in Massachuetts, where he was not permitted to be seen taking off his trousers.

Jamaica Inn (1939)

Pre-production activity in connection with *Jamaica Inn* was a model of cooperation between the PCA, represented by Francis S. Harmon, and the film's producers, Charles Laughton and Erich Pommer. In August 1938, Harmon read the novel by Daphne du Maurier, an historical drama about a gang of smugglers in eighteenth-century Cornwall, and noted the 'sordid character' of the story and delineated the various problems, which included one of the central characters, Francis Davey, being both a minister and the villain of the piece; a horse thief escaping trial; the female lead lying to a magistrate; the stripping and subsequent nudity of the 'idiot'; and substantial profanity. At the same time, Harmon also met in New York with Pommer and, on 18 October 1938, the latter confirmed that the clergyman lead had now become a country squire.

The first shooting script, dated 2 November 1938, was read by Harmon, and on 22 December he reported thirty-three pages with problems, including excessive gruesomeness, the gang's being shown in various stages of undress with one completely nude, the 'pansy' characterization of Dandy, the amount of drinking, the attempted hanging of Jem, the attempted rape of Mary, and profanity throughout. The squire's ultimate suicide was a difficulty in that the Code forbade suicide as a solution to problems occurring in the development of the screen drama. A second shooting script was submitted on 27 December and, four days later, Harmon noted with satisfaction that a number of items listed in his earlier letter had been satisfactorily handled. There were still problems relating to violence, drinking and, primarily, profanity in some twenty scenes.

Tentative Certificate No. 02483 was issued on 30 March 1939, and confirmed 24 May 1939, after the PCA staff had viewed the finished film. Cut by ten minutes and released by Paramount, *Jamaica Inn* opened at the Rivoli Theatre, New York, on 11 October 1939. The local censorship board in Chicago required deletion of the scene showing a man's legs dangling while hanging.

Juggernaut (1937)

Boris Karloff stars as a doctor who poisons a patient in order to gain money to finance his medical researches and commits suicide when exposed.

A print was viewed by the PCA staff on 19 February 1937, and that same day, Vincent G. Hart informed R. M. Savini at Astor Pictures, Inc., that the film did not meet the standards of the Production Code in that it was filled with conspiracy, crime, murder and loose living, without compensating moral values or evidence of punishment at the hands of the law. After a number of conferences, 723 feet were cut, eliminating details of the murder committed by the central character of the doctor and his suicide. On 15 March 1937, Certificate No. 01542 was issued. At that same time, Astor announced that Grand National Pictures, Inc., would take over distribution of the film. Cut to 64 minutes, *Juggernaut* opened at New York's Globe Theatre, on 14 July 1937. According to Denis Gifford, the film was released in the USA as *The Demon Doctor*, but this was probably a reissue title.

Jump for Glory (1937)

This romantic drama stars Douglas Fairbanks Jr as a cat burglar who falls in love with one of his victims, who is later accused of murdering her husband.

The film was viewed on 23 March 1937, and in its present form did not meet the standards of the Production Code. Various crimes by the lead were portrayed without punishment, a 'fence' was portrayed as a sympathetic character, the heroine commits perjury and goes unpunished, and a clergyman is depicted as a comic character. United Artists re-edited the film and included a statement to the effect that the male lead served time in prison for his crimes. Certificate No. 0142 was issued on 4 May 1937. Cut to 85 minutes and retitled *When Thief Meets Thief*, the film was released by United Artists, and opened at the Rialto Theatre, New York, on 14 June 1937.

Jungle Book (1942)

A final shooting script, dated 24 June 1941, was submitted by George L. Bagnall of Alexander Korda Films, Inc. The following day, the PCA responded that it contained one element unacceptable from the standpoint of the Code, and that was the suggestion that Mowgli was naked in the early scenes. If a baby was to be pictured nude, his sexual organs could not be seen, and later, the child was to wear a loincloth. Further, the PCA asked that scenes of Mowgli's fight with a tiger and a panther should avoid any suggestion of cruelty to animals. In September 1941, Korda asked the PCA's opinion as to the depiction of a female wolf nursing Mowgli, and he was strongly urged to dismiss any such notion. Certificate No. 7518 was issued on 26 February 1942, and, released by United Artists, *Jungle Book* opened at New York's Rivoli Theatre, on 4 April 1942.

The Key (1958)

The project was first submitted to the PCA on 9 September 1952 by Warner Bros in the form of a synopsis for the first half of Jan de Hartog's novel *The Distant Shore* (published in the UK as *Stella*). This sombre drama is set in England during the Second World War. The key of the title is the key to Stella's apartment, handed from one tugboat captain to another as each man senses his impending death in action. A conference took place on 18 September 1952, at which time it was confirmed that the novel was unacceptable as a story of illicit sex with no compensating moral values, and because of the character of the principal, Stella.

On 18 September 1957, Geoffrey M. Shurlock wrote to Carl Fore-man that the script dated 27 August 1957 had been read and, as a story of sexual promiscuity bordering on prostitution, was unacceptable. Jack Vizzard was in Europe at the time, and he met with Foreman in October 1957, suggesting two alternate stories, one of a girl living in a highly unconventional situation with men because of the war, but not involved sexually with them; the other a clearcut story of sin and retribution, in which the leading character would lose her man at the film's close. The latter was chosen. Certificate No. 18876 was issued on 10 June 1958. Cut to 125 minutes, the film was released by Columbia Pictures in July 1958.

The Kidnappers (1953)

This is the story of two orphan boys in Canada who, when denied a pet dog, kidnap and care for a baby.

On 19 June 1953, Joseph I. Breen wrote to Julius J. Staub in the New York office of the J. Arthur Rank Organization, Inc., to say that the script dated 22 May 1953 for *Scotch Settlement* (previously titled *The Sinners*) had been read, and met the requirements of the Production Code. He asked only that there be no unacceptable exposure of Danny when he is given a bath. However, when Rank retitled the film *The Kidnappers*, the Title Registration Bureau of the MPAA rejected its use on 20 October 1953. Since the kidnapping of the Lindbergh baby in 1932 no title containing the word 'kidnapping' or its variations had been permitted. The one exception was the screen adaptation of Robert Louis Stevenson's classic, and here the title had to include the author's name. The recent kidnapping of Bobby Greenlease further confirmed the rightness of the Bureau's attitude. Rank argued that the film's story did not relate to adult kidnappers and asked for an exception to be made. As a result, on 16 June 1954, the title *The Little Kidnappers* was registered. Certificate No. 17107 was issued on 29 June 1954 and confirmed 7 July. Cut to 93, minutes, the film was released as *The Little Kidnappers* by United Artists in September 1954.

Kind Hearts and Coronets (1949)

A production that treated murder with humour was obviously one that would present problems for the PCA, despite its approval in 1944 of a film with a similar theme, *Arsenic and Old Lace*. The first written material on *Kind Hearts and Coronets* to be submitted to the PCA was a third treatment, dispatched on 14 April 1948 by Alfred Reginald Allen from his Universal studios office of the J. Arthur Rank Organization, Inc. In reply, on 20 April, Stephen S. Jackson wrote:

> We assume that the 'tongue-in-cheek' treatment accorded the story is intended to obviate any flavor of condoning or sympathizing with the lead's crimes and that the finished picture is meant as a sort of high-class spoofing of murder among the nobility. If this flavor comes through, we believe that it can possibly make up for the fact that there is no direct voice for morality, or condemnation of your lead's actions. It will be absolutely essential, however, that there be nothing objectionable about the finished picture, from this standpoint, otherwise it could not be approved.

Jackson noted an 'unacceptable emphasis on illicit sex and adultery,' and that the character of the Reverend Henry Gascoyne (*sic*) was in violation of the Code: 'Ministers of religion in their character as ministers of religion should not be used as comic characters or villains.'

A script dated 28 May 1948 was submitted to Jackson and on 15 June he replied: 'Frankly, this is such a peculiar story, that we will not be able to give a proper opinion on it until we see the finished picture.' He listed three pages of problems relating to the relationship between

Louis (Dennis Price) and Sibella (Joan Greenwood), together with concerns as to the use of the word 'damn', the characterization of the Reverend Henry, the length of the sequence involving the muder of Ethelred, and the failure to establish clearly that Louis was to be hanged. A final draft script, dated 13 August 1948, invoked a response on 10 September from Joseph I. Breen that most of the elements mentioned in previous letters as being in violation of the Code remained.

On 8 September 1948, screenwriter John Dighton submitted four pages of revision to A. Reginald Allen. They related primarily to the Louis–Sibella relationship. Dighton also noted, 'To establish quite clearly that Louis' memoirs, left in the condemned cell, are going to be his retribution we propose to show an additional piece of action at the end of scene J.20 in which, as Louis leaves the cell, the camera will track in on the table to a close-up of the memoirs, which he has left lying there.' On 15 September Breen expressed his general satisfaction with the changes but noted that the PCA would still need to approve the finished film.

Breen and his staff viewed *Kind Hearts and Coronets* on 17 November 1949 and, the following day, he wrote to Jock Lawrence at the New York office of the J. Arthur Rank Organization, Inc.: 'because it is so highly entertaining, it is with very deep regret that I feel compelled to advise you that this picture, in its present form, is definitely and specifically in violation of our Production Code, and because of this cannot be approved.' Noting improper treatment of adultery and murder, together with the characterization of the minister, Breen suggested either 'thoughtful and judicious editing' or an appeal to Eric Johnson, president, and the board of directors of the MPAA.

On 29 November 1949, Jock Lawrence confirmed further cuts in the dialogue between Louis and Sibella. Producer Michael Balcon agreed to shoot an alternative US ending in which the prison governor actually receives the memoirs. The lines 'and sent the fool of the family into the church' and 'boring old ass, but it keeps the thing in the family', in reference to the minister, would be cut. In the song, 'Eenie, Meenie, Minie, Mo, Catch a Nigger by His Toe', the word 'sailor' would be substituted for 'nigger'. Finally, changes would be made to the character of Louis' father so that he was no longer identifiable as Italian. Breen cabled his doubts that the cuts went far enough.

In the meantime, the PCA staff was sidetracked by an item in Logan Gourlay's gossip column, 'Show Business', in the 8 January

1956 edition of the *Sunday Express*. Gourlay claimed the film had been held up in the USA because of the objection of the 'censor' to the description of the vicar as a 'boring old ass', and commented that the censor 'obviously wants to keep assinity in his own family'. The MPAA's director of information reported that he had already spoken with Gourlay's editor in regard to previous attacks on the PCA, and that additional action should be contemplated.

Leaving aside the problem of Logan Gourlay, the PCA viewed revised reels of *Kind Hearts and Coronets* on 1 February 1950. That same day, Breen wrote to Jock Lawrence that the film might be approved if the 'brutal and detailed' killing of the Duke was cut, together with the testimony of Louis' wife Edith (Valerie Hobson) at the trial. On 17 February 1950, Michael Balcon cabled Lawrence that 'all alterations requested by Breen have been made in dupe negative'. Subject to Lawrence's assurance that such really was the case, Certificate No. 13442 was issued on 21 February 1950. *Kind Hearts and Coronets* was released in the USA by Eagle-Lion Films, Inc., in May 1950, with a running time of 100 minutes, six minutes shorter than its UK length.

King of the Damned (1936)

Tentative Certificate No. 0822 was issued on 20 December 1935, and confirmed on 10 January 1936. Later, on 18 March 1936, Frederick L. Herron, foreign manager of the MPPDA, wrote to Joseph I. Breen to tell him that the film was distinctly a Devil's Island story. It stars Conrad Veidt and features a convict revolt in an island prison. He had checked with the French Foreign Office as to why there had been no protest, and the response was that *King of the Damned* was set in Spanish not French territory. Herron suggested in future that producers be urged always to use Spanish names when making such films, thus avoiding French outrage. Cut by nine minutes, the film was released by Gaumont British Picture Corp. of America, and opened at New York's Roxy Theatre, on 31 January 1936. Scenes involving torture and violence were cut in Kansas, Maryland, New York, Ohio and Pennsylvania.

King's Rhapsody (1955)

Ivor Novello's musical play featured a dissolute Balkan king who marries an innocent and pure princess, despite maintaining a mistress.

Geoffrey M. Shurlock read a synopsis and, on 2 June 1955, wrote to Sol Konecoff at United Artists Corp. that the film dealt with illicit sex and seduction and could not be approved. On 15 June 1955, producer/director Herbert Wilcox responded from London that perhaps the synopsis was 'highly coloured', but there was nothing in the screenplay to suggest illicit sex and seduction: 'All the Novello themes are morally acceptable – even to the point of being a little naive.' Shurlock wrote back on 21 June 1955, expressing sorrow that everyone had got off to a bad start, but pointed out that Novello's *The Dancing Years* had run into Code trouble: 'Apparently the London stage and, possibly, the British screen, are a little more relaxed in their attitude towards this type of story than we have to be in this country.' He sent fondest love from Joe and Mary Breen, together with tentative Certificate No. 17604. *King's Rhapsody* had no contemporary US release.

Knight without Armour (1937)

This romantic drama set during the Russian Revolution centres on a love story between an Englishman (Robert Donat) and a Russian countess (Marlene Dietrich).

Tentative Certificate No. 01293 was issued on 9 October 1936, subject to elimination of two nude shots of star Marlene Dietrich, one in a bathtub and one taking a swim. Producer Alexander Korda indignantly protested, noting similar footage in Frank Capra's *Lost Horizon*, but the PCA replied that the actress, Jane Wyatt, in *Lost Horizon* was wearing a bathing costume (albeit unseen) and she was not Dietrich. As Joseph I. Breen wrote on 1 June 1937, 'I should hesitate very much about okaying a picture with Marlene Dietrich shown apparently nude. Marlene Dietrich nude is one thing, and an unknown character in *Lost Horizon* is another.' On 8 June the PCA staff viewed a print of the film and asked that both shots be shortened, despite Korda's argument that the woman in the swimming sequence was not Dietrich but a stand-in. The cuts were made, and the Code Seal of Approval confirmed on 10 June 1937.

Released by United Artists, and with a running time possibly longer than the UK version, *Knight without Armour* opened at Radio City Music Hall on 8 July 1937. Alexander Korda had invested far too much money in the production, and when it became obvious that it would not recoup its costs, he looked for a scapegoat in the PCA, issuing publicity to the effect that the film had been 'savagely mutilated'.

Lady Godiva Rides Again (1951)

After viewing a print of this comedy about a beauty contest, Joseph I. Breen wrote on 21 January 1952 to Morris Helprin at London Film Productions, Inc., to say that, in its present form, the feature was unacceptable under the provisions of the Production Code in view of the amount of suggested nudity. Like many males in the audience, the PCA found the costume worn by Diana Dors in the bedroom and bathroom scenes a cause of considerable concern. It was too brief and intimate an undergarment. Further, it could not approve the classic type of can-can costume, and a bikini was unacceptable. In response, producer Frank Launder ridiculed 'The Johnson Office' in the 30 January 1952 issue of *The Star*, announcing that Diana Dors's 'lace-trimmed camiknickers' were too much for the American censor. On 23 April 1952, the PCA noted that it had 'written off' the film as no cuts had been made. Later, *Lady Godiva Rides Again* was approved, without eliminations, in New York and Ohio. It was released by Carroll Pictures, but did not play Los Angeles until September 1958, when it was booked as a second feature into seven theatres and ten drive-ins.

Lady Hamilton (1941)

Although shot in Hollywood, at the United Artists Studios, *Lady Hamilton* is generally considered a British film. However, all correspondence with the Production Code Administration refers to the production by its American release title of *That Hamilton Woman*. From the start, producer Alexander Korda was aware that the only manner in which he could present the love affair between Emma Hamilton and Lord Nelson for approval by the PCA was with a framing story showing Emma Hamilton thrown into a Calais jail for the theft of a bottle of wine and telling her story to her cell companions.

With that concept in mind, George L. Bagnall submitted to Joseph I. Breen on 11 September 1940 pages 1–87 of a partial script for the film. Subsequently, Breen met in private with Korda, and on 16 September 1930, he reviewed the meeting: 'As we read it, this is a story of adultery and, as such, to be acceptable under the provisions of the

Production Code, it will be necessary that you inject into it what we call the "necessary compensating moral values".' He made various suggestions, including the elimination of the suggestion that Emma Hamilton had been a prostitute, and the moving of a scene between her and Nelson from the bedroom to a balcony or terrace.

Pages 1–105 of a new, partial script were submitted by Bagnall on 18 September 1940, and Breen responded the following day that the suggested changes had not been made. On 12 October by which time shooting had already commenced, Bagnall submitted a new partial script covering pages 1–160. On 15 October Breen replied with a six-page letter, detailing problems with specific lines and with numerous suggestions as to the problem of the script treating adultery as a romance.

New scene pages were submitted directly by Korda on 25 October and Breen wrote back on 30 October to say that two new scenes would materially help the story from the PCA's viewpoint. The first was between Nelson and Lady Nelson, with the latter being portrayed sympathetically. The second was between Nelson and his father, with the latter asking that his son break off his relationship with Lady Hamilton. Korda acquiesced but did not include the second scene in the original English release version. Breen and his staff viewed the completed production on 28 February 1941, and Certificate No. 6915 was issued on 1 March 1941.

That Hamilton Woman was approved without eliminations by censorship boards in Pennsylvania, Ohio, Kansas, New York and Maryland. Massachusetts required the elimination of one scene showing a silhouette of Lady Hamilton registering for childbirth at a hospital and the dialogue pertaining thereto.

The Lady is Willing (1934)

This comedy stars Leslie Howard as a French private detective who kidnaps the wife of a crooked businessman to foil his schemes.

Columbia initially planned to produce the film as *The Woman Possessed*, but, on 17 April 1933, it was advised by Will Hays that such a title was suggestive and could not be registered for use. The studio encountered a further problem when it submitted a synopsis of the source play, *The Woman I Stole*. The PCA's James Wingate was of the opinion that it could be filmed only if all references to a kidnapping – the play's central theme – were cut. However, on 24 April 1933, Geoffrey M. Shurlock read the film script and felt that it was produceable if the words 'kidnapped' and 'kidnapping' throughout were replaced by 'steal,' 'abduct' or 'abduction'. Redeeming features were a French locale and that the kidnapping was played for comedy, with the victim living in utmost comfort while her kidnappers had to pay to keep her happy. Based on Shurlock's views, Wingate wrote to Columbia on 12 May 1933 that the film could prove 'inoffensive and entertaining'. It was first viewed on 12 October 1933, at which time Wingate wrote a letter of praise to Columbia's Harry Cohn. At a re-viewing on 23 July 1934, two minor cuts of a close shot of the heroine's legs as she steps on bathroom scales and the action of Leslie Howard's hand creeping up the heroine's leg towards her knee were requested. Certificate No. 113 was issued on 25 July 1934. Cut to 66 minutes, the film was released by Columbia and opened at the Palace Theatre, New York, 10 August 1934.

The Lady Vanishes (1938)

Alfred Hitchcock's thriller features the adventures of a group of assorted English travellers aboard a trans-European express train.

On 5 October 1938, Francis S. Harmon wrote to Gaumont British Picture Corp. of America informing them that *The Lady Vanishes* was basically in conformity with the Production Code, subject to deletion of all dialogue indicating that the characters of Mr and Mrs Todhunter were not married and travelling on an illicit holiday. Other items to be deleted included an advertisement for 'Cook's Tours'; the lines of Gilbert to Iris, 'Now which side do you like to sleep' and 'In that case I'll sleep in the middle'; the phrase, 'a private thingummy'; expressions of profanity; Gilbert's line, 'Kick him – see if he's got a false bottom'; and the hotel maid looking under the bed and pulling out a hatbox to the accompaniment of facial expressions by the man present (a suggestive toilet gag). Certificate No. 02144 was issued 28 October 1938, subject to the above cuts. The film was released by 20th Century-Fox in March 1939, cut to 87 minutes. In New York, reference to the drug 'hydrocin' was deleted.

Let George Do It (1940)

The problems facing the US distributors in trying to get Code approval for *Let George Do It* are indicative of why few George Formby films ever played in America. Tentative Certificate No. 02917 was issued on 22 July 1940. On 28 March 1941, Francis S. Harmon wrote to Film Alliance of the United States, Inc., saying that the film had been viewed and was basically satisfactory under the Production Code. However, the songs, 'Mr Wu's a Window Cleaner Now' (in reel 3) and 'Oh, Don't the Wind Blow Cold' (in reel 8) would need excision of many lines. Suggestive dialogue in reels 1, 2, 4, and 7 would need deletion, as would the use of the word 'diddle' in reel 7 (because of a vulgar connotation in the USA). Harmon also questioned whether the distributor would wish to release the film in neutral America with its thinly disguised references to Hitler as 'Hilter'. On 7 April 1941, Film Alliance wisely withdrew its application for Code approval, and the Certificate was cancelled. Cut to 73 minutes, the film was released by Film Alliance later in 1941.

The Life and Death of Colonel Blimp (1943)

The film was viewed by the PCA staff on 29 February 1944 and, the following day, Carl E. Milliken wrote to Eagle-Lion Films, Inc., to say that it was basically in conformity with the Production Code. He asked for deletion of sixteen expressions of profanity ('damn', 'Lord', 'My God' and 'hell'). In May 1944, Eagle-Lion claimed all cuts had been made, but the PCA noted that prints were circulating with the offending words. Certificate No. 03762 was issued on 1 June 1944, on assurance that all cuts had finally been made. Released by United Artists as *Colonel Blimp*, the film was first seen at the Gotham Theatre, New York, 29 March 1945.

London Town (1946)

The script was first submitted to the PCA by Eagle-Lion Films, Inc., in June 1945, with a note to the effect that director Wesley Ruggles was familiar with the workings of the Code and there was not a 'damn' or 'hell' therein. On 16 June 1945, Joseph I. Breen acknowledged that the script met the requirements of the Production Code, and later he approved a series of previews of *London Town*, under the title of *My Heart Goes Crazy*, in the New York area on the nights of 10, 11 and 12 September 1946. Then he saw the film. On 27 February 1947, Breen wrote to A. Reginald Allen at the Universal studios offices of the J. Arthur Rank Organization, Inc., that the breast shots of the girl in the green dress and the girl in the white costume were in violation of the Code. More importantly, Breen noted that the two Sid Field sketches contained inescapable elements of 'sex perversion'.

As a result of Breen's condemnation, Universal asked to be relieved of its obligation to release *London Town* in the USA. On 4 March 1947, Robert S. Benjamin, president of Rank's American operation, pleaded with Breen to reconsider, pointing out the tremendous expense involved in the production, and noting that Wesley Ruggles would fly to California to discuss the matter further. Breen replied that nothing could be accomplished through discussion, but he did talk with Ruggles on 10 March 1947. At Breen's suggestion, Rank filed a formal appeal with the board of directors of the MPAA, which met on 31 March 1947, and confirmed Breen's actions. On 4 April, Certificate No. 11816 was issued, subject to total deletion of Field's photography sketch. However, on 10 September 1947, Rank advised the PCA that it would not release *London Town* in the USA, and it asked for a refund of the fee it had paid for certification.

London Town was eventually seen by American audiences under the title of *My Heart Goes Crazy*, cut to 80 minutes, and released by United Artists in July 1953.

The Long Memory (1952)

This drama follows the fortunes of Davidson, a man wrongfully imprisoned for murder, who, when provoked, sets out to find out who framed him.

On 7 May 1952, Joseph I. Breen wrote to Kenneth Bates at the New York office of the J. Arthur Rank Organization, Inc., to say that the second draft script, dated 8 April 1952, had been read. The basic story was acceptable, but it contained two important elements that could not be approved, namely the adulterous relationship between Pewsy and Gladys, and the indication at the film's conclusion that Davidson and Elsa were living together. He noted problems with profanity, prolonged kissing, a kick to the stomach, the word 'frig', and the suggestion that the chauffeur was homosexual. On 26 May 1952, Joyce M. Briggs at Pinewood Studios wrote that Breen's points had been taken care of and that extreme caution would be taken with the depiction of illicit sex affairs. The letter was unsatisfactory from

Breen's viewpoint, and he refused to issue a tentative Certificate. Without a Certificate, the film was released by Astor Films, Inc., opening at the Paramount Theatre, Los Angeles, on 14 March 1953, cut to 90 minutes.

Look Before you Love (1948)

Margaret Lockwood stars in this drama as a woman who marries a charming fraudster who is then paid to disappear by a millionaire who wants to marry Lockwood himself.

Only after *I Know You*, as the film was initially called, had been shot was it realized that no script had been submitted for PCA approval. It was not until 20 August 1948 that Joseph I. Breen wrote to A. Reginald Allen at the Universal studios office of the J. Arthur Rank Organization, Inc., to say that a script had been read and the basic story met the requirements of the Production Code, except for over-emphasis on extraneous and casual drinking and profanity. However, upon viewing the film on 15 November 1949, the PCA advised Eagle-Lion Films, Inc., that it was both in basic theme and detail in violation of the Code. The sanctity of marriage was improperly handled and there were an extraordinary number of drinking scenes, breast shots and profanity. Without a Certificate, the film received limited released by Embassy Pictures, Inc., in 1950.

Love on the Dole (1941)

Ronald Gow's stage adaptation of Walter Greenwood's earthy novel of a Lancashire working-class family, *Love on the Dole*, opened on Broadway without incident on 24 February 1936, with Gow's wife, Wendy Hiller, in the leading role. The screen adaptation, based on both the novel and the play, and directed in 1941 by John Baxter, faced a far more problematic future in the United States. Aside from its depiction of illicit sex, the film featured language appropriate to the characters but inappropriate to American audiences and a scene in which a central character, Mrs Hardcastle, was seen helping her husband take a bath in the living room. No matter the marital status of the individuals involved, members of the opposite sex could not be depicted in a scene in which one or the other was taking a bath or shower.

On 26 November 1941, the Production Code Administration viewed in New York a ten-reel print of *Love on the Dole*, provided by United Artists. The following day, F. S. Harmon of the PCA wrote to Harry D. Buckley at United Artists, noting 'insufficient compensating moral values for illicit sex', the number of profane and vulgar expressions and the impossibility of recutting the film, and advising United Artists to withdraw its application for the Code Seal.

Despite the PCA's refusal to grant *Love on the Dole* a Certificate, individuals within the organization remained enthusiastic about the production. On 22 October 1942, Joseph I. Breen wrote a personal and confidential letter to Martin Quigley, a major influence with the National Legion of Decency. Breen informed Quigley that a friend in the Republic of Ireland had urged the PCA to reconsider its decision in regard to *Love on the Dole*, and had provided him with copies of Irish Catholic newspapers that praised the film. Breen asked Quigley to take a look at *Love on the Dole*, without letting the PCA staff in New York know what he was doing, and to let Breen know in strictest confidence if there was any way that the film might be released. No record of Quigley's response exists, but it was presumably a negative one.

The New York staff of the PCA returned to the problem of *Love on the Dole* in July 1945, with Gordon S. White and Arthur H. DeBra meeting privately with Louis Jacobson and Samuel Spring of Anglo-American Film, the production's British distributor. The men agreed that the basic problem was that the character of Sally Hardcastle (played by Deborah Kerr) became the mistress of bookie Sam Grundy (Frank Cellier). To overcome the obstacle, Anglo-American agreed to record new dialogue by Frank Cellier. In the scene in which Sally comes down the stairs following the birth of her sister-in-law Helen's baby, as presently filmed, Grundy says to her, 'Anything, Sally ... anything for the askin'.' For the American release, Grundy's voice was heard to continue, 'Why, we'll even get married and be respectable, if that's what you want ... sure, come on, Sally, we'll be wed.' In addition, substantial dialogue was deleted from eighteen pages of the script, together with the scene in which Mrs Hardcastle bathed her husband.

On 26 September 1945, Arthur H. DeBra of the PCA wrote to Daniel Frankel of Four Continents Films, Inc., *Love on the Dole's* new American distributor, noting the new dialogue and eliminations and enclosing the PCA Code No. 04039. There was a potential problem when the Massachusetts State Censor Board required the removal of an additional 1,200 feet of film but, in July 1946, the PCA was able to persuade Massachusetts to pass the film without eliminations. *Love on the Dole* was released by Four Continents Films, Inc., late in 1945, cut to 90 minutes.

The Magic Box (1951)

Produced as the British film industry's contribution to the 1951 Festival of Britain, *The Magic Box*, a tribute to pioneer William Friese-Greene, made no impact in the United States when it was released there by Arthur Mayer–Edward Kingsley, Inc., on 24 September 1952. Producer Ronald Neame submitted his own script and not one by credited screen-writer Eric Ambler, titled *A Man Called Willie Green* (*sic*), directly to the MPAA in November 1950. Joseph I. Breen confirmed it was satis-factory on 27 December 1950. A year later, on 23 December 1951, H. McNaught, production manager of Festival Film Productions, reported to Breen that the subject had been retitled *The Magic Box* and re-quested a provisional Code Seal number for incorporation in the credit titles; Certificate No. 15337 was airmailed to the UK on 28 May 1951.

Major Barbara (1941)

Producer Gabriel Pascal first submitted a script to the PCA in October 1930, indicating he would redub the film in the USA, but urging that the Administration understand the hardship he was under in filming during air-raids. Tentative Certificate No. 03074 was issued. On 13 February 1941, Francis S. Harmon informed Pascal that 'your superb production' had been viewed. Harmon understood the need to include a good deal of the language of the gutter for purposes of character-ization, but he did ask for deletion of Snobby's line beginning, 'You're only a jumped-up, jerked off ... ' (in reel 4), the word 'maggot' in Bill's line (in reel 4), 'Gawd' (in reel 5), and 'carroty-cat' (in reel 5). Further, he pointed out that it was a marked disservice to the Salvation Army to imply that a fifty-thousand-pound donation would guarantee salvation, and, therefore, the General's dialogue in reel 9 would need cutting. A conference took place between Pascal, Harry D. Buckley of United Artists and Harmon late in February 1941, at which it was agreed that cuts would be made. 'Carroty-cat' could remain, and Pascal would record a new soundtrack for sequences in which the General's remarks were to be deleted. On 19 February 1941, the Certificate was confirmed, and, cut to 115 minutes, the film was released by United Artists in May 1941.

Major Barbara was classified 'B' by the National Legion of Decency: 'The G. B. Shaw attitudes of irreverence and cynicism toward religious matters and marriage, together with ideological confusions and sub-tleties, render this film capable of conveying false and dangerous connotations.'

The Man in Grey (1943)

On 14 July 1944, Joseph I. Breen wote to Carl E. Milliken in the New York office of the PCA to say that the film had been viewed by the Los Angeles staff and while borderline, with compensating moral values not sufficiently dramatized, it could be approved. It would be necessary, however, to eliminate profanity, the words 'nigger' and 'slut', and the lines, 'Never know until you try', 'A reputation that would not do discredit to a woman of the streets', and 'May have as many lovers as she wishes'. He also wanted to get rid of 'bad breast shots' in reels 4 and 6. On 15 September 1944, Eagle-Lion Films, Inc., asked if 'woman of the streets', 'slut' and 'kept woman' could be retained. On 2 October Breen agreed to the first and last, but pointed out that 'slut' was on the list of forbidden words and phrases, and would have to be deleted. The film was reviewed on 17 October 1945 and, five days later, Certificate No. 11271 was issued on understanding that the production would be released exactly as viewed. Cut to 93 minutes, it was released by Universal, and opened at the Winter Garden Theatre, New York, on 29 November 1945.

The Man in Grey was rated Class B by the National Legion of Decency, on the basis of 'Revengeful murders; marital irresponsibility; tends to convey credence in clairvoyance'.

The Man Who Could Work Miracles (1936)

Even prior to its UK release, PCA Certificate No. 0804 was tentatively issued for *The Man Who Could Work Miracles* on 12 December 1935. On 11 August 1936, James Wingate of the PCA confirmed to Harry D. Buckley in the New York office of United Artists that the film generally met the requirements of the Code. He asked for the deletion of one use of the word 'hell' and one use of the word 'Lord'. It was the character of the minister, played by Ernest Thesiger, that presented the only major problems. A shot in which he hid a bottle of whisky and a glass was asked to be removed, together with the line, 'Bankers and business men! Save me from them.'

When the film opened at New York's Rivoli Theatre, on 20 February 1937, its running time of 82 minutes was identical to that of the UK release.

The Man Who Knew Too Much (1935)

Alfred Hitchcock's thriller stars Leslie Banks as a father whose daughter is kidnapped by a gang of assassins to prevent him from foiling their assassination plot.

The film was first submitted in January 1935 to the PCA staff in New York, who felt unable to take responsibility and referred it to Joseph I. Breen in Hollywood. On 26 January 1935, Breen summarized the problems for Will Hays. The secondary plot concerned the kidnapping of a twelve-year-old girl. It was established policy to withhold approval of all kidnapping stories unless the kidnapping was the central theme of the story, the person kidnapped was not a child, there were no details of the crime, no profit accrued to the kidnappers, and the kidnappers were punished. The film met all the above requirements except that a child was involved, and Breen was of the opinion that the film could be made acceptable in that regard. Further, the final two reels presented 'slaughter the like of which had not been seen since *Scarface*'. There was too much gunplay and killing to make the film acceptable, and no Hollywood company would have considered production of such a storyline.

In order to bring the film into conformity with the Code, in the first part, the close shot of the girl being kidnapped with a hand held over her mouth was deleted. In the last two reels, the gunfight was severely cut, removing scenes of the police being shot, the street strewn with dead policemen, the policeman dying on a mattress, gangsters firing at the police entering the house, and the scene where the 'gangster with a mustache' was shot. The film was viewed by Vincent G. Hart in New York, and he ordered further deletions. On 13 February 1935, Breen issued Certificate No. 620, and it was forwarded by Hart to

Gaumont British three days later. Released by Gaumont British Picture Corp. of America, the film opened at the Mayfair Theatre, New York, 21 March 1935. The publicized running time was identical to that in the UK In April 1935, the local censorship board in Chicago refused to pass *The Man Who Knew Too Much* for showing in the city, and the PCA sent James Wingate to argue the case on behalf of the producer.

Maria Marten; or, The Murder in The Red Barn (1935)

The film was viewed by the PCA on 19 August 1936 and, that same day, Vincent G. Hart wrote to Olympic Pictures Corporation to confirm that it was in compliance with the provisions of the Production Code, subject to cutting of dialogue over-emphasizing the seduction of the young girl by the squire, Maria's fainting at the family table, over-emphasizing her pregnancy, shortening of the burial of the murdered Maria; and deletion of the words 'wench' and 'slut'. This was done, and Certificate No. 01252 was issued on 21 September 1936. As *Murder in the Red Barn*, the film was released by Olympic, opening at the World Theatre, New York, 18 August 1936, cut to 60 minutes. Virginia eliminated the scene of the hood being placed over the condemned man's head, and Ohio eliminated Maria's line, 'Some things can't be hidden for ever' (reel 4) and a section of the burial of her body (reel 5).

A Matter of Life and Death (1946)

On 18 April 1945, Joseph I. Breen wrote to Eagle-Lion Films, Inc., that the script had been read and the basic story met the requirements of the Production Code. He asked for deletion of profanity, 'any questionable posture' of the two leads, and a couple of suggestive lines. On 25 May 1946, Michael Powell and Emeric Pressburger wrote to Breen that they were on the final editing and re-recording of the film and it was the finest they had ever made. Replying to 'Dear Friends', on 4 June 1946, Breen assured the pair he was awaiting it with great pleasure. Certificate No. 11724 was issued on 11 December 1946, after deletion of the shot of the nude boy on the beach. Retitled *Stairway to Heaven*, the film was released by Universal-International, opening at the Park Avenue Theatre, New York, 25 December 1946, cut by one minute.

Meet me Tonight (1952)

Comprises three short plays by Noël Coward: *Ways and Means* about a pair of confidence tricksters on the Riviera; *Red Peppers* about a couple of music hall artists; and *Fumed Oak* about a henpecked suburban husband who makes a break for freedom.

On 13 February 1952, Joseph I. Breen wrote to Kenneth Bates in the New York office of the J. Arthur Rank Organization, Inc., to say that the partial script – *Fumed Oak* and *Red Peppers* – for the film *Curtain Up* had been read, and the basic story met the requirements of the Production Code. In *Fumed Oak*, he noted the dialogue regarding an immoral relationship between Henry and Doris was unacceptably blunt, and that profanity and references to toilet paper and 'That cistern makes terrible noises' should be deleted. In *Red Peppers*, Breen asked that references to HMS *Peculiar* and HMS *Suggestive* not be delivered with a 'pansy' inflection, that Lily not be shown merely in a brassière, and that profanity, such as 'Oh, put it where the monkey ... ', be deleted. On 26 February 1952, Breen wrote to Bates that the final third of the script, *Ways and Means*, had been read. Profanity and two sex-suggestive lines would need deletion, and the scene in Mrs Lloyd-Ransome's bedroom should be changed in order to avoid the suggestion that she was expecting Murdoch. Tentative Certificate No. 15817 was issued at that time. Retitled *Tonight at 8:30*, the film was released by Universal-International in June 1953, cut to 81 minutes.

Mein Kampf – My Crimes (1940)

A docu-drama, purportedly telling the personal story of Hitler from his birth to the present, *Mein Kampf – My Crimes* was originally produced in France by Les Films Regents SA as *Mein Kampf – Mes Crimes*. It was acquired by Associated British, re-edited and subsequently designated a British film. Associated British licensed the US rights to Crystal Pictures, and the production was viewed by the PCA on 6 September 1940, at which time it was noted that Adolf Hitler and 'numerous personages of Nazi regime' were depicted in unsympathetic character-izations. Three days later, F. S. Harmon wrote to Crystal Pictures, awarding the film Certificate No. 02952, provided that Ernst Roehm's off-stage exclamation, 'To Hell with all of you', was deleted; the scene in which a group of small children appeared nude was trimmed; and deletion was made of the underscored portion of the sentence, 'France, too, is laid in ruins and devoured *by the mad dog*'. The objection to the last phrase is unclear.

With some three minutes cut from the original UK running time of 73 minutes, the film opened as *After Mein Kampf* at New York's Bryant Theatre, 13 September 1940. The only major criticism came from the extreme left-wing, with David Platt in the *Daily Worker* (19 September 1940) describing *After Mein Kampf* as 'false history and incendiary propaganda for American involvement'. On the local level, reaction from censorship boards was negative. In Chicago, the elimination of characters, including Hitler's picture, fading into death heads was required. In Maryland and Massachusetts, scenes of violence involving the Youth Movement raiding the palace of the cardinal and throwing a priest through the window were cut. The same scenes were ordered removed in Pennsylvania, together with anti-Semitic references and sequences showing the Jewish pogrom.

Midnight Menace (1937)

Certificate No. 02634 was tentatively assigned to Film Alliance of the US, Inc., on 30 August 1939. The film, about a Balkan minister's plot to bomb London, was viewed on 5 September 1939, at which time the PCA indicated it could not bestow its approval, directing Film Alliance's attention to the resolution: 'There must be no display, at any time, of machine guns, sub-machine guns or other weapons generally classified as illegal weapons, in the hands of gangsters, or other criminals, and there are to be no off-stage sounds of the repercussions of these guns.' The PCA required the deletion of all action depicting American gangsters in armed conflict in reels 7 and 8, two shots of the partially nude girl on the magazine covers and the use of the word 'hell'.

On 7 September 1939, the PCA reviewed the film and, that same day, Certificate No. 02634 was confirmed. Cut by a mere three minutes, and retitled *Bombs over London*, *Midnight Menace* was released by Film Alliance of the US, Inc., in January 1940. That same month, the PCA issued a warning to the distributor that a print at variance with the one approved had been submitted for censorship approval in Ohio. Film Alliance assured the PCA it was merely an oversight. Retitled *Midnight Menace*, the film was reissued in April 1941.

Mimi (1935)

Mimi, starring Douglas Fairbanks Jr and Gertrude Lawrence, is based on the novel that was the source of the libretto of Puccini's *La Bohème*.

Mimi was first viewed by the New York staff of the PCA early in October 1935, and was deemed objectionable to such an extent that no amount of cutting could make it acceptable. On 16 October 1935, Joseph I. Breen viewed the film and told his New York staff to reject it as little more than a romanticization of an illicit love affair, in which evil is made attractive and presentable, and with no voice for morality. *Mimi* was the first of a group of British International Pictures productions acquired by First Division Exchange, Inc., and when told by Vincent G. Hart on 17 October 1935 that the film was rejected, Exchange expressed outrage in that *Mimi* was the story of *La Bohème*, known throughout the world. An appeal was announced, and, to the apprehension of Breen, the Exchange hired well-known attorney Louis Nizer to argue its case. Breen capitulated, and on 19 November 1935, Certificate No. 0769 was issued. Uncut, the film was released by First Division in November 1935.

Miranda (1948)

This comedy centres on the romantic havoc caused by a mermaid when she turns up in London after being caught by a doctor on a fishing trip.

On 27 June 1947, Joseph I. Breen wrote to A. Reginald Allen at the Universal studios office of the J. Arthur Rank Organization, Inc. that the script, dated 27 May 1947, had been read and the basic story was generally acceptable under the requirements of the Production Code. Breen asked that there be some form of costuming for Miranda's upper body, such as seaweed, and pointed out he could not approve the use only of her hair to cover the breasts or any scene in which she was with Paul and her upper body naked. He listed thirty-three pages of script with problems, asking that the Salvationists be played straight, that Paul and Miranda should occupy separate rooms in the hotel, that there be no suspicion of preganancy in Nurse Cary's remarks, and that there be no reference to being rather naughty with a choirboy, no derisive noises, no open-mouth kissing and, of course, no profanity. After viewing the film, Breen wrote to Eagle-Lion Films, Inc., on 12 May 1948, asking for the following cuts to be made: the male dressmaker scene to be severely cut in reel 2; the scene in the dressmaker's shop to be deleted; the scene between the doctor and the mermaid to be cut in reel 6; and the scene of Miranda with her baby to be eliminated in reel 9. Certificate No. 12579 was issued on 18 February 1949. With a reported running time of 80 minutes, the film was released by Eagle-Lion and opened at New York's Little Carnegie Theatre, 23 April 1949.

Mother Riley Meets the Vampire (1952)

With a naïvety that would have done credit to Old Mother Riley herself, Fernwood Films Limited wrote on 30 January 1952 to the MPAA's Title Registration Office, asking for a 'registration number' for a film titled *Vampire over London*. The Title Registration Office (which exists to ensure that rival producers do not use the same film title) forwarded the request to Joseph I. Breen in Hollywood. On 8 February 1952, he wrote to Fernwood, pointing out that a temporary certificate number could not be issued prior to the reading of a shooting script or synopsis. On 28 February 1952, an undated script was submitted by Fernwood's R. D. Comber, and on 31 March 1952 Breen replied that the basic material seemed to meet with the requirements of the Production Code. He expressed concern at the attire of some of the female characters (including Old Mother Riley), and asked that the patch on Mrs Riley's bloomers be eliminated; that there be no suggestive reaction by Mrs Riley as she searched the box containing her inheritance; that a cosh should not be a blackjack; and that criminals should not be seen handling tommy guns. No Production Code Seal was ever issued for the film, which does not appear to have been screened in the USA until 1973 under the title of *My Son, the Vampire*.

Nell Gwyn (1933)

Nell Gwyn was the first British film to undergo considerable refilming and editing in order to win Production Code approval. The PCA was immediately aware that it had a problem when the film was first submitted, and, after viewing the production in New York in July 1934, Vincent G. Hart sought Breen's advice on how to handle a historical film with a 'kept woman' theme. The Code quite clearly stated that 'Pictures shall not infer that low forms of sex relationship are the accepted or common thing', implying that a film such as *Nell Gwyn* should be rejected. On 28 July 1934, Joseph I. Breen concurred, but pointed out that the showing of a 'kept woman' might be acceptable, depending on the manner in which she was treated.

Breen viewed *Nell Gwyn* on 30 July 1934, and again on 1 August 1933. On the latter day, he wrote to Hart, agreeing that the film should be rejected. Later, he sent a list of deletions which Hart passed on to United Artists on 6 August.

- Reel 2: The scene in the dressing room with the girls talking about the King; the line, 'She dreams of herself in the Duchess' place', and the reply, 'The next time I lie dreaming I shall be'; the shot of Nell pounding on her stomach and the king's line, 'We'll see to that'; the line by Nell, 'We'll roll in the hay till the sun gets low'.
- Reel 3: The king's line, 'When will you show me how much you can please me', and the reply, 'What pleases your majesty', etc.; Nell's speech, 'May you forget you are a king and may I forget something else'; the scene in the tavern between Nell and the King, including all 'bad shots' of Nell's breasts; Nell's line, 'And it goes with the rest of me'; the shot of Nell and the king sitting back to back.
- Reel 4: Nell and the king sitting before the fireplace; the girl returning to the room to kiss the king; the king entering Nell's dressing room; Pepys's line, 'A bold and merry slut'; the line, 'Shameless, scheming foreign hor—tense.'
- Reel 5: Pepys's line, 'It offends me to the guts'; Nell lying in bed after Pepys' line, 'And so to bed'.
- Reel 6: The kiss between Nell and the King; the lines by the French ambassador; the movement of the lips of Nell's maid forming the words, 'French bitch'.
- Reel 7: The girls making up the bed and talking of Nell's loves; the remark of the soldier regarding Ben's wife and five children, 'And plenty more where they come from'; Nell's line to the old sailor, 'Tell her to stop at ten o'clock'; the expression, 'They hate your guts'.
- Reel 8: All incidents pointing up that Nell has been the king's mistress for some time.
- Reel 9: The King's line, 'The only piece of me that isn't dying – let not poor Nellie starve'.

On 25 August 1934, a Mr Crammond of British & Dominion

Pictures promised that on return to the UK he would delete as many lines as possible, and that the film would now end with Nell Gywn's arrest and sending to jail by James as she comes to visit the dying King Charles. All shots in the last sequence would show her in jail. Subsequently, director Herbert Wilcox wired that he was now inserting a new sequence, showing Nell founding an old soldiers' hospital.

The recut version was shipped on the *Ile de France* in October 1934. It included a quote from Pepys at the close, indicating that Nell Gwyn died in poverty and despair. It did not include 700 feet eliminated in response to Breen's suggested cuts. When the epilogue was first viewed by the PCA staff in New York on 9 November 1934, the general feeling was that the epilogue added a sour note, and that a prologue might have been better, emphasizing that this was a British film, a historical tale of other days and customs. Some requested deletions remained, and, as a result, Breen asked that the film be shipped to Los Angeles for viewing. He looked at it on 20 November 1934 and rejected it as unacceptable. The changes did not remove the difficulty with the theme. Further, the founding of the hospital by Nell Gwyn only added to the glorification of prostitution. The entry from Pepys's diary at the film's conclusion was insufficient. United Artists agreed to recut the film. On 12 December 1934, Hart viewed a new version with 300 feet removed. Breen viewed the film five days later, and despite the deletions still felt it was thematically a Code violation.

For the next two months, United Artists and Herbert Wilcox were presented with various suggestions from Breen. He wanted a new, written foreword:

> Nations, like men, have their moral lapses. During the reign of Charles II, the court of England sank to depths of immorality that are a blot on the pages of its history.
>
> Our story deals with the colorful but evil time, whose excesses brought about the downfall of the reigning family three years after the death of Charles. Goaded to desperation, the people drove out their corrupt rulers, and new dynasties occupied the throne of England and laid the foundation of its greatness.

In reel 2, an older woman would linger in the king's dressing room and tell Nell to be careful or she would regret her false step. In reel 5, the Archbishop of Canterbury and the Duke of York would point out Charles's indifference to national and foreign affairs because of Nell.

Her carriage would be attacked by an angry mob. In reel 7, Nell would run to the palace and be jostled and treated roughly by the mob. References from Pepys's diary throughout would indicate the extravagance of the king and unrest in the country.

On 12 March 1935, United Artists and the PCA staff viewed yet another version of the film in which all suggestion of actual prostitution had been removed and other changes made. Breen remained dissatisfied. Now he wanted the title to be changed to *Charles the Second* and a new prologue filmed.

On 18 March British & Dominion agreed to the latter request. It shot a prologue in which the bailiffs were shown seizing Nell Gwyn's belongings from a hovel. One of the men would comment, 'Ever heard of Nell Gywn? Never heard of her? That shows you. And now look at her ... ' After additional commentary, the film proper would fade in. At the close, the bailiff would continue, 'Ah well, it just shows yer, don't it. She was only thirty-six, but look at her. She looks fifty. That's what that life does for yer ... '

Breen viewed the latest version on 4 May 1935 and, the next day, Certificate No. 862 was issued. He suggested reinserting the line, 'Let not poor Nellie starve', because of its historical significance, and cutting of the last line, 'That shows what that life does for yer ... ' United Artists agreed.

Released by United Artists and cut to 70 minutes, *Nell Gwyn* opened at New York's Rivoli Theatre, 19 June 1935.

Never Take Sweets from a Stranger (1960)

The play source, *The Pony Cart* by Roger Garis, opened at New York's Theatre de Lys on 14 September 1954. In November 1954, RKO approached the PCA as to a screen adaptation of the story of a high school principal and his wife who move to a small town and make an issue of a seemingly respectable old man who molests their small child. The studio was advised that child molestation came under the heading of 'sex perversion', and, consequently, was unacceptable under the Production Code. Two independent US producers who also contacted the PCA were similarly warned off.

Five years later, on 18 September 1959, Geoffrey M. Shurlock wrote to Samuel J. Briskin at Columbia Pictures that the script had been read, and a film based on this material could not be approved. He suggested changing the plotline to the murder of a child instead of sex molestation but said that if this was done, it would be necessary to make clear that the killer was not suffering from any illness suggestive that he might be a sex pervert. On 10 November 1959, a revised script was read and the same basic problem remained. At the request of Columbia, however, tentative Certificate No. 19519 was issued.

Under the American title of *Never Take Candy from a Stranger*, the film was viewed by the entire PCA staff on 5 February 1960, and rejected. Columbia appealed the decision, but on 16 May 1960, the Review Board, composed of directors of the MPAA, upheld the PCA's withholding of a Certificate. As a member of the MPAA, Columbia could not, and was not willing to, release the film without a Certificate and so the rights were sold in August 1961 to Sutton Pictures Corporation. It applied for a certificate on 22 August 1961 and was rebuffed. Eventually, retitled *The Molester*, the film was released by Omat, opening, uncut, at the Apollo Arts Theatre, Los Angeles, on 8 March 1963.

Curiously, the National Legion of Decency did not condemn the production as 'morally offensive'. Rather, it was awarded a separate classification as a perennial sociological problem, 'treated with moral caution and without sensationalism'.

Nicholas Nickleby (1947)

On 21 May 1946, Joseph I. Breen wrote to A. Reginald Allen at the Beverly Hills office of the J. Arthur Rank Organization, Inc., to say that the final shooting script, dated 12 April 1946, had been read. It contained one unacceptable element in the suicide by Ralph Nickleby in order to escape arrest by the police. He also asked for deletion of profanity, including 'dem'd', and a belch, that there be no cruelty to animals, and that Mrs. Lenville should not be shown 'decidedly pregnant'. In reply to a query from the UK, Breen confirmed on 11 June 1946 that 'deshed' and 'deshit' were acceptable, and that Ralph Nickleby could commit suicide if it was the result of remorse and not an attempt to escape arrest. Certificate No. 12157 was issued on 6 June 1947, and, cut to 95 minutes, the film was released by Prestige Pictures (a subsidiary of Universal-International) in December of that year.

Odd Man Out (1947)

This drama about the last hours of an IRA man on the run in Belfast stars James Mason and Kathleen Ryan.

On 23 April 1946, Joseph I. Breen wrote to A. Reginald Allen at the Beverly Hills office of the J. Arthur Rank Organization, Inc., that the shooting script had been read. It was definitely in violation of the Production Code in that Agnes (renamed Kathleen in May 1948) kills Johnny to prevent his falling into the hands of the police and then she commits suicide. Aside from that one major problem, Breen also noted that there should be no detailed coverage of the hold-up, no suggestion that Teresa's house was a brothel, that there be a change in the expression, 'Get off your backside', and that the reference to the 'Pope is rich and queer' be changed, because of an 'invidious connotation' of the word 'queer' in the USA On 14 May 1946, producer F. Del Giudice wrote to the PCA that murder-suicide was never the director's intention, and that all other points had been taken care of.

Certificate No. 12158 was issued on 20 February 1947. Uncut, *Odd Man Out* was released by Universal-International, and opened at New York's Criterion Theatre, 23 April 1947. Ohio and Pennsylvania ordered deletion of dialogue in reel 2-A between Molly and Lennie in the air-raid shelter.

Oliver Twist (1948)

Oliver Twist typifies how a British producer could be insensitive to the feelings of a religious or ethnic group, despite early warnings from the PCA. A script dated 12 April 1947 was submitted to the PCA and, on 13 May 1947, Joseph I. Breen informed A. Reginald Allen at the Universal studios office of the J. Arthur Rank Organization, Inc., that the basic story met the requirements of the Production Code. The problems he listed were minor, but in a postscript, he added: 'You will bear in mind the advisability of omitting from the portrayal of Fagin any elements or inference that would be offensive to any specific racial group or religion.'

On 7 September 1948, Francis S. Harmon in the New York office of the PCA took a look at the film, and noted it contained no reference to Fagin's 'race'. He advised Eric Johnson that Rank had indicated initially that there would be no release of the film in the USA within the next six months. After a protest from the Anti-Defamation League of B'nai B'rith that Fagin was a caricature of a Jewish stereotype that would have been approved in Nazi Germany, Harmon was told by Rank that the film would not be released in the USA.

Rank's earlier promise notwithstanding, the company sold the US rights to Eagle-Lion Films, Inc., which submitted it to the PCA for Code approval. Breen viewed *Oliver Twist* on 21 November 1950 and, the following day, he wrote to Rank's Jock Lawrence in New York that it was not acceptable under the provisions of the Production Code because of a 'highly offensive characterization of a Jew'. On 5 December 1950, William C. MacMillen, Jr of Eagle-Lion Classics, Inc., announced he would appeal against the decision. He was supported by the American Civil Liberties Union and by the National Conference of Christians and Jews. The latter appointed a committee of four Christians and two Jews to view the film on 4 January 1951, and the group found no justification for its banning.

In the meantime, the Rank Organization was secretly trying to acquire the rights back from Eagle-Lion, offering to reimburse the company for all its expenses to date. This information was confidentially relayed to the PCA, with Rank also suggesting that the appeal not be heard in that Eagle-Lion was the film's distributor and only the producer, Rank, could authorize changes in the production. Amid growing controversy, the appeal hearing was changed from 20 December 1950 to 9 January 1951. After the meeting, Breen wrote to Eagle-Lion that the film had been re-examined and to remove the offensive characterization it would be necessary to eliminate wherever possible all scenes with Fagin, some sixty-nine in total. To the amazement of all, Eagle-Lion agreed to make the cuts, removing 749 feet of film. In February 1951, the new version was reviewed by the PCA. On 21 February Breen authorized issuance of Certificate No. 12487 for the cut version. Breen was anxious to put the matter to rest, and he chose to reject a cable from David Lean, dated 4 February 1951, in which the director offered to make cuts different from those suggested by the PCA. Lean was fearful that an audience aware of obvious cuts would assume that 'unspeakable anti-Semitic propaganda' had been deleted. The director even offered to shoot a new scene in which a representative Jewish leader would offer the services of his community to hunt down Fagin.

Cut to 105 minutes, *Oliver Twist* was eventually released not by Eagle-Lion but by United Artists, 27 April 1951.

On Approval (1944)

Clive Brooks's adaptation of Frederick Lonsdale's classic drawing room comedy about a trial marriage, *On Approval*, opened at New York's Republic Theatre on 27 January 1945 to lukewarm reviews and without benefit of a Production Code Seal. On 6 February 1945, the US distributor, English Films, Inc. (owned by British-born actor George K. Arthur), submitted the film for PCA approval. On 23 February the PCA responded with a demand for cuts in all reels, including many 'damns', and references to sleeping arrangements such as the comment by the Clive Brook character, 'Well you needn't trouble to lock your door Maria – only the rain will want to come in.' In addition, English Films, Inc. was told not to make any reference to trial marriage in its advertising.

A second screening was arranged in Los Angeles on 14 June 1935 by Eagle-Lion Films, Inc. The PCA issued Certificate No. 11008 on 16 June 1945, subject to the film being cut. Subsequently, it transpired that Eagle-Lion did not own the distribution rights. English Films, Inc., refused to make the necessary cuts and released the film without a Code Seal, advertising it as 'Banned by the Hays Office'. *On Approval* was banned in Ohio on 12 May 1945, and was subject to heavy censorship cuts in Maryland, New York and Massachusetts.

Once Upon a Dream (1949)

On 22 October 1947, Joseph I. Breen wrote to A. Reginald Allen at the Universal studios office of the J. Arthur Rank Organization, Inc., to say that the script dated 6 October 1947 for *Roses for Her Pillow* had been read. A comedy stemming entirely from the suspicion of illicit sex, arising from a wife's adulterous dream, and with situations and dialogue decidedly sex-suggestive, the story was in violation of the Production Code both basically and in detail. A final script, dated 26 May 1948, was submitted but, on 15 June Breen wrote saying that the basic story still presented Code problems. Later that month, Allen met with Geoffrey M. Shurlock and another PCA reader and the group went through the script in detail. Allen passed on their suggestions to Vivian Cox at Gainsborough Pictures. On 7 July 1948, Stephen S. Jackson wrote to Allen to say that a new script, dated 17 June 1948, had been read and, while it was an improvement, there were still sixteen pages with problems. *Once Upon a Dream* was viewed on 31 May 1949 and, the following day, Breen advised Eagle-Lion that he would issue a Certificate on deletion of the unacceptably sex-suggestive tag-line reference to 'sleeping partners'. Cut to 87 minutes, the film was released by Eagle-Lion, and opened at the Trans-Lux 60th Street Theatre, New York, on 14 July 1949. However, it was not until 12 September 1949 that Certificate No. 13486 was issued.

Oscar Wilde (1960)

On 27 May 1960, *Oscar Wilde* was viewed by the PCA and rejected inasmuch as it treated of homosexuality. 20th Century-Fox indicated that it might appeal the decision in June 1960, but instead chose to turn the US rights over to another company, Four City Enterprises, Inc., which released *Oscar Wilde*, uncut, in July 1960. A little over a year later, on 23 October 1961, the film was again submitted to the PCA by Crest Film Distributors, Inc./Films Around the World, Inc. *Oscar Wilde* was reviewed on 25 October 1961, and approved, subject to deletion of a reference to 'whores' in a quarrel between Lord Alfred and his father, Certificate No. 20171 was issued on 18 December 1961.

The reason for a change in attitude was adoption of a new 'reading' of the Production Code. Homosexuality came under the heading of 'sex perversion' in the Code, and was automatically rejected. It was now apparently possible to discuss the subject on screen, but the PCA's reaction continued to be vague and undefined. *Tea and Sympathy* (1956) and *Suddenly Last Summer* (1959) contained subtle references to homosexuality and both had been approved. It was obvious that the hero was homosexual in *Cat on a Hot Tin Roof* (1958). In the coming years, the PCA would approve major studio productions of *The Children's Hour* (1962), *Advise and Consent* (1962) and *The Best Man* (1964), all of which had homosexual content. At the same time, it refused a Certificate, in November 1961, for the British production of *Victim*, in which a homosexual was depicted in a sympathetic light.

Our Girl Friday (1954)

On 4 April 1953, Richard Gordon, president of Renown Pictures of America Incorporated, submitted the script for *Our Girl Friday* under the title of the novel from which it was taken, *The Cautious Amorist*, and requested a tentative Certificate number. Certificate No. 16518 was issued on 17 April 1953, but Joseph I. Breen warned, 'As you can appreciate, the situation created in this story of three men and an attractive woman stranded on a desert island could present very serious problems under our Production Code, if the situation were not properly handled.' He was pleased to note that a reading of the story suggested the men were anxious for the girl's companionship rather than romantically inclined towards her, but he pointed out a number of vulgar lines of dialogue and expressions of profanity that needed to be removed.

Gordon reported Breen's comments to George Minter of Renown Pictures in London, and on 15 May 1953 he submitted a revised script for a film now titled *Our Girl Friday*. On 25 May 1953, Breen replied that the earlier problems remained in the script, and his comments were again passed on to George Minter in London. Eventually, on 31 August 1954, Breen viewed the film and expressed his willingness to confirm the Certificate, subject to the elimination of a scene showing the girl (Joan Collins) stripping to the waist while drying her clothes. Gordon argued that the scene showed the girl alone with her back to the camera, covering herself as she turned; elimination of the scene would interrupt the story continuity. Breen rejected the argument, and, on 30 September, Gordon decided to defer a decision. It was not until October that he agreed to cut the scene, which Breen reviewed in January 1955. On 21 February 1955, Certificate No. 16518 was confirmed, and in May 1955, the film, now titled *The Adventures of Sadie*, was released by 20th Century-Fox.

Pandora and the Flying Dutchman (1951)

With incredible nerve, Albert Lewin wrote to Geoffrey M. Shurlock on 6 October 1949, that the latter would have observed that the most intelligent character in his film version of *The Moon and Sixpence* was named Geoffrey. Similarly, it was no coincidence that the most intelligent character in the script for his new production was also named Geoffrey. 'Do not let this sway your judgement,' Lewin concluded. It did not. On 10 November 1949, Lewin met with Shurlock and another PCA reader, and the trio went over a number of questionable items in the script. The main problem was that Lewin wanted the final scene in the film between the two leads to use their voices but without their bodies being seen. It was very obvious to the PCA that the result would inevitably sound like an off-stage sex affair. A revised script was submitted and, after a meeting on 5 December 1949, Lewin agreed to a rewrite.

On 13 December 1949, Joseph I. Breen wrote to Lewin to say that the revised script had been read and met the requirements of the Production Code. He requested consultation with the American Humane Association in regard to the bullfight, and urged that care be taken to avoid any suggestion that Pandora was nude in any scene or in the painting, and that equal care be taken in showing her intimate garments. Tentative Certificate No. 14697 was issued on 27 June 1950, and confirmed 24 January 1951, subject to deletion of a shot of Pandora's naked legs walking across the deck. The film was released by M-G-M, 30 November 1951, and the US version had a running time of 122 minutes.

Pastor Hall (1940)

Loosely based on the story of Pastor Niemöller, a Lutheran minister who stood up to the Nazi regime in Germany, *Pastor Hall* was screened privately at the United Artists Studios in Hollywood on 9 June 1940. Present were Geoffrey Shurlock of the PCA and UA directors Sam Goldwyn and Walter Wanger. Shurlock found only four areas needing revision: the reference to abortion on the part of the doctor in connection with the pregnancy of Lina (Lina Barrie); the dialogue between the Pastor (Wilfrid Lawson) and Lina in which he compares the girl's condition to that of the Virgin Mary and the Christ Child; the scene in which the Pastor's daughter (Nova Pilbeam) offers herself to the young Nazi Party leader; and all profanity to be deleted.

Shurlock's opinion proved of little relevance, because both Wanger and Goldwyn were opposed to the distribution of *Pastor Hall* in the USA Samuel Goldwyn noted: 'The purchase and release in this country of a purely British picture of this strictly anti-Nazi character would very likely give rise to an accusation of deliberate propaganda on the part of the American picture industry, and might cause a revulsion against such American-made pictures as *Mortal Storm*, *Four Sons*, and others.' Further, Goldwyn argued that *Pastor Hall* should not be released in the USA as a matter of industry policy, and that other companies be asked to consider very seriously the advisability of buying the film.

Ultimately, it was not an American film company but the son of an American president, James Roosevelt, who acquired US rights to *Pastor Hall*, as the first presentation of his new company, Globe Productions. On 19 July 1940, F. S. Harmon wrote to Roosevelt to say that the film was in basic conformity with the Code, provided that 'damned', 'hell' and 'Good Lord' were deleted throughout, and that scenes of prisoners in a concentration camp and Pastor Hall being whipped were minimized. The PCA took a final look at the film on 26 July 1940, and Certificate No. 02913 was issued on 1 August 1930.

Pastor Hall was released in the USA with a prologue delivered by James's mother, Mrs Eleanor Roosevelt, written by Robert E. Sherwood, in which she spoke out against aggression, oppression and the curtailment of freedom of worship but avoided any mention of Germany or Hitler. Despite the cuts, the addition of the prologue resulted in *Pastor Hall* having a running time of 97 minutes in the USA, identical to that in the UK.

Additional scenes and dialogue involving brutality were cut in Pennsylvania, but the film played without additional cuts in New York, Maryland, Kansas, Ohio and Massachusetts.

Piccadilly Incident (1946)

The script for the Anna Neagle vehicle, *Piccadilly Incident*, was submitted to the PCA by M-G-M, and on 26 May 1947, Arthur H. DeBra responded that it basically met the requirements of the Production Code. He noted repeated scenes of casual drinking, but in view of this being a story of life under the stress of the blitz, he was willing to accept them. He did request the deletion of 'hell', 'damn', 'Lord', and 'God', and the lines, 'what this fish diet does for these sailors', and, 'for the bottle party with some fannies'. It was subsequently explained to DeBra that, unlike in the USA, 'fannies' was not a slang term for 'bottoms'. DeBra agreed to the retention of the line, but pointed out that it would not change its interpretation by American audiences. Certificate No. 04404 was issued on 9 June 1947, and, cut from 102 to 88 minutes, the film opened at New York's Elysee Theatre, 4 August 1948. Upon its general release by M-G-M, the title was changed to *They Met at Midnight*.

Pimpernel Smith (1941)

Leslie Howard stars as a Cambridge professor rescuing the victims of Nazi oppression in Germany. On 9 December 1941, the PCA advised Edward Small, on behalf of United Artists, that the film contained a number of items unacceptable from the standpoint of the Production Code. Reel 2: line regarding 'sex situation'. Reel 3: line, 'If you are looking for dames, there are enough to go around', and the word 'damned'. Reels 3 and 4: tapestry showing nude female. Reel 5: dialogue of Smith seeing statue 'in the nude'. Reel 7: the offending tapestry. Reel 8: one gag. Reel 11: the line about a woman being married for thirty years and never manhandled. The cuts were made and the film was re-viewed on 7 January 1942. On 15 January 1942, Certificate No. 8050 was issued. Cut to 100 minutes, and retitled *Mister V*, the film was released by United Artists in February 1942. The local censorship board in Pennsylvania required elimination of dialogue relating to the nude statue in reel 1.

Première (1938)

This crime drama centres on a backstage murder committed during the Paris première of a show. The film was viewed by the PCA staff on 19 April 1939, and it presented a problem in that the chorus girls displayed six to eight inches of bare thigh above the tops of their stockings. Urging a uniform interpretation of the Code, Joseph I. Breen wrote to the New York office on 22 April 1939 to say that approval should be withheld until the scenes with these 'girls' had been deleted. The US distributor, Alliance Films Picture Corp., argued that the chorus sequence was integral to the plot and could not be deleted. On 4 May 1939, Breen confirmed the action of the New York staff in requiring the cuts. Alliance undertook some re-editing, but after a viewing on 19 May it was found that several of the offending shots remained. The company appealed to the board of directors of the MPPDA on 21 June. On 30 June the board met and, because this was a British film, it agreed to work with the distributor on the understanding that no precedent would be set. Certificate No. 02593 was issued on 19 July 1939, after elimination of 177 feet of offending film and leaving only 38 feet showing the bare thighs. Cut to 62 minutes and retitled *One Night in Paris*, the film was released by Alliance and opened at New York's Central Theatre on 19 July 1940.

The Prince and the Showgirl (1957)

A script, titled *The Sleeping Prince*, was first submitted to the PCA by Marilyn Monroe Productions, and on 12 June 1956, Geoffrey M. Shurlock responded that the story violated one or two basic elements of the Production Code in taking seduction as a subject for comedy and implying that low forms of sex relationship were the accepted thing. An 'utterly bewildered' Terence Rattigan wrote to Laurence Olivier on 15 June 1956: 'Surely the awakening of a man from a low view of love to a higher one is not only not immoral, but a perfectly fit and proper subject for a comedy.' Shurlock met with Walter McEwen and Finlay McDermid of Warner Bros, and it was agreed to make a change in the opening to remove the relationship between the two leads from the area of pandering, and that the suggestion of a sex affair at the end of the second act be dropped. On 7 December 1956, Olivier personally sent new lines to Shurlock, and they were promptly approved. Certificate No. 18458 was issued on 24 April 1957, and, uncut, the film was released by Warner Bros on 6 July 1957. On 13 June 1957, Shurlock sent a fan letter to Olivier, telling him how much he had enjoyed the film, asking that he thank Rattigan for 'the inimitable grace' with which he handled problems.

Prison Without Bars (1938)

For this British remake of the French film about a girls' reformatory, tentative Certificate No. 02229 was issued on 16 August 1938. However, when Francis S. Harmon first viewed the film in September 1938, he was deeply concerned at the implication of a lesbian relationship between the mannish girl thief and the blonde for whom she stole cigarettes and liquor. There was nothing in the dialogue to support such an inference and, unlike in *Mädchen in Uniform*, the 'perverted relationship' was unclear. Joseph I. Breen urged Harmon that, if it worried him, he should consider the implication was there and act accordingly. On 11 October 1938, Harmon wrote a five-page letter to Harry D. Buckley at United Artists, noting numerous problems in reels 1, 2, 4, 6, 7, and 8, including the suggestion of a lesbian relationship between Renée and Alice. Re-edited reels were viewed on 15 November 1938, with the lesbian overtone removed, but other problems remaining. Vincent G. Hart felt that the film should not be approved, but he was overruled by Harmon and James Wingate, who felt the cuts justified confirmation of the Certificate (which took place the next day). Cut to 80 minutes, the film was released by United Artists, and opened at the Globe Theatre, New York, 18 April 1939.

The Private Life of Don Juan (1934)

The film was first viewed by Vincent G. Hart in New York on 13 September 1934. He asked for deletion of dialogue in reels 2, 3, 4, 5, 6, 7 and 9. He also asked for a cut in reel 6 in the scene between Don Juan and a waitress and the scene in which the woman keeper of the inn asks Don Juan to marry her. On 4 October 1933, United Artists agreed to some of the cuts, but asked that dialogue deletions not be made in reels 2 and 6 for technical reasons. Hart rescinded his requested cut in reel 6 between Don Juan and the waitress, but asked that the second verse of a song be deleted. Certificate No. 0135 was issued on 5 October 1934.

Because most British films were viewed and approved in New York, Joseph I. Breen was not aware of the film's suggestive dialogue until he saw reports of deletions required by censorship boards in Massachusetts and Ohio. Outraged, he wrote to Hart on 26 November 1934, asking why these deletions had not also been required by the PCA. They were obvious Code violations. Hart responded that some cuts had been made by him but not acted upon by United Artists.

Breen decided to take over examination of the film, and it was viewed by his staff in Los Angeles on 17 and 20 December 1934. Breen declared it a definite Code violation. He noted that one staff person had dubbed it 'The Saga of the Coxman'. It was the story of the sexual aberrations of a philanderer: 'The whole thing is treated as a huge joke,' fumed Breen. On 31 December 1934, Breen advised Hart that he wanted substantial cuts in reels 1, 2, 4, 6, 7, 8, and 9. On 9 January 1935, United Artists wrote to all its branches that the cuts, totalling 151 feet, should be made in all prints. In the meantime, the film had opened at the Rivoli Theatre, New York, 9 December 1934.

Except for Kansas, all US states with censorship boards required cuts. *The Private Life of Don Juan* was also rejected for exhibition in Australia, and in the Canadian provinces of Alberta, British Columbia and Quebec.

The Private Life of Henry VIII (1933)

The film was first viewed in New York on 25 September 1933. Vincent G. Hart viewed it on 3 October and described it as 'one of the finest pictures I have witnessed this year'. He noted some references to God, but these were made in supplication, and he was of the opinion that no objection should be made. On reissue, the film was viewed by the PCA staff on 11 July 1935, and four days later, Hart asked for deletion of dialogue relating to the 'King's in one of his merry moods'; the king vigorously kissing Jane Seymour on the shoulder and neck; the reference to the king as 'a breeding bull'; the king adjusting his crotch before entering Catherine's bedroom; the dialogue between the king and Anne in reference to the origins of children; the barber's line to the king, referring to 'when the well runs dry'; and the wife's comment to the cook that 'What a man wants is regular meals'. The deletions were made and Certificate No. 0612 was issued on 21 August 1935. The film was again reissued in 1937 – by Film Classics, Inc. – and at that time, the PCA asked that the version conform to the 1935 reissue. On the first reissue, the film was condemned by the National Legion of Decency.

The Private Life of Henry VIII first opened in the United States at New York's Radio City Music Hall, 12 October 1933.

Pygmalion (1938)

George Bernard Shaw's play contained potential problems under the Production Code, but the approval process was relatively simple in that producer Gabriel Pascal made it perfectly clear, on 18 February 1938, that he was shooting a different version for the US market. Based on the first reel of the film alone, it is obvious that the American release version differs substantially from that seen in the UK, with not only different dialogue but different camera set-ups and even a different score, with William Axt replacing Arthur Honegger.

On 22 March 1938, Francis S. Harmon wrote to Gabriel Pascal that a script had been read. He asked for deletion of profanity throughout, substitution of the word 'baggage' (because of its US meaning in reference to women), deletion of the word 'slut', care in the handling of the bathing of Eliza, and a cut in the dialogue between Doolittle and Pickering to avoid the suggestion that the former would sell his daughter for fifty pounds. The film was viewed on 7 September 1938, and the above problems noted, together with a reference to Eliza's being illegitimate and Doolittle's living with her stepmother outside marriage. Because of these problems, Breen rejected the film as 'unacceptable' on 9 September 1938.

M-G-M indicated it might bring over the players to remake part of the film, but Pascal admitted he had 'covering shots' on several of the scenes. After changes had been made, Certificate No. 4845 was issued on 26 November 1938. Cut to 87 minutes, the film was released by M-G-M and opened in New York at the Astor Theatre, on 7 December 1938. In 1938, Pascal approached Breen as to whether the illegitimacy scene might be reinstated for a reissue, but the latter refused.

Quartet (1948)

On 23 October 1947, A. Reginald Allen at the Universal studios office of the J. Arthur Rank Organization, Inc., submitted ten W. Somerset Maugham stories to Joseph I. Breen, with a note that Gainsborough was planning to develop a number into motion pictures. The original idea was to produce a compilation of five stories under the title of *Quintet*, selected from the following: 'Red', 'The Sanatorium', 'The Alien Corn', 'The Facts of Life', 'The Kite', 'The Round Dozen', 'The Unconquered', 'The Happy Couple', 'The Force of Circumstance', and 'The Colonel's Lady'. Breen immediately rejected 'The Kite.' On 30 October 1947, he replied that he could not in any circumstances approve a film based on 'The Facts of Life', in that it was a story of illicit sex without any compensating moral values. That same day, 'The Colonel's Lady' was similarly rejected as a story of adultery without compensating moral values, and 'The Alien Corn' was approved subject to George's death at the climax being accidental and not a suicide.

On 8 December 1947, Allen submitted screen adaptations of 'The Sanatorium', 'Red' and 'The Facts of Life'. Breen noted a basic change in the storyline of 'The Facts of Life' on 15 December and approved it as meeting the provisions of the Production Code, provided it was made absolutely clear that there was no sex affair between Nicky and Jeanne; he also required elimination of various expressions of profanity. A second script for 'The Facts of Life' was submitted on 18 March 1948, followed by revised script pages on 8 April. The following day Breen responded, pointing out the need to delete 'Good Lord', 'damned' and 'damn'. A script for 'The Alien Corn' was submitted on 12 February 1948 and, six days later, Breen confirmed it met the requirements of the Production Code, subject to the deletion of three uses of the word 'damn'. A final script for 'The Colonel's Lady' was submitted on 18 February 1948, and, on 23 February, Breen replied that it was still unacceptable because of the suggestion that Daphne was being kept by George.

It was not until 1 April 1948 that A. Reginald Allen advised that *Quintet* was now *Quartet*, consisting of 'The Colonel's Lady', 'The Facts of Life', 'Alien Corn', and 'The Kite'. 'Red' was dropped from the group. No correspondence exists in relation to 'Red' or 'The Kite', but a tentative Certificate No. 12905 was issued around this time.

Nothing happened for almost a year, and then, on 24 February 1949, Breen cabled Robert S. Benjamin at the J. Arthur Rank Organization, Inc., in New York that the first three episodes of *Quartet* were approved, but 'The Colonel's Lady' remained unacceptable because of its theme of adultery. Breen suggested cuts that might be made, but, that same day, Jock Lawrence of Rank cabled him that such demands were 'difficult for us to comprehend' in that Daphne and the Colonel were pictured as no more than good friends. He pointed out that the film was scheduled to open at New York's Sutton Theatre on 28 March 1949, under the sponsorship of the Overseas Press Club of America. Any cuts would virtually require junking the film and would cause embarrassment for all concerned. The screening apparently went ahead without the cuts.

With the announcement that Eagle-Lion would release *Quartet*, Joseph I. Breen wrote to his son, an executive with that company, asking for specifics as to changes that had been made in the film. Breen Jr replied on 30 March 1949 that cuts had been made in the UK, all but one relating to 'The Colonel's Lady'. That same day, Certificate No. 12905 was issued for the film, which, with a running time identical to that in the UK, was released by Eagle-Lion.

A Question of Adultery (1958)

In July 1957, when the PCA first received 'a rather well-written and not over-sensationalized script' dealing with artificial insemination, it was decided to take up the subject with the American Medical Association. The PCA had already approved a German film, *Alraune*, dealing with artificial insemination, but as science fiction. At issue was whether artificial insemination fell under the heading of 'sex hygiene', forbidden under the Code. The AMA provided some documentation on the legal, medical and moral status of the process, and noted it was opposed by both the Catholic Church and the Church of England. The legal issue was dismissed by the PCA as irrelevant on the basis that murder was forbidden by law but still permitted on screen.

In August 1957, Geoffrey M. Shurlock met with producer Raymond Stross, and it was agreed it would be possible to produce a film on the subject, approvable under the requirements of the Code. On 20 December 1957, Stross submitted his final script and, on 2 January 1958, Shurlock replied that the basic story was acceptable, noting various scenes and lines of dialogue with problems relating to sexual intimacy, questionable comments and over-exposure of cleavage. On 8 January Stross wrote that the film would complete shooting in less than ten days, and that it had 'genuine integrity'. No Certificate was ever issued, and the film was released by NTA Pictures, Inc., in February 1959, uncut. The local censorship board in Kansas required deletion of the words 'bastard' and 'intercourse', which it identified as 'obscene and indecent language'.

The Rake's Progress (1945)

This drama stars Rex Harrison as a cad whose pre-war career of swindling and adultery is eventually expiated by his death in the war. On 8 January 1945, Joseph I. Breen wrote to the British Information Service in New York that the script had been read. The material was definitely and specifically in violation of the provisions of the Production Code because of illicit sex and adultery. On 26 January 1945, he submitted a detailed analysis of the script, listing twenty-three pages with problems. The film was first viewed on 16 April 1946, after which Breen wrote to Universal that it would be necessary to omit the chamber pot, 'God' and sequences in the bar between the husband and Vivian which condoned adultery. On 23 April 1946, the film was reviewed, and Breen asked for removal of a shot of the placing of a commode atop the steeple, kissing in the punt, the expression by the girl as the policeman toots his horn, the scene in the hotel room where the husband finds his wife, the scene of two men in the pub, and the father's lines to his son at the seashore home. Certificate No.

11658 was issued on 12 July 1936, subject to all prints being as viewed on 10 July. With a running time of 109 minutes, the film was released as *Notorious Gentleman* by Universal-International in October 1946.

The Rat (1937)

This drama stars Anton Walbrook as a French jewel thief, 'The Rat', who takes the blame for a murder committed by his ward but is exonerated in court when another woman claims he spent the night with her.

Tentative Certificate No. 01780 was issued on 7 October 1937. After viewing the film on 17 November, Joseph I. Breen decided that although a central character perjures herself to exonerate the hero, the ends of justice were properly served, proving the Code statement that 'Crime need not always be punished, just so long as it is shown to be wrong'. The Certificate was confirmed on 30 November 1937. Released by RKO, the film opened at the Globe Theatre, New York, on 27 February 1938.

The Red Shoes (1948)

On 7 August 1947, Joseph I. Breen wrote to A. Reginald Allen at the Universal studios office of the J. Arthur Rank Organization, Inc., to confirm that the basic story met the requirements of the Production Code. He pointed out that he could not approve the costumes of the can-can dancers if they showed bare thighs and garters above the top of their stockings. He also noted there should be nothing objectionable about the embrace in the cab between Vicky and Julian, and one 'damn' should be omitted. Certificate No. 12673 was issued on 30 August 1948, with a note that the 'damn' remained in the print for technical reasons and the PCA's approval of its use here did not constitute a precedent. Uncut, *The Red Shoes* was released by Eagle-Lion Films, Inc., in October 1948.

Rembrandt (1936)

On 5 November 1936, Vincent G. Hart in the New York office viewed the film and reported to United Artists that it conformed with the provisions of the Production Code. He asked that Charles Laughton's line to the beggar, 'You have had all the women you want', be deleted. Certificate No. 01250 was enclosed. The PCA staff appears to have been lax in its attention to the film, causing a number of complaints, and on 28 December 1936, Joseph I. Breen admitted to Kenneth Clark at the MPPDA in New York, 'We, in this office, have not seen the picture in question, but we have heard much about it – much criticism – which is not pleasant.' Cut to 75 minutes, *Rembrandt* was released by United Artists, and opened at Grauman's Chinese Theatre, Hollywood, on 22 December 1936. The local censorship board in Massachusetts required the elimination of the dialogue in reel 6, beginning, 'Why did she submit to this man's desires?'

The Ringer (1952)

The Ringer was first submitted to the PCA by Monogram, and viewed on 23 September 1952. The following day, Joseph I. Breen wrote that the film was unacceptable under the provisions of the Production Code. It was a story of a murderer and notorious criminal who kills his planned victim, escapes capture and plans to continue his life of crime elsewhere. The character of Sam Hackitt was a problem in that he was living with and had children by Mrs Hackitt, to whom he was not married. There were also references to drug trafficking and un-acceptable uses of 'hell' and 'damn'.

Morris Helprin of London Films cabled on 11 December 1952, asking what might be done to make the film acceptable, pointing out it was tongue-in-cheek and intended as satire. Breen sent him a copy of his letter to Monogram, and wrote that he could not accommodate himself to Helprin's argument. Tentative Certificate No. 16340 was issued on 21 January 1953 and, the following day, Helprin advised that corrections and eliminations had been made, and a short commentary by Cora Ann recorded for the end of the film, indicating that the Ringer did not escape.

On 30 November 1953, Breen pointed out that he still had not seen the film, and confirmed its Code Seal of Approval. The following month, he learned from London Films that it had been sold to NBC. Manhattan Films International stated they had theatrical rights, but refused to pay for the Code Seal. Uncut and without a Seal, the film was released by Ellis Films, and opened at the United Artists Theatre, Los Angeles, on 10 December 1953.

Sabotage (1936)

Tentative Certificate No. 01184 was issued on 11 June 1936. The film was viewed by the New York staff on 7 December 1936, and approved subject to the deletion of two uses of 'hell', and one use each of 'for God's sake' and 'bastard'. The deletions were made and the Certificate was confirmed on 6 January 1937. It was very obvious that the New York office was slipshod in its handling of the film. When *Sabotage* opened in Los Angeles, C. R. Metzger of the PCA office there viewed it at the Filmarte Theatre on 25 January 1937. He noted a number of Code violations: there is levity in regard to an illegitimate child, the heroine kills her husband and there is no due process of law, the hero, a police officer, shields the heroine from arrest, and there is a shot of a knife sticking out of the husband's body. Someone else who viewed the film was B. B. Kahane, a senior executive at Columbia Pictures, and, on 4 March 1937, he demanded of Joseph I. Breen why such a film had been approved. Breen passed on Kahane's letter, together with other protests, to Will Hays on 5 March 1937. There was nothing to stop the release of the film – under the title of *The Woman Alone* – by the Gaumont British Picture Corp. of America. It opened in New York, at the Roxy Theatre, on 26 February 1937.

St Martin's Lane (1938)

F. S. Harmon of the PCA viewed a print of *St Martin's Lane* in New York on 8 August 1938 and, the following day, he wrote to Budd Rogers of Alliance Films Corporation confirming that the film was in basic conformity with the Code. Harmon requested the deletion of the word 'God' and the phrase 'on the make' from Vivien Leigh's lines, together with the comment by Charles Laughton, when Leigh comes to his room to spend the night, 'You'll find conveniences beyond the curtain', because audiences might construe this as a reference to a toilet. After the viewing of a new print that day, on 25 November 1936, PCA Certificate No. 02227 was issued. Following Vivien Leigh's starring in *Gone with the Wind*, Paramount took over distribution rights to *St Martin's Lane* in November 1939, renaming it *Partners of the Night*. However, by the time the film opened at New York's Paramount Theatre, on 14 February 1940, it had been retitled *Sidewalks of London*.

Saraband for Dead Lovers (1948)

On 9 December 1946, Joseph I. Breen wrote to A. Reginald Allen at the Universal studios office of the J. Arthur Rank Organization, Inc., saying that the script dated 15 November 1946 had been read. The illicit sex affairs between the Countess Platen and the Duke of Hanover and the Countess Platen and Konigsmark made the story unacceptable He noted thirteen pages with problems. The initial response – on 10 January 1947 – from producer Michael Balcon was that this was the most important film of the current year. He would respond to the pages with problems, but he was unwilling to undermine the structure of the film. In a more conciliatory tone, Balcon wrote on 31 January that he believed he could make the story acceptable without any important sacrifices.

After reading a revised script, Breen wrote to Allen on 8 July 1947 that the story was still unacceptable because of the lack of a very strong voice for morality and the Countess Platen's sexual intimacy with three men. On 23 July the PCA came up with ideas for an American version, removing the suggestion that the countess was the old duke's mistress, strengthening the voice for morality, keeping Frau Busche out of the picture as much as possible, and changing two bedroom scenes that were indicative of adultery. On 14 August 1947, Breen wrote to Allen that revisions, dated 13 August, had been read and met the requirements of the Production Code. Certificate No. 12180 was issued on 30 June 1949. Uncut, the film was released as *Saraband* by Eagle-Lion Films, Inc.; it opened at New York's Little Carnegie Theatre on 12 June 1949.

The Scarlet Pimpernel (1935)

The film was viewed on 24 January 1935 and, the following day, Joseph I. Breen issued Certificate No. 578, noting he was approving the film with reluctance. The policy of the PCA was that the bodice on any actress should be sufficiently high to avoid exposure of her cleavage. Here, in the better part of two reels, Merle Oberon's bodice was cut so low that there was ample display of her breasts. The film was released by United Artists, opening at Radio City Music Hall, New York, on 7 February 1935, cut to 85 minutes.

The Secret Agent (1936)

On 13 November 1935, the PCA wrote to Gaumont British Picture Corp. of America that the script had been read, and there were certain elements needing modification in order to bring the film into conformity with the Code. Throughout, Mexicans were offensively characterized as bandits and killers. There was a need to establish that Ashenden and Elsa occupied separate hotel rooms, and no action should take place in the bathroom. The running gag of the Mexican throwing coins and chocolates to girls was offensive. The use of a Swiss chocolate factory would give offence to the Swiss. Forty-one scenes with problems were listed, including profanity, an impressionistic shot of a gibbet, the portrayal of casino gambling, and suggestive dialogue. Tentative Certificate No. 0825 was issued on 20 December 1935.

The film was viewed on 14 May 1936, and a request was made for the elimination of the bathroom scene with Elsa and Marvin, the gibbet scene, and the exposure of 'R''s body in the Turkish bath. Re-edited reels 2 and 9 were viewed on 5 June 1936, and the Certificate confirmed. The film was released by Gaumont British Picture Corp. of America, opening at the Roxy Theatre, New York, on 12 June 1936, cut to 75 minutes.

The Shop at Sly Corner (1947)

In order to satisfy the Code, minor editing was undertaken substantially altering the storyline. Stephen S. Jackson viewed the film on 26 January 1948 and, at his request, Republic Pictures, Inc., agreed to edit scenes showing the suicide of the elderly antique dealer (Oscar Homolka) in such a way that it would now appear he died of a heart attack. A line by the doctor (Derek Farr) to the antique dealer that he, too, would have murdered the blackmailer was deleted in order to avoid justification for and creation of sympathy for murder. On a lesser note, 'Lord' was deleted throughout. Jackson viewed the edited film on 3 February 1948, and Certificate No. 13003 was issued on 20 May 1948. Retitled *Code of Scotland Yard*, the film was released by Republic on 30 August 1948, cut to 60 minutes.

The Stars Look Down (1939)

M-G-M arranged a private screening of *The Stars Look Down* for Joseph I. Breen on 2 April 1940 and, that same day, he wrote to Louis B. Mayer: 'I regret to be compelled to advise you that the picture, in its present form, is definitely unacceptable under the provisions of the Production Code, because it is a story of illicit sex, and adultery, without any compensating moral values of any kind.' Breen recommended judicious cutting, suggesting the elimination of a shot of raindrops on the window and the fade-out of the scene of Jenny in the arms of her sweetheart. Further, the adulterous relationship between Jenny (Margaret Lockwood) and Joe (Emlyn Williams) could be corrected by eliminating shots of a lighted upstairs window, by Joe coming down the stairs, and, at the door, waving up the stairs as the door is partially open. Editors at M-G-M worked over a considerable period of time recutting the film, for which Certificate No. 6774 was issued on 26 June 1941.

Breen also warned Mayer that local censorship boards would probably delete the scenes of the looting of a butcher's shop and the devastation in the mine, but the film was passed without additional cuts in Ohio, New York, Pennsylvania, Kansas, Maryland and Massachusetts.

The Stars Look Down was cut to 97 minutes for its US release by M-G-M in July 1941. Trade paper critics unkindly suggested that the cutting of another ten or fifteen minutes might help the film further.

Strange Boarders (1938)

This thriller stars Tom Walls as a secret service agent investigating an espionage ring based in a boarding house.

Tentative Certificate No. 02143 was issued on 15 June 1938. The film was viewed by the PCA staff in Los Angeles on 20 July 1938, at which time a cutter for Larry Darmour Productions was asked to re-edit the film to eliminate suggestive dialogue in regard to a couple's honeymoon night. Almost simultaneously, the film was viewed by the PCA staff in New York, who asked for only one deletion, the butler's line to Tom Walls, 'Excuse me, sir, the honeymoon didn't come up to scratch?' in reel 2. As confusion reigned, Joseph I. Breen agreed the PCA was at fault in viewing the film on both coasts and informed Gaumont British that in future it should submit films only to the New York office, unless Will Hays gave approval for Los Angeles to have jurisdiction. The film was re-viewed by the entire Los Angeles staff on 1 August 1938, at which time Gaumont British was asked to delete the butler's line, a man's four reactions to four shots of a woman's leg as she undressed, a woman running down the hallway, dialogue in the bedroom, a toilet gag, and the dialogue after the man kisses his wife goodnight (all in reel 5). On assurances the cuts had been made, the Certificate was confirmed on 15 August 1938. Cut to 73 minutes, the film was released by Gaumont British Picture Corp. of America on 1 August 1938.

Sweeney Todd, the Demon Barber of Fleet Street (1936)

The film was viewed in April 1939 and, at that time, the original US distributor, Arthur Ziehm, was asked to delete footage in order to reduce all gruesomeness to a minimum. To be cut were the silhouette shot of Todd cutting the throat of one of his victims, Todd rolling the body of the piemaker into the fireplace, Todd dangling a razor in front of the sailor's throat, and, because arson was not permitted, Todd's going around with a lighted torch and setting fire to the building. (A cut was asked from his piling up furniture to a shot of the building in flames.) Certificate No. 02514 was issued on 18 April 1939, on the understanding that all cuts had been made in all prints. Cut to 66 minutes, and retitled *The Demon Barber of Fleet Street*, the film was released by Select Attractions, Inc., and opened at New York's Central Theatre on 29 September 1939.

The Tales of Hoffmann (1951)

Because the introductory credits were to be included in one long rolling title, London Films requested a tentative Certificate No. for *The Tales of Hoffmann*. The company made its request not to the PCA but to Gordon White of the MPAA. The latter passed the request on to Joseph I. Breen, who agreed, on 22 January 1951, to assign tentative No. 15097 to the film. He also pointed out that, as he recalled, the second act of the Offenbach opera contained a storyline, involving Hoffmann's passion for courtesan Giulietta, that might present a basic Code problem. Breen viewed the finished film on 8 March 1951, and reported to Morris Helprin of the New York office of London Films, Inc., that the scene in the banquet hall, immediately following the first singing of the Barcarole, included shots of scantily attired men and women 'lolling and twisting while in close embrace on what looks like circular tables'. Breen considered that material unacceptable as overly lustful and offensively sex-suggestive. On 17 April 1951, Helprin reported that the entire Bacchanal sequence had been cut, and Certificate No. 15097 was confirmed 27 June 1951. The censorship board in Massachusetts subsequently demanded the deletion of the line, 'Then you can go to hell', from reel 11. Running 138 minutes, and, apparently, longer than its UK general release version, *The Tales of Hoffmann* received its world première at New York's Bijou Theatre on 4 April 1951; it was released by Lopert Film Distributing Co., Inc.

Ten Minute Alibi (1935)

M-G-M, RKO and Warner Bros all considered Anthony Armstrong's play, *Ten Minute Alibi* (which opened on Broadway in October 1933), for screen adaptation, but Joseph I. Breen advised that it was not suitable for filming. In that crime was presented in such a way as to inspire others to imitate and the technique of murder was presented in detail, the story was in specific violation of the Code.

Ten Minute Alibi was subsequently filmed by British Lion, and the production was viewed on 7 April 1936 by the PCA's Vincent G. Hart. He advised the US distributor, Olympic Picture Corp., that the film 'is in definitive violation of our Production Code'. Breen was concerned that he had advised US producers to avoid *Ten Minute Alibi* and yet a British company had felt no qualms in bringing it to the screen. He had the foreign department of Paramount Pictures take up the matter with the Hon. J. Brooke Wilkinson of the British Board of Film Censors, and the latter explained that while it was quite true that the film depicted a murder with the killer going free, it was his feeling that the murdered man represented evil, the murderer virtue, and so elementary justice was satisfied.

Elementary justice and the British Board of Film Censors might be satisfied, but Breen was not. On 5 October 1936, he viewed a new version of *Ten Minute Alibi*, in which the story was presented totally as a dream. The film now concluded with a charwoman waking up the young killer and saying, 'Dreams are such nonsense.' This was followed by a close shot of the man repeating the word, 'nonsense'. The next day, Breen wrote to Vincent G. Hart in New York:

The new ending, in our judgment, was so patently phony and so crudely a makeshift as to leave us firmly unconvinced. It smacks very much of the old formula where we indulged in all kinds of crimes for six and a half reels and then sought to make the objectionable material palatable by a gesture in the right direction during the last fifty feet of film.

A new distributor, Imperial Pictures, Inc., became involved, and its Clifford Sanforth met with Breen, bringing with him three pages of deletions and new scenes. Because the leading man, Phillips Holmes, was back in Hollywood, Sanforth had the notion to film a sequence there in which the killer would be seen on trial, sentenced to death and about to be hanged. At that point, he would be awakened from his dream by the charlady. For whatever reason, nothing came of this proposal. Eventually, the film was acquired by Michael Mindlin who received approval from the New York State Censorship Board on 30 November 1936 and opened it without a Certificate.

They Drive by Night (1938)

They Drive by Night was viewed by Joseph I. Breen on 2 October 1939 and, that same day, he wrote to Warner Bros that he would be glad to forward a Certificate once the shots of a bookcase, with the camera emphasizing the book, *Sex in Relation to Society*, were removed, such shots suggesting that Hoover (Ernest Thesiger) was a sex murderer. On 10 October 1939, Warner Bros, advised the PCA that it was impossible to get the negative out of Britain and that it did not plan a US release. Subsequently, the studio used the title for a 1940 film directed by Raoul Walsh. In countries in which the British film had already been released, the US production was retitled *Road to Frisco*.

They Were Not Divided (1950)

This story of two soldiers, one British and one American, covers the five years from their enlistment to their deaths.

On 29 April 1949, Joseph I. Breen wrote to Jock Lawrence in the New York office of the J. Arthur Rank Organization, Inc., that the final shooting script, dated 22 March 1949, had been read. The basic material was acceptable under the provisions of the Production Code, but there were thirty unacceptable words that would need deletion. He asked for no naming of a brand of cigarettes and the deletion of a nude bathing sequence. The film was viewed on 12 June 1950, and Breen pointed out half-a-dozen expressions of profanity that remained, together with the protracted nude swimming sequence. Deletion of the profanity created no problems, but the nude swimming sequence was a pivotal part of the plot, the first time the boy (played by Ralph Clanton) and the girl (Stella Andrews) meet. To no avail, Rank argued that General Eisenhower, no less, was wanting this film, which was being held up by the PCA. Rank suggested that cutting the line 'Are you like me?' would eliminate the suggestion that the couple were nude. Breen disagreed, pointing out that this was not only a nude bathing scene but a mixed nude bathing scene. An appeal was planned but, at the last minute, Jock Lawrence recut the film in November 1950, taking out all references to nudity, making it appear only that the boy had dived into the pool in which the girl was already present. Also deleted was later dialogue referring to a scar on the girl's back which would imply the boy had seen her nude. On 15 November 1950, Breen reviewed the offending sequence and found it acceptable. Certificate No. 13813 was issued on 16 November 1950. Cut to 91 minutes, the film was released by Eagle-Lion Classics, Inc., in March 1951.

Things to Come (1936)

Tentative Certificate No. 0803 was issued on 12 December 1935. The film was viewed on 9 March 1936, at which time the Certificate was confirmed, subject to the elimination of the scene of a woman bathing a nude child. The PCA also asked for deletion of 'My God' in a speech by Passworthy, but, because of technical difficulties in removing it, agreed that it might stay. Four other references to God were permitted to remain in that they were not used in a profane sense. Joseph I. Breen disagreed with the actions of his New York staff, writing on 5 May 1936 that Hollywood producers were now asking why they were not allowed similar references to God. The film was released by United Artists, opening at the Rivoli Theatre, New York, on 17 April 1936, cut to 96 minutes.

The Third Man (1949)

Geoffrey M. Shurlock and Jack Vizzard met in conference with producer David O. Selznick, director Carol Reed and writer Graham

Greene on 18 August 1948, at which time the basic story was judged acceptable. The group agreed that there would be no dialogue pointing up an illicit sex relationship between Anna and Harry Lime; the sequence in the bedroom would be played without emphasis on the bed; when Anna was arrested, she would be shown in nothing less than a slip and there would be no suggestive reactions from the soldiers; and Martin's shooting of Harry Lime at the end would be on a direct shouted order from Calloway, with no flavour of either a mercy killing or deliberate murder. On 22 October 1948, Joseph I. Breen wrote to Selznick to say that the script, dated 20 September 1948, had been read. The soldiers would not watch Anna dress. The early killing should not be suggestive of outright murder and Harry Lime must still have a gun in his hand. There should be no suggestion in the bedroom of sexual intimacy between Anna and Harry Lime. The question about Oscar Wilde from an 'effeminate young man' was unacceptable.

Certificate No. 14125 was issued on 16 September 1949. The film was released by Selznick Releasing Organization, Inc., opening at the Victoria Theatre, New York, on 2 February 1950, uncut. In the USA, the opening remarks read by Carol Reed were replaced by ones spoken by Joseph Cotten.

The 39 Steps (1935)

The film was viewed on 2 July 1935, at which time Gaumont British was asked to delete the close shot of the girl taking off her stockings while handcuffed to Hammond; Hammond's line, 'Now for the operating table'; two shots of Hammond rolling over and placing his hand on the girl's leg; and all profanity. The deletions were made under protest, and Certificate No. 0550 was issued on 11 July 1935. The film was released by Gaumont British Picture Corp. of America, opening at the Roxy Theatre, New York, on 13 September 1935, cut by two minutes. It was reissued in 1942 by Artlee Corporation.

This'll Make You Whistle (1936)

This musical comedy stars Jack Buchanan as a playboy who poses as a forger to shock the guardian of a fiancée he wants to ditch.

The film was viewed by Vincent G. Hart in the New York office of the PCA on 15 June 1937. He listed a number of cuts that were needed: all sequences of women undressing, including the entire bedroom scene with Jack Buchanan under the bed; all discussion of the 'colored baby', and scenes in which the baby was displayed (under the miscegenation clause of the Code); all dialogue with double meaning, including the strip poker act; Buchanan goosing the dowager; excessive drinking; and the rhumba dancers and the solo dance, because of the 'burlesque bumps'. The film was rejected and, on 6 July 1937, Gaumont British Picture Corp. of America intimated it was planning an appeal.

On 24 September 1937, the film was viewed by Joseph I. Breen and the cutter for Hollywood producer Larry Darmour, but the cutter advised that deletions would completely destroy the entertainment value of the production. Early in 1938, a British cutter named Merrill White arrived in Hollywood, and he began working on the film, with the PCA re-viewing it up to twelve times. At last, on 6 April 1938, a weary Breen agreed to the issuance of a Certificate after the cutting of excessive drinking; a burlesque on the sanctity of marriage; the implication of miscegenation (taken care of with a new printed insert shot in Hollywood, indicating that the child was no longer the result of Uncle Sebastian's years in Africa but had been borrowed from the cook); 'vulgar, profane and double meaning dialogue'; 'much – but not all – of the "undressing scenes"'; indecent and obscene movements in the dances; risqué song lyrics; the bedroom scene (cut to a minimum); and all scenes of the strip poker game. Two scenes remained – a flash scene of a girl with garters showing above her stockings and a flash scene of a girl in a bathtub – that Breen did not like, but he agreed to let them go. He was passing the production with great reluctance, his real motivation being one of 'utter irritation' with White, who was a 'first-class nuisance'. 'If this be treason make the most of it,' Breen wrote to Francis S. Harmon in New York on 6 April 1938.

At this point, Gaumont British decided the film was unsuitable for US release. However, in July 1938, rights were acquired by C & M Pictures, Inc. When it submitted the film for approval, it was discovered that many deletions had not been made, but, eventually, on 28 July 1938, Certificate No. 4541 was issued. Then, on 16 September 1938, C & M decided to reject the Certificate and release the film without cuts, opening it at the 55th Street Playhouse in New York on 30 October 1938. Breen was furious. 'We get *rooked* with a number of these pictures made by non-member companies,' he wrote to Harmon on 4 October 1938, complaining that after a great deal of work on the part of the PCA, the end result was no payment of the fee.

Thunder Rock (1942)

Michael Redgrave stars in this allegory about an isolationist who rediscovers his commitment to fight fascism.

The PCA viewed the film at the request of M-G-M in May 1943 and found it in compliance with the Production Code, subject to deletion of one 'damn', five uses of 'hell', and two uses of 'Goddam'. However, on 11 June 1943, the studio advised it had decided not to release the production. Tentative Certificate No. 03873 was issued on 5 September 1944 and, two days later, Lester Thompson wrote to English Films, Inc., to say that the script had been read. He asked for deletion of profanity, together with two lines by Streeter: 'You've got me all wrong. I'm no crusader. All a Chinaman means to me is "Did he starch my shirt when I told him to." Japs, Chinks, I don't give a damn'; and, 'Pick your nose, examine your navel.' The Certificate was confirmed on 15 February 1945, and the film, cut to 90 minutes, was released by English Films, Inc., opening at New York's World Theatre on 14 September 1944.

Re-viewed on 12 October 1944, the film was classified 'B' by the National Legion of Decency: 'In the film's presentation of its message of courage and optimism there are traces of deism and naturalism whereby the impressions are gathered that God is a being far from this struggling world, and that man by himself can make the better world of the future.'

Tiger Bay (1959)

The film was viewed on 30 December 1959, and Continental Distributing, Inc., was advised that a Certificate could be issued if an early scene between Horst Buchholz and Yvonne Mitchell, in which 'bitch' was used several times, was deleted. The distributor demurred, but, unable to make a sale to the US military without a Certificate, it agreed to make the cut. Certificate No. 19730 was issued on 12 August 1960. The film was released by Continental in December 1960 and, in all probability, the cuts were not made for the film's general release and the Code Seal not affixed.

Tom Brown's Schooldays (1951)

On 20 June 1950, Joseph I. Breen wrote to Richard Gordon, Renown Pictures' representative in New York, that the script, dated May 1950, had been read and the material met the requirements of the Production Code. Minor problems were profanity, the advisability of Flashman's kicking Tom, and the need to avoid the suggestion that the boys were swimming nude. Tentative Certificate No. 14842 was issued on 13 September 1950. The film was released by United Artists on 9 November 1951, uncut. Neither UA nor Renown bothered to pay the PCA fee or obtain final approval of the film, and only after protest by Breen was the matter resolved and the Certificate confirmed on 25 November 1953.

Tony Draws a Horse (1950)

The emphasis in both the original play and film was on how Tony visualized the horse, and it was also the focal point of the PCA's response to the proposed production. When submitted in play form, Joseph I. Breen wrote, on 3 November 1949, to Jock Lawrence in the New York office of the J. Arthur Rank Organization, Inc., to inform him that the picture drawn by Tony was completely unacceptable for the screen. It would also be necessary to cut the dialogue in regard to the maid's immoral relationship with a soldier, and there was a problem in Clare's condoning of immorality. On 16 February 1950, a revised final shooting script, dated 9 January 1950, was read, and the basic story found to be acceptable. It was stressed that Tony's drawing should not be vulgar, and that the use of the word 'poop' was unacceptable. Dialogue in reel 2 between Dr and Mrs Fleming had to be cut in reference to the drawing being biologically correct. However, Universal, which had initially acquired the US rights, decided not to go ahead with the film, and it was released by a new distributor, Pinnacle Productions, Inc., without cuts and without a Certificate. *Tony Draws a Horse* opened at the Park Avenue Theatre, New York, on 14 May 1951.

The Trials of Oscar Wilde (1960)

On 1 March 1960, Geoffrey M. Shurlock wrote to tell Paramount Pictures that a synopsis, dated 19 February 1960, had been read, and

'Inasmuch as this story deals factually with Oscar Wilde's trials and conviction for homo-sexuality, it is in violation of the Code, and a picture based on it would not be approved by us.' The PCA viewed the film on 20 June 1960, and confirmed its ruling. *The Trials of Oscar Wilde* opened at the Paris Theatre, New York, in July 1960, uncut. The title was changed to *The Man with the Green Carnation* in August 1960, under which title it opened at the Paramount Theatre, Hollywood, on 23 September 1960. It was released on a states rights basis.

Turn the Key Softly (1953)

The story of what becomes of three women released from prison on the same morning and what becomes of them.

On 1 December 1952, Joseph I. Breen wrote to Kenneth Bates in the New York office of the J. Arthur Rank Organization, Inc., that the script, dated 3 November 1952, had been read. It contained items unacceptable from the standpoint of the Production Code, namely the characterization of Stella as a prostitute and the sex affair between Monica and David. There were fourteen pages with problems, including the showing of a bed, lustful kissing and vulgar emphasis on Mrs Quilliam's entering a ladies' room. Joyce M. Briggs, story editor at Pinewood Studios, responded that the producer had now made Stella 'a gold digger of weak but not bad character', and other items were being taken care of. The film was viewed on 11 August 1953, and Breen commented that the sex affair between Monica and David remained unacceptable. He also noted that the film bore Certificate No. 140707, despite no such number having been issued. On 27 November 1953, Rank responded that the film had been sold to a small, independent distributor, that it would be released without a Certificate and that the offending number would be removed from all prints. It was released by Astor Films, Inc., opening at the Pantages Theatre, Hollywood, on 17 March 1954, uncut.

24 Hours (1954)

This thriller features an American airforce pilot on leave who is framed for the murder of his wife by a gang of blackmailers and seeks the real murderer while on the run from the police. On 4 December 1950, Joseph I. Breen wrote to Alex Gottlieb to say that the script had been read and it was the PCA's unanimous judgment that the material was wholly and completely unacceptable under the requirements of the Production Code: it was a story of excessive violence, sex-suggestiveness and general depravity. On 11 November 1950, Jack Vizzard and Albert Van Schmus met with Gottlieb and major script changes were made on some twenty-four pages. Katie and Johnny would no longer live together; there would be no suggestion that Katie had been a prostitute; Sparrow would not be portrayed as a sex pervert; and Slauson could no longer be characterized as a complete sadist. At this point, the film was retitled *Goodbye to Katie*.

On 29 December 1950, a revised script was read and the basic material met the requirements of the Code. On 13 March 1953, a new script was read, and it contained a number of unacceptable items, including removal of fingerprints from a gun, the unfair portrayal of a charity worker, reference to narcotics, the slapping of Jenny, the brutality in a fight between Bill and Harry, and the implication that Slauson was involved in pornography. Tentative Certificate No. 16595 was issued on 8 June 1953, and confirmed on 1 July 1954. Retitled *Terror Street*, the film was released by Lippert Pictures, Inc., on 4 December 1954, uncut. It was released in Britain as *36 Hours*.

24 Hours of a Woman's Life (1952)

This romantic drama set on the French Riviera stars Merle Oberon as a woman who tries to cure a gambler of his compulsion.

On 19 June 1950, George W. Kreusser of Cusick International Films submitted the final shooting script for *23 Hours of a Woman's Life*, intended for production in London and Monte Carlo in August. On 26 June 1950, Joseph I. Breen reported that the story met the requirements of the Production Code, but noted a problem with the considerable amount of suggestive dialogue. He stressed the importance of introducing a definite 'voice for morality' in condemnation of Linda's willingness to run away with a man to whom she is not married, and commented that Sinclair's concluding speech was unacceptable in its suggestion that anything we do is all right, provided we feel like doing it. On 27 June Monogram Pictures Corp. submitted what was probably the same script and, that same day, Breen responded with an identical letter.

A script dated 27 September 1950 and titled *Just for the Night* was read by the PCA staff, who deemed the story unacceptable by reason of its improper treatment of adultery and justification of an illicit love affair between the leading male and female characters. It was noted that the element of adultery was not present in the earlier version of the script, and Breen passed on the comments of his staff to Monogram on 6 October 1950. On 6 and 16 October the PCA staff met with Scott R. Dunlap and Ben Schwalb of Monogram, and at those meetings it was agreed that the character of Sinclair, the yacht owner, should become the voice for morality. Six months later, on 4 April 1951, the PCA staff held a meeting with producer Ivan Foxwell, and he outlined a proposed treatment, eliminating the sex affair between Sir James and the film actress. Linda and Max would stop at a hotel because of the inability of their automobile to negotiate a hill, and scenes between the two would be played in the restaurant rather than a hotel room. Monogram submitted a new shooting script on 2 July 1951 and, two days later, Breen airmailed Ivan Foxwell, expressing delight at the changes in the basic story. He also pointed out that the prologue in which Stirling justified a boring wife running off with 'some gay stranger' would need to be eliminated; it was nothing more than 'a plea for what would amount to social chaos'. Finally, on 16 July 1951, Foxwell wrote to tell Breen that the scene between Stirling and Linda had been rewritten to eliminate any suggestion that they had slept together. A final shooting script of that day's date was read by Breen and approved.

Allied Artists registered the titles *Monte Carlo Affair* and *Affair in Monte Carlo* in August 1952. On 21 January 1953, Certificate No. 16341 was issued. Cut to 74 minutes, *Affair in Monte Carlo* was released by Allied Artists in September 1953.

29 Acacia Avenue (1945)

On 12 December 1949, Joseph I. Breen advised Oliver Unger at Distinguished Films, Inc., that he could not approve this film in its present form because of the improper treatment of adultery and illicit sex. He suggested various possible changes, but concluded that, even with all the eliminations, it was quite possible that he could not issue a Code Seal of Approval. Released by Oxford Films, Inc., and cut to 65 minutes, the film opened as *The Facts of Love* at New York's Embassy Theatre on 30 October 1949. It was rejected for screening in Ohio, and substantial cuts were required in Massachusetts, Maryland and Pennsylvania.

Venetian Bird (1952)

Richard Todd stars as a British agent searching for a former war hero who has become an assassin.

A shooting script submitted on 13 September 1951 by Kenneth Bates of the New York office of the J. Arthur Rank Organization, Inc., evoked a four-page negative response from Joseph I. Breen on 27 September 1951. Breen pointed out that the major problem was that Rosa's house was obviously a brothel and she and her friends were prostitutes. Such lines as 'Are you here on business or pleasure?', 'Professional or private visit?', 'I keep my men in bed, not under it', and 'Freud and I are in the same business: the relief of inhibitions', could not be approved, neither could the profanity throughout the script. A revised script was submitted by Bates on 19 February 1952 and, ten days later, Breen noted some new minor problems. A year later, on 17 March 1953, United Artists provided the PCA with a print of *Venetian Bird*, which it expected to retitle *The Assassin*. On 24 March 1953, Certificate No. 15831 was issued. Cut to 90 minutes, *The Assassin* was released by United Artists in April 1953.

Vessel of Wrath (1938)

Charles Laughton stars in this comedy-drama as a drunken beach-comber reformed by a missionary's sister.

A third script for *Vessel of Wrath*, formerly titled *Give a Dog a Name*, was submitted to the PCA by Budd Rogers of Alliance Films Corporation. On 15 October 1937, the PCA replied, in a five-page letter, stating a number of points: 'ministers of religion should not be used as comic characters or as villains', provisions regarding nudity also applied to natives, all profane expressions should be deleted, etc. Subsequently, F. S. Harmon, James Wingate and Vincent Hart from the PCA all worked personally with producer, Erich Pommer, to help revise the film. On 19 August 1938, a provisional Code Seal No. 02232 was issued. The Code Seal was confirmed on 5 October 1938 and, at that time, F. S. Harmon was moved to write a personal letter to Pommer, congratulating him on the re-editing of the film.

For the record, that same day Harmon also wrote to Budd Rogers:

We desire to state ... that we agreed to Ginger's use of the exclamation 'Aw, nuts in May!' solely for the reason that earlier in the picture Ginger was shown looking into the schoolroom where Miss Jones was shown teaching English to the native children by having them repeat after her, 'We are gathering nuts in May, nuts in May!' Approval of this expression in this picture does not constitute a precedent for such approval under different circumstances where the phrase would obviously have an objectionable connotation.

Cut to 88 minutes, *Vessel of Wrath* was released under the title *The Beachcomber* in November 1938. Some dialogue in double reels 2 and 3 was subsequently ordered to be eliminated in Ohio, in January 1939.

Wanted for Murder (1946)

A script for this film was first submitted to the PCA on 26 October 1938, by Mack Littman on behalf of producer Marcel Hellman. It was described by the PCA as the story of a sex degenerate who lures young girls into London parks and strangles them. On 31 October 1938, Francis S. Harmon wrote to Littman to say that the script contained violations of the Production Code both in basic theme and in important details. Seven years later, a new script was submitted in its final shooting format by Jason S. Joy at 20th Century-Fox. On 11 July 1945, Joseph I. Breen reported that the basic story appeared to comply with the requirements of the Code. There were a few minor problems, including the need to remove the suggestion that the woman trying to pick up Victor was a prostitute, the use of 'Oh, my God' on three occasions, and, most importantly, the avoidance of any hint of suicide in the drowning of Victor. Tentative Certificate No. 11049 was issued that day. On 18 July 1945, Marcel Hellman replied that Victor committed suicide because of his insanity, and, on 2 August Breen concurred that such action was acceptable under the Code. The Certificate was confirmed on 19 August 1946, and, cut to 92 minutes, the film was released by 20th Century-Fox in December 1946.

Warning to Wantons (1949)

On 23 January 1948, Stephen S. Jackson wrote to A. Reginald Allen at the Universal studios office of the J. Arthur Rank Organization, Inc., informing him that the script had been read. It failed to comply with the requirements of the Code in that Rene and Pauli live together outside of wedlock and engage in an illicit sex affair on the first night they meet. The relationship was not treated with full compensating moral values. Further, there were other problems, including the use of the word 'slut' three times, a striptease and the characterization of Gilbertier as a 'pansy'. To meet Code requirements, George Archibald at Pinewood Studios wrote, on 9 December 1948, that a special American version would be made, with, for example, 'you' substituted for 'slut'. Tentative Certificate No. 13617 was issued on 28 December 1948. The title was changed in the USA to *Warning All Wives* in January 1949, but the Certificate was never confirmed and there is no evidence of a contemporary US release.

Western Approaches (1944)

Western Approaches was first submitted to the PCA by Paramount Pictures in March 1945 as *Atlantic Adventure*, but it was withdrawn in August of that year when the company announced it would not release the film. In the original title, Tentative Certificate No. 04089 was issued on 28 November 1945 to English Films, Inc. It was cancelled on 14 March 1946, and, as *The Raider*, and cut to 70 minutes, the film was first released by English Films, Inc., without a Certificate, on 27 September 1946. On 29 November 1946, Nat Sanders of English Films met the PCA's Arthur H. DeBra and was advised that Certificate No. 04285 would be issued if he would delete 'hell', 'damned', 'damn', and 'God'. Sanders refused, and the new Certificate was cancelled on 5 April 1948. Massachusetts, New York, Ohio, and Pennsylvania all required elimination of the above words, and New York also added 'bastard'.

Whisky Galore (1949)

On 13 July 1948, Joseph I. Breen wrote to A. Reginald Allen at the Universal studios office of the J. Arthur Rank Organization, Inc., to say that the treatment, dated 2 June 1948, for *Tight Little Island* or *Liquid Treasure* had been read, and the basic story met the requirements of the Code. He asked for avoidance of any suggestion that the islanders are guilty of anything approaching a serious crime. On

5 August 1948, a revised shooting script, dated 16 July 1948, was read, and Breen required there be no possibility of a sex affair between Peggy and Odd in the sand dunes: they should be standing and not lying on the beach. Certificate No. 13321 was issued on 19 September 1949, and retitled *Tight Little Island*, the film was released by Universal-International, opening at the Trans-Lux 6oth Street Theatre, New York, on 25 December 1949, uncut.

A Window in London (1939)

Tentative Certificate No. 03353 was issued on 27 March 1942. The previous day, the PCA had informed the Lamont Pictures Company that, in its present form, the film contained a serious violation of the Production Code. The magician Zoltini shoots his wife, and there is no indication that the murderer pays the penalty for his crime. It was suggested that the distributor put in at the end of the film an insert of a newspaper story, showing that the murderer was taken into police custody. On 2 April 1942, additional deletions were listed by the PCA's Carl E. Milliken, including the slapping of Pat on her posterior by Peter, and Peter's reference to 'night starvation'. On 27 April 1942, Milliken confirmed that these cuts had been made, and that the insert ending had been included. The Certificate was then confirmed. Cut to 62 minutes, the film was released as *Lady in Distress* by Times Pictures, Inc., and opened in New York at the Globe Theatre on 14 February 1942.

Wings of the Morning (1937)

After viewing the film, Joseph I. Breen wrote to Jason S. Joy at 20th Century-Fox, on 28 December 1936, to say that much of the action showing Henry Fonda in the bathtub would need to be entirely eliminated. Certificate No. 2992 was issued that day. Released by 20th Century-Fox, the film opened at Radio City Music Hall, New York, on 11 March 1937; it was cut to 66 minutes for general release. All action involving Henry Fonda's believing Annabella to be a boy and undressing her, together with the couple sleeping in the hay together, was subject to local censorship cuts.

The Woman in Question (1950)

A script was submitted to the PCA on 20 March 1950 by Kenneth Bates in the New York office of the J. Arthur Rank Organization, Inc. Four days later, Joseph I. Breen responded that the basic story was unacceptable in that the central character, Astra, was portrayed as little better than a prostitute, with a positive implication of adultery with Murray. He listed twenty-seven pages of script with problems in action or dialogue. On 18 April 1950, director Anthony Asquith wrote directly to Breen, notating various changes he was making to the script, and concluding: 'We assure you that it has never been, or ever will be, our intention to make a film which is in any way suggestive or immoral.' Breen replied on 25 April 1950, with a few additional changes. On 20 July 1950 Asquith wrote that the film had now finished shooting and that he had complied to the best of his ability with Breen's requests, making an alternative US version.

That same day, a tentative Certificate No. 14748 was issued, and, a year later, on 26 July 1951, it was confirmed to Harry Cohn at Columbia. On 18 February 1952, the film opened at New York's Park Avenue Theatre. In December 1952, with a running time identical to that in the UK, it was released by Columbia Pictures as *Five Angles on Murder*. The local censorship board in Massachusetts required the elimination of the expressions, 'St Christopher!' and 'the two-faced tramp'.

The Wooden Horse (1950)

On 24 August 1949, Joseph I. Breen wrote to Jock Lawrence in the New York office of the J. Arthur Rank Organization, Inc., that the shooting script of this prisoner-of-war drama, dated 22 July 1949, had been read and the basic story met the requirements of the Production Code. There were, however, many problems, including Nigel's line, 'Heaven help his wife on their wedding night'; the dialogue in regard to the sex life of Eskimos was unacceptable, together with the story of the two bulls; there should be no implication that the house at No. 17 was a brothel; there should be no implication that the blonde is a prostitute; Peter should not stand on a toilet bowl or pull the chain; and there should be no excessive brutality in the fight between Peter and the sentry. The scenes in the wash-house were particularly troublesome. The intimate parts of the men's bodies were to be kept covered at all times, and, if under showers, there was to be an adequate solid screen in front of them, starting above the waist. No Certificate was issued, and the film, cut to 98 minutes, was released by Snader Productions on 28 August 1951.

A Yank at Oxford (1938)

On 20 August 1937, Joseph I. Breen wrote to M-G-M to say that the script had been read and the basic story met the requirements of the Production Code. He asked for deletion of the words 'rear end' and 'posterior', and noted that the one questionable element was a married woman, Elsa Craddock, pursuing college boys, references to which would need revision throughout. Certificate No. 4009 was issued on 3 January 1938, and the film was released by M-G-M, opening at the Capitol Theatre, New York, on 24 February 1938, with a running time of 100 minutes. Breen was much taken with the production, cabling his congratulations to producer Michael Balcon on 30 December 1937: 'The Yank is magnificent.' In a follow-up letter, dated 3 January 1938, Breen wrote: 'I really mean this. The picture is quite outstanding.'

Zarak (1957)

This Indian empire adventure stars Victor Mature as an Afghan chieftain and Michael Wilding as his Army antagonist.

On 29 October 1955, Geoffrey M. Shurlock wrote to producer Irving Allen that the script for *Zarak Khan* had been read. It contained extremes of cruelty, brutality and slaughter which definitely were unacceptable, including the whipping to death of Zarak, the beating of Zarak by Haji, the slashing of Zarak's nose, the stoning of Zarak, Zarak kicking Ingram in the head, Zarak striking Ismeet, the killing of Mahmud, and the bayoneting of the native policemen. There was a further problem with Salma's attire or lack of it. Tentative Certificate No. 17789 was issued that day. A rough cut was viewed on 19 August 1956, at which time the PCA pointed out problems with Anita Ekberg's costume, that her character and Zarak were living together outside marriage, there was too much emphasis on violence, and two open-mouth kissing scenes. It was agreed to wait until the British Board of Film Censors viewed the film, and then base the PCA action on the

British response. On 6 November 1956, a re-edited version was viewed, in which Columbia had cut two lashing scenes to a minimum, trimmed the first and second dances by Ekberg, eliminated two heavy embracing scenes on the balcony, and deleted the line, 'Closed up for the night'. The Certificate was confirmed on 31 December 1956, and, cut by one minute, the film was released by Columbia in January 1957. The film was classified 'B' by the National Legion of Decency: 'Despite substantial changes made by the producers of this film, the version presently exhibited still retains grossly suggestive costuming, dancing and situations.'

Appendix 1

Other British Films Released in the USA with a Production Code Certificate

Listed here are films not included in the main body of the book. Information is provided as to original American distributor, original American release date, original American running time, Certificate number and date of confirmation.

Abdul the Damned (1935), released by Alliance Films, Inc., December 1935, uncut. Certificate No. 1837 confirmed 6 December 1935.

The Abominable Snowman (1957), released by 20th Century-Fox, October 1957, cut to 85 minutes. Certificate No. 18535 confirmed 27 September 1957.

Accused (1936), released by United Artists, opening at the Criterion Theatre, New York, 17 December 1936, uncut. Certificate No. 01138 confirmed 4 December 1936.

Accused (1957), released as *Mark of the Hawk* by Universal-International, March 1958, uncut. Certificate No. 18853 confirmed 8 November 1957.

Action for Slander (1937), released by United Artists, 1938. Certificate No. 01654 confirmed 17 August 1937.

Action of the Tiger (1957), released by M-G-M, November 1957, uncut. Certificate No. 18354 confirmed 21 May 1957. Cuts required at script submission stage.

Adam and Evalyne (1949), released by Universal-International, December 1949, uncut. Certificate No. 13567 confirmed 24 October 1949. Cuts required at script submission stage.

The Admirable Crichton (1957), released as *Paradise Lagoon* by Columbia Pictures,

1958, uncut. Certificate No. 18403 confirmed 15 May 1957. Cuts required at script submission stage.

The Adventurers (1951), released as *The Great Adventure* by Lippert Pictures, Inc., opening at the New York Theatre, New York, 29 April 1952, cut to 76 minutes. Later retitled *Fortune in Diamonds*. Certificate No. 14741 confirmed 29 August 1951.

Alibi (1942), released by Republic Pictures, Inc., April 1943, cut to 66 minutes. Certificate No. 9173 confirmed 25 March 1943, subject to deletion of suggestive dialogue and implication that the Margaret Lockwood character was a prostitute and/or kept woman.

All over the Town (1949), released by Prestige Pictures, August 1949, uncut. Certificate No. 13295 confirmed 29 June 1949.

Always a Bride (1953), released by Universal-International, 27 May 1954. Certificate No. 16759 confirmed 13 October 1953. Cuts relating to hashish, a light attitude towards marriage and comedic aspects of adultery required at script submission stage.

The Amateur Gentleman (1936), released by United Artists, opening at the Roxy Theatre, New York, 24 April 1936, cut to 97 minutes. Certificate No. 0896 confirmed 11 February 1936.

The Amazing Quest of Mr Ernest Bliss (1936), released as *Romance and Riches* by Grand National Pictures, Inc., opening at the Strand Theatre, Brooklyn, 5 May 1937, cut to 56 minutes. Certificate No. 01452 confirmed 7 January 1937.

The Angry Hills (1959), released by M-G-M, June 1959, uncut. Certificate No. 19150 confirmed 11 December 1958. Cuts and legitimization of sexual relationship between Lisa and Mike required at script submission stage.

Another Man's Poison (1951), released by United Artists, 16 January 1952, cut by two minutes. Certificate No. 15257 confirmed 27 November 1951. Minor cuts, including a gag with a dog urinating, required at script submission stage.

Appointment with Venus (1951), released as *Island Rescue* by Universal-International, 30 June 1952, uncut. Certificate No. 15354 confirmed 20 December 1951. Cuts required at script submission stage.

As You Like It (1936), released by 20th Century-Fox, opening at Radio City Music Hall, New York, 5 November 1936, uncut. Reissued by United Artists, 1949. Certificate No. 01249 confirmed 23 September 1936.

Atlantic Ferry (1941), released as *Sons of the Sea* by Warner Bros, December 1941, cut to 90 minutes. Certificate No. 7720 confirmed 1 October 1941, subject to deletion of one 'damned'.

The Bandit of Zhobe (1959), released by Columbia Pictures, April 1959, uncut. Certificate No. 19061 confirmed 2 February 1959. Cuts required at script

submission stage, including request that 'the slaughter be kept to a reasonable minimum'.

Barbados Quest (1955), released as *Murder on Approval* by RKO, May 1956,
uncut. Certificate No. 18025 confirmed 4 April 1956.

Barnacle Bill (1957), released as *All at Sea* by M-G-M, January 1958, uncut.
Certificate No. 18718 confirmed 23 December 1957. PCA required that the
girls not wear bikini-type bathing suits.

The Barretts of Wimpole Street (1957), released by M-G-M, February 1957, uncut.
Certificate No. 18177 confirmed 24 September 1956. PCA expressed concern that there be nothing incestuous in Barrett's love for Elizabeth and
that portrayal of the former as 'a synthetically pious, Bible-spouting villain'
made a mockery of religion and prayer.

Before I Wake (1955), released as *Shadow of Fear* by United Artists, June 1956,
cut by two minutes. Certificate No. 17464 confirmed 29 December 1955.
Cuts required at script submission stage, and PCA noted it was offensive
to have April clutching a St Christopher medal while plotting to kill
Florence.

The Beggar's Opera (1953), released by Warner Bros, 26 September 1953, uncut.
Certificate No. 16384 confirmed 13 August 1953. Ealing Studios protested
that it had registered *The Beggar's Opera* with the Title Registration Bureau
and that no Certificate should have been issued to Warner Bros for a film
of that title.

Behemoth The Sea Monster (1959), released as *The Giant Behemoth* by Allied Artists,
Inc., March 1959, uncut. Certificate No. 19083 confirmed 12 March 1959.

The Bells Go Down (1943) was to have been released by United Artists, but
there is no evidence of a contemporary US release. Certificate No. 03508
tentatively issued 16 October 1942.

The Beloved Vagabond (1936), released by Columbia Pictures, opening at the
Globe Theatre, New York, 6 February 1937, cut to 68 minutes. Certificate
No. 2920 confirmed 12 December 1936.

Beyond Monbasa (1956), released by Columbia Pictures, June 1957, uncut.
Certificate No. 17934 confirmed 4 October 1956.

Beyond This Place (1959), released as *Web of Evidence* by Allied Artists, Inc.,
September 1959, cut to 88 minutes. Certificate No. 19250 confirmed 8 April
1960. Cuts required at script submission stage, including unseemly exposure
of boy in bathtub and open-mouth kissing.

The Big Blockade (1942) was acquired for release as *Blockade* by Hal Roach, but
there is no evidence of a contemporary US release. Certificate No. 03214
was tentatively issued 26 August 1941, on the understanding that profanity
would be deleted.

Bitter Springs (1950), released by Bell Pictures, Inc., 1 October 1951, cut to 73 minutes. Tentative Certificate No. 13913 issued 6 June 1949 but never confirmed. Cuts required at script submission stage.

Bitter Sweet (1933), released by United Artists, opening at the Rivoli Theatre, New York, 23 August 1933, cut to 89 minutes. The paperwork is lost but a Certificate is believed to have been issued.

The Black Sheep of Whitehall (1941) was planned for release by Hal Roach, May 1942, cut to 45 minutes, but there is no evidence of a contemporary US release. Certificate No. 03215 confirmed 26 August 1941.

Blackmailed (1951), released by H. H. Films, Inc., and Bell Pictures, Inc., 15 October 1951, cut to 73 minutes. Tentative Certificate No. 14840 issued 15 September 1950 but never confirmed. Cuts required at script submission stage, including scene of criminals removing fingerprints.

Blanche Fury (1948), released by Eagle-Lion Films, Inc., 11 September 1948, uncut. Certificate No. 12213 issued to Universal-International, 22 April 1948, cancelled and reissued to Eagle-Lion Films, Inc., 17 June 1948. Cuts required at script submission stage.

Blind Date (1959), released as *Chance Meeting* by Paramount Pictures, March 1960, uncut. Certificate No. 19481 confirmed 27 November 1959, on the understanding that a scene in artist's studio showing the silhouette of a girl on the wall be removed.

The Blind Goddess (1948), released by Universal-International, June 1949, uncut. Certificate No. 12872 confirmed 16 June 1949. Original script rejected in that suicide at the climax was condoned and justified. Approved revised script had Lord Newton knocked down and killed by a bus.

Blithe Spirit (1945), released by United Artists, opening at the Winter Garden Theatre, New York, 3 October 1945, cut by two minutes. Certificate No. 11215 confirmed 28 September 1945. Classified 'B' by the National Legion of Decency for 'suggestive dialogue and situations'.

Blood of the Vampire (1958), released by Universal Pictures, Inc., November 1958, uncut. Certificate No. 19145 confirmed 25 August 1958.

Blossom Time (1934), released as *April Blossoms* by M-G-M, opening at the Belmont Theatre, New York, 28 January 1937, cut to 80 minutes. Certificate No. 1524 confirmed 12 September 1935.

Breach of Promise (1941), released as *Adventure in Blackmail* by English Films, Inc., opening at the Strand Theatre, New York, 5 August 1943, cut to 70 minutes. Certificate No. 03639 confirmed 23 July 1943, subject to the deletion of 'Good Lord' and 'Haven't I seen that behind before'.

Break in the Circle (1955), released by 20th Century-Fox, April 1957, cut by nine minutes. Certificate No. 18541 confirmed 1 April 1957. Minor cuts required at script submission stage.

Break The News (1938), released by Trio Films, Inc., opening at the Bryant Theatre, New York, 2 January 1941, cut to 72 minutes. Certificate No. 03021 confirmed 23 December 1940.

Brief Ecstasy (1937), released as *Dangerous Secrets* by Grand National Pictures, Inc., opening at the Central Theatre, New York, 24 October 1938, cut to 59 minutes. Certificate No. 4679 confirmed 8 September 1938, after the deletion of an implication of an illicit sex affair in reel 1.

Britannia Mews (1949), released as *The Forbidden Street* by 20th Century-Fox, opening at the Roxy Theatre, New York, 13 May 1949, cut by three minutes. Certificate No. 13228 confirmed 30 December 1948. Cuts required at script submission stage, largely to avoid suggestion that The Blazer might be a prostitute.

Brown on Resolution (1935), released as *Born for Glory* by Gaumont British Picture Corp. of America, opening at the Globe Theatre, New York, 19 October 1935, cut by ten minutes. Released as *Torpedo Raider* by Monogram Pictures, Inc., 1940, cut to 55 minutes. Certificate No. 0566 confirmed 26 July 1935, after cutting of reel 1.

The Browning Version (1951), released by Universal-International, November 1951, uncut. Certificate No. 15627 confirmed 28 March 1951.

Bulldog Drummond at Bay (1937), released by Republic Pictures, Inc., 31 July 1937, cut to 63 minutes. Certificate No. 01645 confirmed 2 June 1937. Minor changes were required, including the deletion of 'hell' throughout and avoidance of undue cruelty in the killing of the love-birds with poison gas.

Bulldog Sees It Through (1940) was scheduled for release as *Bulldog Strikes Again* by Fine Arts Film and Studio Corp., 1942, but the company went out of existence shortly after the issuance of the Code Seal of Approval and there is no evidence of a contemporary US release. Certificate No. 0357 confirmed 27 April 1942, subject to the deletion of 'damned' in reel 7.

Burma Victory (1945), released by Warner Bros, 1945, uncut. Certificate No. 11332 confirmed 4 December 1945.

Busman's Holiday (1940), released by M-G-M, August 1940, cut to 83 minutes. Certificate No. 6280 confirmed August 1, 1940. Minor cuts required at script submission stage.

A Canterbury Tale (1944), released by Eagle-Lion Films, Inc., 21 January 1949, cut to 95 minutes. Certificate No. 10904 confirmed 12 June 1945, subject to deletion of all profanity and references to marijuana.

Captain Boycott (1947), released by Individal Pictures (a subsidiary of Universal-International), January 1948, uncut. Certificate No. 12150 confirmed 17 October 1947, subject to deletion of word 'slut'. Cuts required at script submission stage.

The Captive Heart (1946), released by Prestige Pictures, opening at Studio 65, New York, 26 April 1947, cut to 86 minutes. Certificate No. 11953 confirmed 27 August 1946.

The Card (1952), released as *The Promoter* by Universal-International, October 1952, cut to 88 minutes. Certificate No. 15548 confirmed 19 August 1952. Minor cuts required at script submission stage.

Carry On Sergeant (1958), released by Governor Films, Inc., November 1959, uncut. Certificate No. 19423 confirmed 14 August 1959.

Children on Trial (1946), released by English Films, Inc., opening at the Gotham Theatre, New York, 8 November 1947. One year later, Certificate No. 04696 was confirmed 9 November 1948, subject to deletion of 'You're a cheap, dirty, little tart' and 'Good Lord'.

The Chiltern Hundreds (1949), released as *The Amazing Mr Beecham* by Eagle-Lion Films, Inc., 1950, uncut. Certificate No. 13670 confirmed 23 February 1950. Among eliminations required was Lord Lister's exposition on the sex life of the salmon.

The Chinese Bungalow (1940), released as *Chinese Den* by Film Alliance of the United States, Inc., 25 March 1941, uncut. A month later, the US title was changed to *The Chinese Bungalow*. Certificate No. 03080 confirmed 14 March 1941, on understanding that Sing did not commit suicide at film's conclusion, deletion of profanity and Sing's statement that 'just revenge is never murder', etc.

Circle of Danger (1951), released by Eagle-Lion Films, Inc., April 1951, uncut. Certificate No. 15015 confirmed 17 August 1951. Cuts required at script submission stage.

The Clairvoyant (1935), released by Gaumont British Picture Corp. of America, opening at the Roxy Theatre, New York, 7 June 1935, cut to 72 minutes. Certificate No. 0526 confirmed 24 June 1935.

Climbing High (1938), released by 20th Century-Fox, opening at the Globe Theatre, New York, 4 June 1939, cut to 71 minutes. Certificate No. 02145 confirmed 23 December 1938.

Cloak Without Danger (1956), released as *Operation Conspiracy* by Republic Pictures, Inc., 1957. Certificate No. 18634 confirmed 14 June 1957.

The Clouded Yellow (1950), released by Columbia Pictures, opening at the Park Avenue Theatre, New York, 12 November 1951, uncut. Certificate No. 14606 confirmed 15 January 1951. Minor cuts requested at script submission stage.

The Cockleshell Heroes (1955), released by Columbia Pictures, April 1956, cut to 94 minutes. Certificate No. 17642 confirmed 14 February 1956, subject to deletion of 'bastard' from reel 12.

Come On George (1939), released by United Artists, 1942. Certificate No. 7470 confirmed 9 January 1942. Eliminations from the print required by the PCA include dialogue concerning the old man who followed horses with a bucket and shovel, corset-clad girls, George Formby's scratching his posterior after a kid has put fleas down his trousers, a nurse displaying too much flesh, and her comment to Formby, 'I'll take down your particulars'.

Cone of Silence (1960), released as *Trouble in the Sky* by Universal-International, opening at the Hillstreet Theatre, Los Angeles, 3 May 1961, cut to 76 minutes. Certificate No. 19739 confirmed 26 August 1960.

Confidential Lady (1939) was planned for released by Warner Bros, but in October 1939, they advised the PCA that they could not get the negative out of Britain and there would be no American release. Certificate No. 5762 confirmed 2 October 1939, subject to deletion of 'hell,' 'damn' and 'Oh, nuts'.

Conspirator (1949), released by M-G-M, 24 March 1950, uncut. Certificate No. 13717 confirmed 31 March 1949.

Convict 99 (1938) received Certificate No. 02148, 15 June 1938, but in January 1939, Gaumont British Picture Corp. of America advised the PCA that it did not intend to release the film in the USA, and the Certificate was cancelled.

The Courtneys of Curzon Street (1947) was scheduled for US release as *The Courtneys*. Certificate No. 15137 was confirmed 16 February 1951, but cancelled 18 April 1952 when Lopert Distributing Corp. failed to pay the $500 fee.

The Cruel Sea (1953), released by Universal-International, 19 August 1953, cut by five minutes. Certificate No. 16500 confirmed 15 April 1953 on the understanding that 'damn' and 'bastard' throughout had been deleted, with the exception of 'Damn the war', which was permitted to remain.

The Curse of Frankenstein (1957), released by Warner Bros, July 1957, uncut. Certificate No. 18481 confirmed 2 May 1957, subject to the deletion of a gruesome shot in the laboratory. Classified 'B' by the National Legion of Decency: 'This picture contains material which is judged to be morally questionable for entertainment purposes.'

Curtain Up (1952), released by Fine Arts Films, Inc., opening at the Trans-Lux 60th Street Theatre, New York, 31 January 1953. Certificate No. 15851 confirmed 28 November 1952, after deletion of expression 'a hell of a head' and objectionable painting of a naked woman wearing a cocked hat.

The Dam Busters (1955), released by Warner Bros, opening at the Egyptian Theatre, Hollywood, 17 June 1955, cut to 101 minutes. Certificate No. 17528 confirmed 21 July 1955.

Dangerous Moonlight (1941), released as *Suicide Squadron* by Republic Pictures, Inc., April 1942, cut to 83 minutes. Certificate No. 8133 confirmed 23 February 1942.

Dangerous Voyage (1954), released as *Terror Ship* by Lippert Pictures, Inc., 3 September 1954, uncut. Certificate No. 17123 confirmed 14 July 1954.

Dark Eyes of London (1939), released as *The Human Monster* by Monogram Pictures, Inc., 9 March 1940, uncut. Certificate No. 02754 confirmed 7 February 1940, subject to trimming of the murders of Grogan and Dumb Lew.

The Dark Man (1951), released by Fine Arts Films, Inc., opening at four Los Angeles theatres, 21 February 1952, cut to 73 minutes. Certificate No. 14742 confirmed 14 May 1951. Minor cuts required at script submission stage.

The Day They Robbed the Bank of England (1960), released by M-G-M, July 1960, uncut. Certificate No. 19475 confirmed 18 November 1959. Minor cuts required at script submission stage.

The Day Will Dawn (1942), released as *The Avengers* by Paramount Pictures, opening at the Rivoli Theatre, New York, 24 November 1942, cut by ten minutes. Certificate No. 8872 confirmed 28 September 1942, subject to deletion of profanity throughout.

Dear Octopus (1943), released as *The Randolph Family* by English Films, Inc., 10 March 1945. Certificate No. 04061 confirmed 16 October 1945, subject to deletion of profanity throughout and five suggestive lines.

The Demi-Paradise (1943), released as *Adventure for Two* by United Artists, opening at the Winter Garden Theatre, New York, 13 December 1945. Certificate No. 03979 confirmed 13 April 1945, subject to deletion of three uses of 'hell' in reel 12.

Desert Victory (1943), released by 20th Century-Fox, 16 April 1943, uncut. Certificate No. 03584 confirmed 7 April 1943.

Dinner at the Ritz (1937), released by 20th Century-Fox, November 1937, uncut. Certificate No. 01791 confirmed 21 October 1937.

The Divine Spark (1935) was to have been released by Gaumont British Picture Corp. of America but there is no record of the film in its 1935–36 schedule; it did release another Marta Eggerth vehicle as *Lover Divine*, but this is the 1934 British feature, *The Unfinished Symphony*. Certificate no. 0690 confirmed 1 October 1935.

The Divorce of Lady X (1938), released by United Artists, opening at Radio City Music Hall, New York, 31 March 1938. Certificate No. 01416 confirmed 28 January 1938. Requested dialogue deletions were not made because of 'mechanical difficulties'.

Doctor at Sea (1955), released by Republic Pictures, Inc., March 1956, uncut. Certificate No. 17845 confirmed 8 February 1956. A 'bad breast exposure' of Brigitte Bardot was impossible to cut.

Doctor in the House (1954), released by Republic Pictures, Inc., March 1955, cut to 88 minutes. Certificate No. 17283 confirmed 26 November 1954. Cuts were made at the script submission stage.

The Doctor's Dilemma (1958), released by M-G-M, January 1959, uncut. Certificate No. 19065 confirmed 2 December 1958.

Don't Take It to Heart (1944), released by Eagle-Lion Films, Inc., opening at the Esquire Theatre, Los Angeles, 10 March 1949, cut by three minutes. Certificate No. 10906 confirmed 7 June 1945.

The Door with Seven Locks (1940), released as *Chamber of Horrors* by Monogram Pictures, Inc., 12 August 1940, cut by two minutes. Certificate No. 02911 confirmed 19 July 1940, after deletion of a reference to etchings and a portion of the sequence with a girl in the bathroom.

Dracula (1958), released as *Horror of Dracula* by Universal-International, June 1958. Certificate No. 18981 confirmed 24 July 1958.

Dunkirk (1958), released by M-G-M, September 1958, cut to 113 minutes. Certificate No. 18714 confirmed 23 May 1958.

Dusty Ermine (1936), released as *Hideout in the Alps* by Grand National Pictures, Inc., 23 July 1937, cut to 75 minutes. Certificate No. 01516 confirmed 13 July 1937.

D'Ye Ken John Peel? (1935), released as *Captain Moonlight* by Atlas Film Exchange, 1940, cut to 60 minutes. Certificate No. 0712 confirmed 11 October 1935.

East Meets West (1936), released by Gaumont British Picture Corp. of America, opening at the Roxy Theatre, New York, 30 October 1936, uncut. Paperwork is missing but a Certificate is believed to have been confirmed.

East of Piccadilly (1941), released as *The Strangler* by PRC, 3 April 1942, uncut. Certificate No. 03260 confirmed 10 March 1942, subject to deletion of profanity throughout, 'sluts' in reel 6 and suggestive dialogue relating to immorality and 'bedding pansies'.

Easy Money (1948), released by Eagle-Lion Films, Inc., opening at the Beacon Theatre, New York, 13 February 1949, uncut. Certificate No. 12798 confirmed 30 June 1949.

Elephant Boy (1937), released by United Artists, opening at the Rialto Theatre, New York, 5 April 1937. Certificate No. 01077 confirmed 3 March 1937.

Emil and the Detectives (1935), released by Olympic Pictures Corporation, opening as the first presentation at the Showshop (formerly the President Theatre), New York, 14 April 1938. Certificate No. 01318 confirmed 20 October 1936.

English Without Tears (1944), released by Universal-International, opening at the Embassy Theatre, New York, 8 June 1949, cut to 78 minutes. Certificate No. 03890 confirmed 12 October 1944.

Escape Route (1953), released by Lippert Pictures, Inc., 16 January 1953, uncut.

Certificate No. 16311 confirmed 26 December 1952. Minor cuts required at script submission stage.

Everybody Dance (1936), released by Gaumont British Picture Corp. of America, 1937, cut to 68 minutes. Certificate No. 01272 confirmed 5 April 1937.

Everything is Thunder (1936), released by Gaumont British Picture Corp. of America, opening at the Strand Theatre, Brooklyn, 19 November 1936, cut by four minutes. Certificate No. 01045 confirmed 1 September 1936, after deletion of scenes and dialogue suggesting Anna was a prostitute and addition of dialogue indicating couple were married 'according to the conventions of society'.

F. P. One (1933), released by Fox, opening at the Roxy Theatre, New York, 15 September 1933. Reissued by Gaumont British Picture Corp. of America, 1938. Certificate No. 1643 confirmed 8 October 1935.

Farewell Again (1937), released as *Troopship* by United Artists, opening at the Little Carnegie Theatre, New York, 25 April 1938, uncut. Certificate No. 01418 confirmed 20 May 1937.

Father Brown (1954), released as *The Detective* by Columbia Pictures, September 1954, uncut. Certificate No. 16966 confirmed 29 June 1954.

Father O'Flynn (1935), released by J. H. Hoffberg Co., Inc., opening at the Squire Theatre, New York, 25 December 1938, cut to 66 minutes. Certificate No. 02332 confirmed 22 November 1938, after deletion of a scene in which a priest has a drink in his hand.

The First of the Few (1942), released as *Spitfire* by RKO, opening at the Rivoli Theatre, New York, 12 June 1943, cut to 90 minutes. Certificate No. 9204 confirmed 3 March 1943, after deletion of three uses of 'damned' and sex-suggestive line by David Niven to the barmaid, 'Just a test pilot'.

The Flemish Farm (1943), released by Eagle-Lion Films, Inc., 1945. Certificate No. 10903 confirmed 7 June 1945, subject to deletion of 'damn', 'hell', 'God', and 'son of a ... '.

Flesh and Blood (1951) received Certificate No. 15150, 9 April 1951, but it was cancelled 18 April 1952, because of the failure of Lopert Films Distributing Corp. to pay the $500 fee. The film was released by Snader Productions later in 1952, by which time it had already been seen on US television.

Floodtide (1949), released by Eagle-Lion Films, Inc., 1950. Certificate No. 13536 confirmed 23 Febraury 1950. All profanity was deleted or rerecorded, except for one 'Lord!', which could not be re-recorded as the actor involved had since died.

The Foreman Went to France (1942), released as *Somewhere in France* by United Artists, opening at the Globe Theatre, New York, 11 July 1943, cut to 84 minutes. Tentative Certificate No. 03216 issued 26 August 1941, but not confirmed.

Fortune is a Woman (1957), released as *She Played with Fire* by Columbia Pictures, May 1958, uncut. Certificate No. 18400 confirmed 12 April 1957, after deletion of description on how to commit arson without detection and indication of an adulterous affair.

Freedom Radio (1941), released by Columbia Pictures, 20 May 1941, cut to 79 minutes. Certificate No. 03100 confirmed 15 May 1941.

Gaiety George (1946), released by English Films, Inc., May 1948, cut to 89 minutes. Certificate No. 04567 confirmed 28 May 1948, subject to shortening of scene in which Daphne does the 'can-can'.

The Gang Show (1937) was intended for release by RKO, but there is no evidence of a contemporary US release. Paperwork is missing but a Certificate is believed to have been confirmed, subject to deletion of sequence with Boy Scout masquerading as a clergyman.

The Gentle Sex (1943) received Certificate No. 10919, which was cancelled on 24 June 1947. There is no evidence of a contemporary US release.

Gentleman of Venture (1940), released by RKO, opening at the Little Carnegie Theatre, New York, 22 February 1941, uncut. Certificate No. 03009 confirmed on 25 November 1940, after judicious re-editing to avoid central male character's committing suicide and statement he is guilty of murder.

Gideon's Day (1958), released by Columbia Pictures, February 1959, uncut. Certificate No. 18802 confirmed 14 January 1958, subject to deletion of profanity throughout.

Gilbert and Sullivan (1953), released by United Artists, October 1953, cut to 105 minutes. Certificate No. 16400 confirmed 15 January 1954.

Glamorous Night (1937), released by Republic Pictures, Inc., 1937. Certificate No. 01662 confirmed 14 June 1937, subject to deletion of one 'damn', the maid's line, 'and you'd never guess where your tiara is', and Melitza's reply, 'What an original place to wear it'.

The Golden Disc (1958), released by Allied Artists, Inc., 3 August 1958, uncut. Certificate No. 19098 confirmed 27 June 1958.

The Golden Salamander (1950), released by Eagle-Lion Classics, Inc., opening at the Vogue Theatre, Hollywood, 4 April 1951, uncut. Certificate No. 13864 confirmed 2 October 1950. At script submission stage, PCA requested omission of a belch and the line, 'In this country Allah is great and dyspepsia is his prophet' as offensive to 'Mohammedans'.

Goodbye, Mr Chips (1939), released by M-G-M, opening at the Astor Theatre, New York, 15 May 1939, uncut. Certificate No. 5086 confirmed 28 April 1939. Noting that the book would make 'a delightfully clean picture', PCA requested deletions at the script submission stage, including 'stinker', 'fat ass', a goosing gag, and 'frog' (as offensive to the French).

Goodnight Vienna (1932), released as *Magic Night* by United Artists, opening at the Rivoli Theatre, New York, 2 November 1932. Certificate No. 0614 confirmed 21 August 1935, subject to deletion of two shots of scantily clad men in reel 1, and suggestive dialogue and profanity throughout. In 1940, United Artists advised that its rights had expired and the new distributor, Select Attractions, Inc., planned to reinsert the cut footage if it could be obtained from the UK.

The Goose Steps Out (1942) was scheduled for release by United Artists, but there is no evidence of a contemporary US release. Certificate No. 03376 confirmed 15 April 1942.

Grand National Night (1953), released as *Wicked Wife* by Allied Artists, Inc., 25 October 1955, cut to 75 minutes. Certificate No. 17698 confirmed 12 September 1955. Minor cuts required at script submission stage, including profanity and two references to divorce by Philip.

The Great Barrier (1937), released as *Silent Barriers* by Gaumont British Picture Corp. of America, opening at the Criterion Theatre, New York, 25 March 1937, uncut. Certificate No. 01468 confirmed 9 March 1937, after deletion of 'hell' (twice), 'dago', 'for God's sake', and dialogue and action suggesting Steve spent the night with the young girl in his room.

Great Day (1945), released by RKO, July 1946, cut to 68 minutes. Certificate No. 11621 confirmed 23 April 1946, subject to deletion of a slap on the posterior in reel 4.

Great Expectations (1946), released by Universal-International, opening at Radio City Music Hall, New York, 22 May 1947, cut by three minutes. Certificate No. 12128 confirmed 3 March 1947.

The Green Scarf (1954), released by Associated Artists Productions, Inc., opening at the Egyptian and Paramount Theatres, Los Angeles, 6 May 1955. Certificate No. 17496 confirmed 12 April 1955.

Grip of the Strangler (1958), released as *The Haunted Strangler* by M-G-M, May 1958, uncut. Certificate No. 18998 confirmed 10 March 1958. Specific changes requested included cutting of depraved reaction of audience at hanging, abbreviation of jail lashing and elimination of bust exposure during champagne spilling and in dressing room. M-G-M agreed to do what it could but without cutting the negative.

Hamlet (1948), released by Universal-International, opening at Park Avenue Theatre, New York, 29 September 1948, uncut. Certificate No. 12473 confirmed 25 May 1948. PCA expressed hesitance at suggesting further cutting of the text, but asked for deletion of Hamlet's line, 'That's a fair thought to lie between maid's legs.'

Happy Ever After (1954), released as *Tonight's the Night* by Allied Artists, Inc., December 1954, uncut. Certificate No. 16877 confirmed 29 June 1954. Cuts required at script submission stage, including profanity, open-mouth kissing, cries of 'Fire, Fire', and indication of an illicit sex affair between Serena and Jasper.

Happy Go Lovely (1951), released by RKO, 18 July 1951, cut to 88 minutes. Certificate No. 14659 confirmed 10 April 1951. Cuts required at script submission stage, including use of the word 'frog' and comedy regarding Frost and his kilt.

Harry Black and the Tiger (1958), released by 20th Century-Fox, September 1958, cut by ten minutes. Certificate No. 18993 confirmed 13 August 1958. Cuts required at script submission stage, including avoidance of gruesomeness in the tiger's attack on humans and only suggesting, not showing, the beating of a dog.

The Hasty Heart (1949), released by Warner Bros, opening at the Strand Theatre, New York, 20 January 1950, cut by two minutes. Certificate No. 13890 confirmed 1 June 1949. Cuts required at script submission stage, including running gag of men looking under Lachie's kilt to see if he is wearing underwear.

Head Over Heels (1937), released as *Head Over Heels in Love* by Gaumont British Picture Corp. of America, 30 January 1937, cut to 87 minutes. Certificate No. 01185 confirmed 17 February 1937, subject to various minor deletions.

Her Favourite Husband (1950), released as *The Taming of Dorothy* by Eagle-Lion Classics, Inc., November 1950, cut to 75 minutes. Certificate No. 14849 confirmed 6 November 1950.

High Flight (1957), released by Columbia Pictures, April 1958, cut to 85 minutes. Certificate No. 18319 confirmed 16 October 1957. Cuts required at script submission stage.

Hindle Wakes (1952) was to have been released in the USA as *Holiday Week*, but there is no evidence of a contemporary US release. Certificate No. 16516 confirmed 17 April 1953, subject to deletion of last line in the film, 'That was a grand week we had – and I shall never regret it.'

His Excellency (1952), released by Joseph Brenner Associates, opening at the 55th Street Playhouse, New York, 1 February 1956. Certificate No. 15343 confirmed 28 May 1951, subject to deletion of fifteen expressions of profanity.

His Lordship (1937), released as *Man of Affairs* by Gaumont British Picture Corp. of America, opening at the Criterion Theatre, New York, 19 February 1937, uncut. Certificate No. 01186 confirmed 14 January 1937, subject to deletion of 'Oh, Lord' and 'damn'.

Holiday Camp (1947), released by Universal-International, January 1948, uncut. Tentative Certificate No. 12388 issued April 1947, confirmation date unknown. Major cuts required at script submission stage, removing suggestion of illicit sex affair, and excessive and unnecessary drinking throughout, etc.

Honours Easy (1935), released as *Jilted* by Alliance Films Corp., 1936. Certificate No. 01088 confirmed 5 June 1936, subject to deletion of profanity, various shots of Greta Nissen dressing and undressing and two suggestive lines.

The Horse's Mouth (1958), released by Lopert-United Artists, November 1958, cut to 93 minutes. Certificate No. 19408 confirmed 20 July 1959.

The Hound of the Baskervilles (1959), released by United Artists, June 1959, cut to 84 minutes. Certificate No. 19213 confirmed 26 June 1959.

Hunted (1952), released as *Stranger in Between* by Universal-International, August 1952, uncut. Certificate No. 15512 confirmed 6 August 1952. Cuts required at script submission stage, including 'tart', lustful flavour of Magda's speech and toning down of bedroom scene between Magda and Lloyd.

The Hypnotist (1957), released as *Scotland Yard Dragnet* by Republic Pictures, Inc., 1957. Certificate No. 18755 confirmed 16 October 1957. Cuts required at script submission stage, including illicit sex affair between Suzie and Val and suicide of Pelham in order to escape police capture.

I Know Where I'm Going (1945), released by Prestige Pictures, August 1947, uncut. Certificate No. 11820 confirmed 27 September 1946, subject to deletion of six expressions of profanity and assurance that the Gaelic language in the film contained no profanity.

I Live in Grosvenor Square (1945), released as *A Yank in London* by 20th Century-Fox, February 1946, cut to 107 minutes. Certificate No. 04096 confirmed 20 February 1946.

I Met a Murderer (1939), released by York Pictures, Inc., opening at the 55th Street Playhouse, New York, 1 October 1939. Certificate No. 02900 confirmed 21 June 1940.

I See a Dark Stranger (1946), released by Eagle-Lion Films, Inc., 17 March 1947, cut to 98 minutes. Certificate No. 11954 confirmed 2 October 1946. Cuts required at script submission stage.

Ice Cold in Alex (1958), released by 20th Century-Fox, opening at the Paradise and Hawaii Theatres, Los Angeles, 21 December 1960 cut to 80 minutes. Certificate No. 19618 confirmed 7 March 1960.

An Ideal Husband (1948), released by 20th Century-Fox, opening at the Roxy Theatre, New York, 14 January 1947, uncut. Certificate No. 12764 confirmed 6 January 1948. Minor cuts required at script submission stage.

I'll Get You for This (1951), released as *Lucky Nick Cain* by 20th Century-Fox, March 1951, cut to 87 minutes. Certificate No. 14696 confirmed 11 December 1950. Cuts required at script submission stage, including sex-suggestive dialogue, unattached women not to be prostitutes, rooms above the café not to be a brothel, sympathetic leads not to be shown killing police officers, and no machine guns shown in hands of criminals.

I'm All Right, Jack (1959), released by Lion International Films, Inc., 1960, cut by one minute. Certificate No. 19662 confirmed 13 July 1960, subject to elimination of nudist camp sequences.

The Importance of Being Earnest (1952), released by Universal-International, December 1952, uncut. Certificate No. 15780 confirmed 21 October 1952. Minor cuts required at script submission stage.

An Inspector Calls (1954), released by Associated Artists Productions, Inc., opening at the El Rey Theatre, Los Angeles, 20 May 1955, uncut. Certificate No. 17498 confirmed 13 April 1955.

Inspector Hornleigh (1939), released by 20th Century-Fox, opening at the Rialto Theatre, New York, 14 June 1939, cut to 76 minutes. It was later cut to 61 minutes. Certificate No. 02506 confirmed 11 April 1939, subject to deletion of two indistinct utterances that sounded like 'God'.

Inspector Hornleigh on Holiday (1939), released by 20th Century-Fox, 1 December 1939, cut to 77 minutes. Certificate No. 02707 confirmed 30 November 1939, subject to deletion of one line.

The Interrupted Journey (1949), released by Lopert Films, Inc., June 1951, uncut. Certificate No. 14513 confirmed 14 April 1950.

Into the Blue (1950) received Certificate No. 15110 on 16 February 1951, subject to deletion of 'What the hell' in reel 4. The Certificate was cancelled 18 April 1952, when Lopert Films, Inc., failed to pay the $575 fee, and there is no evidence of a contemporary US release.

The Iron Duke (1934), released by Gaumont British Picture Corp. of America, opening at Radio City Music Hall, New York, 24 January 1935, uncut. Later cut to 80 minutes. Certificate No. 0296 confirmed 16 January 1935.

It's in the Air (1938), released by B.S.B. Film Corporation, opening at the Little Carnegie Theatre, New York, 9 December 1940, cut to 74 minutes. Certificate No. 02965 confirmed 23 September 1940, subject to deletion of 'Good Lord!' and various 'damns' and 'damned'.

It's Love Again (1936), released by Gaumont British Picture Corp. of America, opening at the Roxy Theatre, New York, 22 May 1936, cut to 79 minutes. Certificate No. 0823 confirmed 16 May 1936, after deletion of line referring to the 'bull' and the 'heifer' in the title song; Jessie Matthews walking around the room in her 'scanties'; the crotch shot from her dance routine; and the reference to 'witch' in the telephone conversation.

Jack of All Trades (1936), released as *The Two of Us* by Gaumont British Picture Corp. of America, opening at the Chaloner Theatre, New York, 11 February 1938, cut to 55 minutes. Certificate No. 01136 confirmed 6 July 1937.

Just Like a Woman (1938), released by Alliance Films Corporation, 1939. Certificate No. 02584 confirmed 12 July 1939, subject to deletion of scene in which minister attempts to button his clerical collar in a silly manner.

Just William's Luck (1947), released by United Artists, January 1949, cut by three minutes. Certificate No. 04733 confirmed 5 January 1949.

Kathleen Mavourneen (1937), released as *Kathleen* by J. H. Hoffberg Co., Inc., opening at the Squire Theatre, New York, 23 January 1938, cut by seven minutes. Certificate No. 02024 confirmed 18 March 1938.

Keep Smiling (1938), released as *Smiling Along* by 20th Century-Fox, opening at Central Theatre, New York, 19 February 1939, cut to 83 minutes. Title change was necessitated in that *Keep Smiling* was title of a Jane Withers film, released in the UK as *Miss Fix-It*. Certificate No. 4966 confirmed 8 December 1938.

Kipps (1941), released as *The Remarkable Mr. Kipps* by 20th Century-Fox, March 1942, cut by thirty minutes. Certificate No. 03182 confirmed 11 July 1941, subject to deletion of 'damn' and 'damn fine'.

The Lambeth Walk (1939), released by M-G-M, 1940, cut to 87 minutes. Certificate No. 5853 confirmed 10 November 1939, after deletion of 'ruddy hell'.

Land Without Music (1936), released as *Forbidden Music* by World Pictures Corp., opening at the Waldorf Theatre, New York, 21 December 1938. Certificate No. 02370 confirmed 28 December 1938, subject to elimination of shot showing sex organs of a child being bathed.

The Last Journey (1935), released by Atlantic Pictures Corp., opening at the Globe Theatre, New York, 7 June 1936, cut to 55 minutes. Certificate No. 097 confirmed 3 April 1936, subject to deletion of profanity, dialogue between fireman and engineer, a woman reformer drinking from a bottle of whiskey, and the escape of two pickpockets.

The Last Page (1952), released as *Manbait* by Lippert Pictures, Inc., opening at the Vogue Theatre, Hollywood, 24 January 1952, cut to 78 minutes. Certificate No. 15432 confirmed 22 January 1952. Minor cuts required at script submission stage.

The Late Edwina Black (1951), released as *Obsessed* by United Artists, 7 September 1951, cut by one minute. Certificate No. 15256 confirmed 28 August 1951, subject to re-editing of reel 5 to remove indication of illicit sex affair between sympathetic leads.

The Lavender Hill Mob (1951), released by Universal-International, October 1951, uncut. Certificate No. 15054 confirmed 26 July 1951.

Lilli Marlene (1950), released by RKO, 1951, cut to 74 minutes. Certificate No. 15332 confirmed 12 July 1951, after recutting to eliminate light treatment of marriage.

Limelight (1936), released as *Backstage* by Gaumont British Picture Corp. of America, opening at the Fox Theatre, Brooklyn, 25 June 1937, cut to 65 minutes. Certificate No. 01525 confirmed 19 March 1937, after cutting to eliminate exploitation of the breasts of the chorus girls, suggestive dialogue including a reference to 'the home for fallen governesses' and drinking scenes.

Little Red Monkey (1955), released as *The Case of the Red Monkey* by Allied Artists, Inc., July 1955, uncut. Certificate No. 17454 confirmed 7 March 1955.

Living Dangerously (1936), released by Alliance Films Corporation, December 1936, cut by two minutes. Certificate No. 01358 confirmed 10 November 1936, after re-editing to avoid presentation of illegal drug traffic, attractive presentation of adultery, the district attorney assisting a murderer to establish false evidence, and murder being justified and apparently going unpunished. The film was condemned by the National Legion of Decency.

The Lodger (1932), released as *The Phantom Fiend* by Olympic Pictures, Inc., opening at the Criterion Theatre, New York, 19 April 1935, cut to 67 minutes. Certificate No. 942 confirmed 31 May 1935.

London Melody (1937), released as *Girl in the Street* by Gaumont British Picture Corp. of America, opening at the Continental Theatre, New York, 25 May 1938, cut to 69 minutes. Certificate No. 01663 confirmed 15 June 1937.

Lonely Road (1936), released as *Scotland Yard Commands* by Grand National Pictures, Inc., opening at the Strand Theatre, Brooklyn, 15 March 1937, cut to 61 minutes. Certificate No. 01441 confirmed 30 December 1936, after deletion of profanity and all shots in which machine guns were seen in the hands of criminals.

Look Back in Anger (1959), released by Warner Bros, September 1959, cut by one minute. Certificate No. 19388 confirmed 24 September 1959, subject to deletion of nudity in bedroom scene.

The Lost Hours (1952), released as *The Big Frame* by RKO, 25 April 1953, cut to 66 minutes. Certificate No. 15686 confirmed 3 November 1952.

Love from a Stranger (1937), released by United Artists, opening at the Rivoli Theatre, New York, 17 April 1937, uncut. Certificate No. 01554 confirmed 31 March 1937.

Love in Exile (1936), released by Gaumont British Picture Corp. of America, opening at the Criterion Theatre. New York, 9 December 1936, cut to 63 minutes. Certificate No. 01282 confirmed 23 February 1937.

Love Story (1944), released as *A Lady Surrenders* by Prestige Pictures, Summer 1946, uncut. Certificate No. 10908 confirmed 3 October 1946.

The Luck of the Navy (1938), released as *North Sea Patrol* by Alliance Films Corporation, opening at the Central Theatre, New York, 28 December 1939, cut to 64 minutes. Certificate No. 02642 confirmed 8 September 1939, subject to deletion of shot of semi-naked sailor with girl's head tattooed on his chest, reference to a 'pansy' and the sound coming from the butler's gas mask.

Mademoiselle Docteur (1937), released as *Under Secret Orders* by Guaranteed Pictures Co., Inc., 1943. Certificate No. 03247 confirmed 14 October 1941.

Madness of the Heart (1949), released by Universal-International, October 1950, cut to 90 minutes. Certificate No. 13589 confirmed 19 September 1949. Cuts required at script submission.

Madonna of the Seven Moons (1944), released by Universal, opening at the Garden Theatre, New York, 22 May 1946, cut to 88 minutes. Certificate No. 10933 confirmed 23 November 1945, subject to deletion of Mrs Fiske in her underwear (reel 3), 'Mother of God' (reel 4), the fade-out in the bedroom scene (reel 5), the entire bedroom scene (reel 6), the fade-out in the garden scene (reel 10), 'Good Lord' and 'hell' (reel 11), and the shot of the man and girl on the bed (reel 12).

The Maggie (1954), released as *High and Dry* by Universal-International, 1954, uncut. Certificate No. 17097 confirmed 17 June 1954. Minor cuts required at script submission stage.

The Magic Bow (1946), released by Universal-International, opening at the Carthay Circle Theatre, Los Angeles, 12 March 1947. Certificate No. 12124 confirmed 25 November 1946. Minor cuts required at script submission stage.

The Malta Story (1953), released by United Artists, July 1954, uncut. Certificate No. 17089 confirmed 29 June 1954, subject to elimination of three uses of 'damn' and two uses of 'hell'.

The Man at the Gate (1941), released as *Men of the Sea* by PRC, 30 April 1944, cut to 48 minutes. Certificate No. 03787 confirmed 31 March 1944.

The Man in the Mirror (1936), released by Grand National Pictures, Inc., 24 April 1937, cut to 71 minutes. Certificate No. 01543 confirmed 15 March 1937, subject to elimination of line, 'If everybody who lent books left the country, there would be few of us left' and cutting and shortening of belching and drinking scenes.

The Man in the Road (1956), released by Republic Pictures, Inc., opening at the El Rey and Iris Theatres, Los Angeles, 24 July 1957. Certificate No. 17850 confirmed 21 December 1956.

The Man in the Sky (1957), released as *Decision against Time* by M-G-M, July 1957, uncut. Certificate No. 18429 confirmed 24 January 1957.

The Man in the White Suit (1951), released by Universal-International, April 1952, cut to 85 minutes. Certificate No. 15096 confirmed 11 December 1951. Minor cuts required at script submission stage.

The Man Who Changed His Mind (1936), released as *The Man Who Lived Again* by Gaumont British Picture Corp. of America, opening at the Rialto

Theatre, New York, 15 December 1936, cut to 64 minutes. Title changed in 1938 to *Doctor Maniac*. Certificate No. 0954 confirmed 15 September 1936.

The Man Who Never Was (1956), released by 20th Century-Fox, February 1956, uncut. Certificate No. 17582 confirmed 23 January 1956. Minor cuts required at script submission stage.

The Man Who Watched Trains Go By (1952), released as *Paris Express* by McDonald Pictures, Inc., June 1953, uncut. Certificate No. 16196 confirmed 3 March 1953. Cuts required at script submission stage.

The Man Within (1947), released as *The Smugglers* by Eagle-Lion Films, Inc., 31 January 1948, uncut. Certificate No. 12367 confirmed 1 August 1947. Cuts required at script submission stage.

Mandy (1952), released as *Crash of Silence* by Universal-International, March 1953, uncut. Certificate No. 15852 confirmed 4 November 1952.

Manuela (1957), released as *Stowaway* by Paramount Pictures, September 1957, cut to 87 minutes. Certificate No. 18722 confirmed 29 July 1957. Classified 'B' by the National Legion of Decency for 'suggestive sequences' and 'low moral tone'.

Mask of Dust (1954), released by Lippert Pictures, Inc., opening at the Vogue Theatre, Hollywood, 26 January 1955, cut to 68 minutes. Certificate No. 17104 confirmed 9 November 1954.

The Master of Ballantrae (1953), released by Warner Bros, August 1953, uncut. Certificate No. 16016 confirmed 18 November 1952. Cuts required at script submission stage to eliminate 'blood bath' flavour.

The Master of Bankdam (1947), released by Universal-International, opening at the Embassy Theatre, New York, 15 October 1949. Certificate No. 13921 confirmed 21 June 1949, subject to elimination of illicit sex affair between Joshua and Annie.

Menace (1934), released as *While London Sleeps* by Ideal Pictures, Inc., July 1936, cut to 58 minutes. Certificate No. 01125 confirmed 26 February 1937, after deletion of profanity, placing of explosives under the rails, shots of a man holding the lifeless form of his wife, and close shot of injured passenger with bloodstained face.

The Middle Watch (1939), released as *Night Patrol* by Fine Arts Film & Studio Corporation, 1942. Certificate No. 03375 confirmed 12 June 1942, subject to deletion of profanity.

The Mikado (1939), released by Universal, opening at the Rivoli Theatre, New York, 1 June 1939, uncut. Certificate No. 02383 confirmed 24 March 1939.

The Million Pound Note (1954), released as *Man with a Million* by United Artists, July 1954, cut to 83 minutes. Certificate No. 16891 confirmed 14 September 1954.

Millions Like Us (1943), released by Eagle-Lion Films, Inc., 1945. Certificate No. 10901 confirmed 5 June 1945, on understanding that 'hell' would be deleted throughout.

The Miniver Story (1950), released by M-G-M, October 1950, uncut. Certificate No. 14268 confirmed 7 April 1950.

Mr Reeder in Room 13 (1938), released as *Mystery of Room 13* by Alliance Films Corporation, 1940. Certificate No. 02914 confirmed 18 July 1940, on understanding that Alliance would do what it could to cut end of film showing forgers firing at police.

Moby Dick (1956), released by Warner Bros, July 1956, uncut. Certificate No. 17465 confirmed 13 July 1956.

Monkey into Man (1940), released by World Pictures Corp., March 1940, cut to 67 minutes. It may also have been released as *Symphony of Life*. Certificate No. 02782 confirmed 16 February 1940, on understanding that Dr Julian Huxley had approved use of his name in connection with film.

The Morals of Marcus (1935), released by Gaumont British Picture Corp. of America, opening at the Globe Theatre, New York, 11 January 1936, cut to 72 minutes. No Certificate is on file, but it is believed that one was issued. Many cuts were required, including shot of half-nude girl in harem pool, 'you son of a pig', Carlotta's breasts outlined in her nightgown, and the title of her book, *What Young Girls Ought To Know*.

Morning Departure (1950), released as *Operation Disaster* by Universal-International, 13 January 1951, uncut. Certificate No. 14246 confirmed 16 January 1951. Cuts required at script submission stage.

The Mouse That Roared (1959), released by Columbia Pictures, November 1959, uncut. Certificate No. 19205 confirmed 4 September 1959.

The Mudlark (1950), released by 20th Century-Fox, January 1951, uncut. Certificate No. 14628 confirmed 13 November 1950. Minor cuts required at script submission stage, including reduction of emphasis on John Brown's drinking.

The Mummy (1959), released by Universal-International, July 1959, uncut. Certificate No. 19340 confirmed 29 June 1959. Cuts required at script submission stage, primarily relating to gruesomeness.

Murder in Reverse (1945), released by Four Continents Films, Inc., 1946. Certificate No. 04335 confirmed 1 May 1947, subject to minor cuts.

Murder in Soho (1939), released as *Murder in the Night* by Film Alliance of the United States, Inc., 1940. Certificate No. 02880 confirmed 15 November 1940, after deletion of three shots of drinking and insertion of a newspaper headline to the effect that the hostess-heroine had confessed to the killing and was under arrest.

The Mutiny on the Elsinore (1937), released by Alliance Films Corporation, opening at the Criterion Theatre, New York, 15 February 1939, cut to 73 minutes. Certificate No. 02336 confirmed 15 November 1938, subject to deletion of profanity and two references to 'nigger'.

My Brother Jonathan (1948), released by Allied Artists, Inc., 29 June 1949, cut to 102 minutes. Certificate No. 13647 confirmed 8 February 1949, subject to deletion of two uses of 'damn'.

My Brother's Keeper (1948), released by Eagle-Lion Films, Inc., February 1949, uncut. Certificate No. 12912 confirmed 13 July 1949. Cuts required at script submission stage, including change at ending removing suggestion that a criminal committed suicide in order to escape justice.

My Heart is Calling (1934), released by Gaumont British Picture Corp. of America, opening at the Roxy Theatre, New York, 12 April 1935, cut to 70 minutes. Certificate No. 591 confirmed 29 January 1935.

My Learned Friend (1943) was scheduled for release by United Artists, but there is no evidence of a contemporary US release. Certificate No. 03614 confirmed 30 April 1943.

My Sister and I (1948) was scheduled for release by 20th Century-Fox, but there is no evidence of a contemporary US release. Tentative Certificate No. 13348 was issued 29 July 1948, with the PCA noting a basic objection to Hypatia's suicide.

The Navy Lark (1959) was the recipient of tentative Certificate No. 19445 on 2 September 1959, but it was cancelled 20 October 1960, on confirmation that 20th Century-Fox would not release the film in the USA.

The Net (1953), released as *Project M.7* by Universal-International, December 1953, uncut. Certificate No. 16466 confirmed 26 March 1953. Minor cuts required at script submission stage.

The Night Has Eyes (1942), released as *Terror House* by PRC, opening at the New York Theatre, New York, 1 June 1943, cut to 62 minutes. Reissued January 1949 as *Moonlight Madness* by Cosmopolitan Pictures, Inc. Certificate No. 03589 confirmed 16 April 1943, subject to deletion of two 'damns' and one 'hell'.

Night of the Demon (1957), released as *Curse of the Demon* by Columbia Pictures, February 1958, uncut. Certificate No. 18459 confirmed 26 July 1957. Minor cuts required at script submission stage.

Night Train to Munich (1940), released as *Night Train* by 20th Century-Fox, January 1941, cut to 90 minutes. Certificate No. 02933 confirmed 23 August 1940.

Nine Men (1943) was scheduled for release by United Artists, but there is no evidence of a contemporary US release. Tentative Certificate No. 03539 issued 2 December 1942.

1984 (1956), released by Columbia Pictures, September 1956, uncut. Certificate No. 17708 confirmed 11 April 1956.

Non-Stop New York (1937), released by Gaumont British Picture Corp. of America, opening at the Globe Theatre, New York, 28 November 1937, cut by two minutes. Reissued as *Lisbon Clipper Mystery* in 1943. Certificate No. 01624 confirmed 23 September 1937, subject to deletion of profanity.

Noose (1948), released by Monogram Pictures, Inc., 9 July 1950, cut to 72 minutes. Certificate No. 14574 confirmed 3 May 1950.

Not Wanted on Voyage (1936), released as *Treachery on the High Seas* by Film Alliance of the United States, Inc., September 1939, cut to 88 minutes. Certificate No. 02646 confirmed 22 September 1939, after elimination of dialogue between Johnny, Brainy and the policeman in which Johnny lies to police about May's criminal activities.

O.H.M.S. (1937), released as *You're in the Army Now* by Gaumont British Picture Corp. of America, 1 March 1937, cut to 71 minutes. Certificate No. 01470 confirmed 14 January 1937.

Obsession (1949), released as *The Hidden Room* by Eagle-Lion Films, Inc., opening at the Broadway Embassy Theatre, New York, 3 January 1950, cut by five minutes. Certificate No. 13968 confirmed 23 February 1950. Minor cuts required at script submission stage.

The October Man (1947), released by Eagle-Lion Films, Inc., March 1948, cut to 91 minutes. Certificate No. 12149 confirmed 31 December 1947. Cuts required at script submission stage.

On the Night of the Fire (1939), released as *The Fugitive* by Universal, July 1940, cut to 75 minutes. Certificate No. 6339 confirmed 27 May 1940.

Once in a Million (1936), released as *Week-End Millionaire* by Alliance Films Corporation, opening at the Chaloner Theatre, New York, 25 March 1937, cut to 62 minutes. Certificate No. 01333 confirmed 30 October 1936, after deletion of 'son of a … ', Mrs F. glancing at Pierre's posterior and three suggestive lines.

One of Our Aircraft is Missing (1942), released by United Artists, opening at the Globe Theatre, New York, 1 November 1942, cut to 86 minutes. Certificate No. 8798 confirmed 18 September 1942, subject to deletion of 'hell' and 'damn' in reel 4 and 'damned' in reel 5.

Our Fighting Navy (1937), released as *Torpedoed!* by Gaumont British Picture Corp. of America, opening at the Globe Theatre, New York, 25 September 1939, cut to 66 minutes. Reissued as *Fighting Navy* in 1941. Certificate No. 02659 confirmed 20 September 1939, subject to deletion of all profanity.

Our Mr Shakespeare (1948), released by English Films, Inc., 1948. Certificate No. 04570 confirmed 15 April 1948.

Ourselves Alone (1936), released as *River of Unrest* by Alliance Films Corporation, 1939, uncut. Certificate No. 01331 confirmed 28 October 1936, after deletion of all profanity.

The Outsider (1939), released by Alliance Films Corporation, opening at the Little Carnegie Theatre, New York, 17 March 1940, uncut. Certificate No. 02510 confirmed 12 April 1939.

Owd Bob (1938), released as *To the Victor* by Gaumont British Picture Corp. of America, 1 March 1938. Certificate No. 01937 confirmed 23 February 1938.

Pagliacci (1936), released by Gaumont British Picture Corp. of America, 1939. Certificate No. 02269 confirmed 16 January 1939, subject to deletion of remark by Tonio, 'I'll say they're pretty', as the showgirl pulls up her stocking.

Painted Boats (1945), released as *The Girl of the Canal* by Bell Pictures, Inc., October 1947, cut to 47 minutes. Certificate No. 04122 confirmed 13 March 1946, after elimination of one 'damn' and cutting of scene in the woods between Ted and Mary, with its inference of illicit sex.

Paradise for Two (1937), released as *The Gaiety Girls* by United Artists, opening at the Rivoli Theatre, New York, 30 March 1938, cut to 72 minutes. Certificate No. 01823 confirmed 23 February 1938.

The Passing of the Third Floor Back (1935), released by Gaumont British Picture Corp. of America, opening at the 55th Street Playhouse, New York, 30 April 1936, cut to 79 minutes. Certificate No. 0718 confirmed 23 October 1935, after deletion of 'slut', (twice), 'bellied', 'guts', 'hell', 'Lord', and the sentence, 'It's bound to happen sooner or later'.

The Passionate Friends (1949), released as *One Woman's Story* by Universal-International, opening at the Rivoli Theatre, New York, 17 May 1949, cut by four minutes. Certificate No. 13526 confirmed 8 March 1949. Cuts required at script submission stage, including elimination of suicide ending and adultery between central characters.

Passport to Pimlico (1949), released by Eagle-Lion Films, Inc., opening at the Trans-Lux 60th Street Theatre, New York, 26 October 1949, cut to 67 minutes. Certificate No. 13221 confirmed 28 July 1949. Cuts required at script submission stage, including business of sparrows leaving 'a little white mark' and expression, 'To hell with Burgundy'.

Peg of Old Drury (1935), released by Paramount Pictures, opening at the Bijou Theatre, New York, 11 April 1936, cut to 66 minutes. Certificate No. 02326 confirmed 7 November 1938, after deletion of line, 'like this livin' here', and suggestion of an illicit sex affair between Peg and Michael. The low-cut dresses worn by Peg were deemed borderline under Code rules governing exposure.

Penn of Pennsylvania (1941), released as *The Courageous Mr Penn* by J. H. Hoffberg Co., Inc., opening at the 55th Street Playhouse, New York, 23 December 1943. Certificate No. 03389 issued 23 April 1942, but cancelled 18 May 1943, after distributor failed to screen film for PCA.

Penny Princess (1952), released by Universal-International, March 1953, uncut. Certificate No. 15554 confirmed 5 November 1952. Cuts required at script submission stage, including running gag of customs official and his girlfriends.

Perfect Strangers (1945), released as *Vacation from Marriage* by M-G-M, opening at Loew's State, New York, 14 March 1946, cut by six minutes. Certificate No. 11265 confirmed 15 November 1945, subject to deletion of 'damned good'.

The Perfect Woman (1949), released by Eagle-Lion Films, Inc., opening at the Esquire Theatre, Los Angeles, 16 June 1950, cut to 83 minutes. Certificate No. 13666 confirmed 26 September 1949. Cuts required at script submission stage.

The Pickwick Papers (1952), released by Arthur Mayer–Edward Kingsley, Inc., 3 April 1954, uncut. Certificate No. 15940 confirmed 15 March 1954. Minor cuts required at script submission stage.

The Planter's Wife (1952), released as *Outpost in Malaya* by United Artists, 21 November 1952, cut by three minutes. Certificate No. 15818 confirmed 26 February 1952. Cuts required at script submission stage, including elimination of suggestion of nudity in bedroom scene (husband in nothing less than shorts) and no emphasis on the sex organs of a small, carved male figure.

Port Afrique (1956), released by Columbia Pictures, October 1956, uncut. Certificate No. 17924 confirmed 1 August 1956.

Portrait from Life (1948), released as *The Girl in the Painting* by Universal-International, 20 August 1949, uncut. Certificate No. 13973 confirmed 29 June 1949.

Portrait of Alison (1953), released as *Postmark for Danger* by RKO, January 1956, cut to 77 minutes. Certificate No. 17592 confirmed 12 January 1956. Minor cuts required at script submission stage.

Prelude to Fame (1950), released by Universal-International, November 1950, cut to 77 minutes. Certificate No. 14388 confirmed 17 November 1950. Minor cuts required at script submission stage.

The Prime Minister (1941), released by Warner Bros., October 1941, cut to 93 minutes. Certificate No. 7454 confirmed 19 June 1941.

Private's Progress (1956), released by Distributors Corporation of America, August 1956, cut to 96 minutes. Certificate No. 18212 confirmed 15 August 1956, after deletion of some profanity; for 'technical reasons', not all could be removed.

The Proud Valley (1940), released as *The Tunnel* by Supreme Productions, Inc., 1941. Certificate No. 03226 confirmed 15 September 1941, subject to deletion of profanity throughout and a toilet gag in reel 3.

Puppets Of Fate (1933), released as *Wolves of the Underworld* by Regal Films, Inc., opening at the Chaloner Theatre, New York, 10 January 1936, cut to 57 minutes. Paperwork is missing but Certificate No. 0656 is known to have been issued.

The Purple Plain (1954), released by United Artists, April 1955, uncut. Certificate No. 17357 confirmed 5 April 1955. Minor cuts required at script submission stage.

Q Planes (1939), released as *Clouds over Europe* by Columbia Pictures, opening at Radio City Music Hall, New York, 15 June 1939, uncut. On general release cut to 78 minutes. Certificate No. 5391 confirmed 12 May 1939.

Quatermass II (1957), released as *Enemy from Space* by United Artists, September 1957, uncut. Certificate No. 18128 confirmed 28 May 1956, subject to deletion of 'My God'.

Quiet Wedding (1941), released by Universal, 21 November 1941, cut to 63 minutes. Certificate No. 03147 confirmed 11 July 1941. Cuts required at script submission stage, including ridiculing of a magistrate and vicar, and description of a policeman as 'a good fairy'.

Radio Follies of 1935 (1934), released as *Radio Follies* by Alliance Films Corporation, 1936. Certificate No. 01089 confirmed 9 June 1936, subject to minor cuts, including a 'scantily-clad negro girl'.

Reach for the Sky (1956), released by Rank Film Distributors of America, Inc., May 1957, cut to 123 minutes. Certificate No. 18471 confirmed 4 February 1957, subject to deletion of 'bastard'.

Return of a Stranger (1937), released as *The Face Behind the Scar* by Film Alliance of the United States, Inc., opening at the Central Theatre, New York, 29 February 1940. Certificate No. 02709 confirmed 24 November 1939.

Return of the Frog (1938), released by Select Attractions, Inc., October 1939, cut to 70 minutes. Certificate No. 02630 confirmed 30 August 1939, subject to minor dialogue deletions.

The Return of the Scarlet Pimpernel (1937), released by United Artists, opening at the Rivoli Theatre, New York, 10 April 1938, cut to 80 minutes. Certificate No. 01657 confirmed 17 March 1938, after deletion of profanity throughout.

The Revenge of Frankenstein (1958), released by Columbia Pictures, July 1958, uncut. Certificate No. 19022 confirmed 1 July 1958. Cuts required at script submission stage, primarily relating to gruesomeness.

Rhodes of Africa (1936), released as *Rhodes* by Gaumont British Picture Corp. of America, opening at the Roxy Theatre, New York, 28 February 1936, cut to 89 minutes. Reissued as *Diamond Empire* in 1944. Certificate No. 0824 confirmed 10 February 1936.

Rob Roy, the Highland Rogue (1953), released by RKO, February 1954, uncut. Certificate No. 16185 confirmed 25 November 1953.

The Rocks of Valpre (1935), released as *High Treason* by Olympic Pictures Corp., January 1937, cut to 62 minutes. Certificate No. 0706 confirmed 9 October 1935.

The Romantic Age (1949), released as *Naughty Arlette* by Eagle-Lion Films, Inc., February 1951, cut to 77 minutes. Certificate No. 14007 confirmed 14 March 1951. Cuts required at script submission stage.

Rome Express (1932), released by Universal Pictures, 1933, with three minor cuts relating to profanity. On reissue by Universal in 1936, the film was submitted to the PCA and same cuts confirmed, together with pictures of nude and semi-nude girls on magazine covers and shot of woman entering George's compartment. Certificate No. 2761-R issued 6 October 1936.

Romeo and Juliet (1954), released by United Artists, December 1954, uncut. Certificate No. 17210 confirmed 16 September 1954.

The Rough and the Smooth (1959), released as *Portrait of a Sinner* by American International Pictures, Inc., May 1961, cut by three minutes. Certificate No. 19804 confirmed 30 December 1960, subject to deletion of 'bitch' (twice) and 'whore'.

Rough Shoot (1953), released as *Shoot First* by United Artists, May 1953, uncut. Certificate No. 16547 confirmed 13 July 1953.

A Royal Divorce (1938), released by Select Attractions, Inc., 1939. Certificate No. 02635 confirmed 13 September 1939, subject to deletion of 'excessive and lustful' kissing between Napoleon and Josephine.

A Run for Your Money (1949), released by Universal-International, 8 April 1950, uncut. Certificate No. 13765 confirmed 27 February 1950. Cuts required at script submission stage.

The Safecracker (1958), released by M-G-M, January 1958, uncut. Certificate No. 18726 confirmed 10 October 1957. Minor cuts required at script submission stage.

Said O'Reilly to McNab (1937), released as *Sez O'Reilly to McNab* by Gaumont British Picture Corp. of America, opening at the Varsity Theatre, Lincoln, Nebraska, January 1938. Certificate No. 01819 confirmed 16 November 1937.

Sailing Along (1938), released by Gaumont British Picture Corp. of America, opening at the Criterion Theatre, New York, 15 April 1938, cut to 80 minutes. Certificate No. 01845 confirmed 4 April 1938.

Sailors Three (1940), released as *Three Cockeyed Sailors* by United Artists, June 1941, cut to 75 minutes. Certificate No. 7116 confirmed 12 February 1941.

Saint Joan (1957), released by United Artists, June 1957, uncut. Certificate No. 18409 confirmed 24 May 1957. Cuts required at script submission stage.

The Saint's Return (1953), released as *The Saint's Girl Friday* by United Artists,

March 1954. Certificate No. 16644 confirmed 8 September 1953. Cuts required at script submission stage.

San Demetrio – London (1943), released by 20th Century-Fox, April 1947, cut to 76 minutes. Certificate No. 10406 confirmed 22 August 1944, subject to deletion of 'hell' (twice).

Sapphire (1959), released by Universal-International, November 1959, uncut. Certificate No. 19398 confirmed 7 July 1959.

The Scapegoat (1959), released by M-G-M, August 1959, uncut. Certificate No. 19160 confirmed 10 February 1959. Cuts required at script submission stage, including casual treatment of drug addiction and illicit sex relationship between John and Bela.

School for Husbands (1937), released by J. H. Hoffberg Co., Inc., opening at the Little Carnegie Theatre, New York, 6 February 1939, uncut. Certificate No. 02441 confirmed 23 February 1939, subject to a number of dialogue deletions.

School for Scoundrels (1960), released by Continental Film Distributing, Inc., July 1960, uncut. Tentative Certificate No. 19566 issued 19 January 1960, but cancelled 30 June 1961.

The Scotland Yard Mystery (1934), released as *The Living Dead* by First Division Exchanges, Inc., 1935. Certificate No. 0800 confirmed 24 December 1935, subject to deletion of 'damn' and 'Oh, Lord'.

Scott of the Antarctic (1948), released by Eagle-Lion Films, Inc., 20 April 1949, cut to 107 minutes. Certificate No. 12715 confirmed 22 September 1949. Cuts required at script submission stage, including glorified suicide of Oates and real or apparent cruelty to animals.

The Sea Shall Not Have Them (1954), released by United Artists, June 1956, uncut. Certificate No. 17775 confirmed 13 October 1955. Cuts required at script submission stage.

Seagulls over Sorrento (1954), released as *Crest of the Wave* by M-G-M, December 1954, cut by two minutes. Certificate No. 16799 confirmed 8 January 1954. Minor cuts required at script submission stage.

Secret Journey (1939), released as *Among Human Wolves* by Film Alliance of the United States, Inc., 1 December 1940, cut to 59 minutes. Certificate No. 02987 confirmed 18 November 1940, subject to deletion of three uses of 'hell'.

Secret Lives (1937), released as *I Married a Spy* by Grand National Pictures, Inc., opening at the Central Theatre, New York, 8 July 1938, cut to 59 minutes. Certificate No. 4370 confirmed 1 June 1938, subject to deletion of scenes showing Lena with inadequate clothing and implication that she had slept with a German spy. In October 1938, the PCA took note of a protest from the French Embassy of the film's depiction of its military in a negative fashion.

Secret Mission (1942), released by English Films, Inc., 29 August 1944, cut to 75 minutes. Certificate No. 03776 confirmed 3 August 1944. Minor cuts required at script submission stage.

The Seekers (1954), released as *Land of Fury* by Universal-International, March 1955, cut to 87 minutes. Certificate No. 17154 confirmed 6 August 1954, subject to elimination of scenes of native girl with bare breasts and swimming in nude. Cuts also required at script submission stage.

Sensation (1937), released by Film Alliance of the United States, Inc., 1941. Certificate No. 02928 confirmed 16 December 1940, after deletion of profanity, unnecessary drinking scenes and a toilet gag.

Service for Ladies (1932), released as *Reserved for Ladies* by Paramount Pictures, 20 May 1932, cut to 71 minutes. On reissue by Paramount in 1935, Certificate No. 1606-R issued 30 September 1935.

Seven Sinners (1936), released by Gaumont British Picture Corp. of America, opening at the Roxy Theatre, New York, 21 August 1936. Certificate No. 0955 confirmed 7 August 1936, subject to two minor deletions.

Seven Waves Away (1957), released as *Abandon Ship!* by Columbia Pictures, May 1957, uncut. Certificate No. 18080 confirmed 18 March 1957. Cuts required at script submission stage.

The Seventh Veil (1945), released by Universal, opening at the Winter Garden Theatre, New York, 25 December 1945, cut by two minutes. Certificate No. 11358 confirmed 4 January 1946, subject to re-editing of sequence in which Layden suggests going off with the heroine. Classified 'B' by the National Legion of Decency for 'lack of adequate moral compensation'.

She Shall Have Music (1935), released by Gaumont British Picture Corp. of America, 1936, cut to 78 minutes. Certificate No. 01181 confirmed 5 November 1936, after major deletions of lines from two songs, chorus girls inadequately attired, an 'artistic dance' featuring 'undue amount of nudity', and a comedian thumbing his nose.

The Sheriff of Fractured Jaw (1958), released by 20th Century-Fox, January 1959, uncut. Certificate No. 19147 confirmed 2 December 1958.

Shipyard Sally (1955), released by 20th Century-Fox, February 1940, cut by two minutes. Certificate No. 02661 confirmed 21 September 1939.

The Show Goes On (1937), released by Gaumont British Picture Corp. of America, opening at the Metropolitan Theatre, Brooklyn, 11 August 1938, cut to 70 minutes. Certificate No. 01846 confirmed 12 August 1938, after deletion of shot of girl undressing.

The Silent Battle (1939), released by Monogram Pictures, Inc., 1 March 1942, cut to 73 minutes. Certificate No. 03146 confirmed 3 June 1941.

The *Silken Affair* (1956), released by Distributors Corporation of America, November 1957, cut to 89 minutes. Certificate No. 18155 confirmed 27 November 1956. Cuts required at script submission stage.

Silver Blaze (1937), released as *Murder at the Baskervilles* by Astor Films, Inc., 1940. Certificate No. 02983 confirmed 22 October 1940, after deletion of profanity, and acknowledgement that the air-gun here was of such fantastic character that its use could be approved.

The Silver Fleet (1943), released by PRC, 1 July 1945, cut to 78 minutes. Certificate No. 03966 confirmed 23 March 1945, subject to deletion of 'damn' in reel three.

Simon and Laura (1955), released by Universal-International, July 1956, uncut. Certificate No. 18006 confirmed 20 March 1956, after substitution of 'darn' and 'heck' for 'damn' and 'hell'.

Single-Handed (1953), released as *Sailor of the King* by 20th Century-Fox, August 1953, uncut. Certificate No. 16141 confirmed 6 March 1953. Cuts required at script submission stage.

The Spy in Black (1939), released as *U-Boat 29* by Columbia Pictures, opening at the Globe Theatre, New York, 6 October 1939, cut to 77 minutes. Certificate No. 5703 confirmed 14 September 1939, subject to minor deletions.

Spy of Napoleon (1936), released by Syndicated Pictures, Inc., opening at the Central Theatre, New York, 18 August 1939. Certificate No. 01515 confirmed 19 February 1937.

The Squeaker (1937), released as *Murder on Diamond Row* by United Artists, opening at the Rialto Theatre, New York, 11 November 1937, uncut. Certificate No. 01659 confirmed 22 September 1937.

Squibs (1935), released by Olympic Pictures Corporation, 1935 (unconfirmed). Certificate No. 0709 confirmed 10 October 1935.

Star of the Circus (1938), released as *The Hidden Menace* by Alliance Films Corporation, 15 January 1940, cut to 59 minutes. Certificate No. 02616 confirmed 14 August 1939.

State Secret (1950), released by Columbia Pictures, previewing October 1950 as *State Secret* and opening April 1951 as *The Great Man Hunt*. Certificate No. 14712 confirmed 28 September 1950. Minor cuts required at script submission stage.

Storm in a Teacup (1937), released by United Artists, opening at the Little Carnegie Theatre, New York, 21 March 1938, cut by two minutes. Certificate No. 01653 confirmed 3 August 1937, after minor deletions.

The Story of Esther Costello (1957), released by Columbia Pictures, August 1957, cut by two minutes. Certificate No. 18370 confirmed 25 July 1957. Classified 'B' by the National Legion of Decency for 'suggestive sequences' and because it tended 'to create sympathy for immoral actions'. Cuts required at script submission stage.

The Stranger Came Home (1954), released as *The Unholy Four* by Lippert Pictures, Inc., September 1954, uncut. Certificate No. 16942 confirmed 16 July 1954.

Strangers on a Honeymoon (1936), released by Gaumont British Picture Corp. of America, opening at the Criterion Theatre, New York, 11 March 1937, cut to 66 minutes. Certificate No. 01183 confirmed 11 December 1936.

Street Corner (1953), released as *Both Sides of the Law* by Universal, January 1954, uncut. Certificate No. 16657 confirmed 29 July 1953, subject to deletion of 'bastard' (reel 1) and 'God' (reels 2 and 12).

Sunset in Vienna (1937), released as *Suicide Legion* by Film Alliance of the United States, Inc., opening at the Arena Theatre, New York, 17 July 1940, cut to 54 minutes. Certificate No. 02757 confirmed 22 May 1940.

Suspected Person (1942), released by PRC, opening at the New York Theatre, New York, 10 January 1944, uncut. Certificate No. 03705 confirmed 5 October 1943.

A Tale of Five Cities (1951), released as *A Tale of Five Women* by United Artists, February 1952, cut to 86 minutes. Certificate No. 15258 confirmed 12 December 1951.

Talk of the Devil (1936), released by Gaumont British Picture Corp. of America, 1 June 1937, cut to 76 minutes. Certificate No. 01599 confirmed 26 April 1937, subject to deletion of 'damn'.

Talking Feet (1937), released by J. H. Hoffberg Co., Inc., 1938. Certificate No. 02283 confirmed 29 September 1938.

The Tawny Pipit (1944), released by Prestige Pictures, 6 September 1947, uncut. Certificate No. 10902 confirmed 5 June 1945.

Tell Me Tonight (1932), released as *Be Mine Tonight* by Universal, opening at the Paramount Theatre, New York, 13 April 1933. A Certificate was issued but its number is unknown. On reissue by Universal in 1936, Certificate No. 2757-R issued 3 October 1936.

Ten Days in Paris (1939), released by Columbia Pictures, July 1941, cut to 76 minutes. Certificate No. 02867 confirmed 7 April 1941.

The Tenth Man (1936), released by Gaumont British Picture Corp. of America, November 1937, cut to 64 minutes. Certificate No. 01338 confirmed 2 November 1936, subject to deletion of profanity.

That Dangerous Age (1949), released as *If This Be Sin* by United Artists, 8 September 1950, cut to 72 minutes. Certificate No. 13891 confirmed 25 October 1949.

They Flew Alone (1942), released as *Wings and the Woman* by RKO, August 1942, cut to 92 minutes. Certificate No. 03393 confirmed 19 May 1942.

They Made Me a Fugitive (1947), released as *I Became a Criminal* by Warner Bros, February 1948, cut to 78 minutes. Certificate No. 12816 confirmed 4 December 1947, on understanding that all references to illegal drugs be omitted. Cuts required at script submission stage.

They Met in the Dark (1943), released by English Films, Inc., 1945, cut to 94 minutes. Certificate No. 03802 confirmed 24 May 1945.

They Were Sisters (1945), released by Universal, opening at the Winter Garden Theatre, New York, 23 July 1946, cut to 92 minutes. Certificate No. 11807 confirmed 19 June 1946, after various cuts.

Third Man on the Mountain (1959), released by Buena Vista, November 1959, uncut. Certificate No. 19125 confirmed 5 October 1959.

Third Party Risk (1955), released as *The Deadly Game* by Lippert Pictures, Inc., November 1955, cut to 63 minutes. Retitled *Big Deadly Game* for television release. Certificate No. 17077 confirmed 7 February 1955. Cuts required at script submission stage.

The 39 Steps (1959), released by 20th Century-Fox, July 1960, uncut. Certificate No. 19544 confirmed 3 February 1960.

This Happy Breed (1944), released by Prestige Pictures, opening at Little Carnegie Theatre, New York, 12 April 1947, uncut. Certificate No. 10736 confirmed 31 January 1945, subject to deletion of unacceptable words and phrases.

Time Bomb (1953), released as *Terror on a Train* by M-G-M, 18 September 1953, uncut. Certificate No. 16043 confirmed 9 September 1952. Cuts required at script submission stage.

The Titfield Thunderbolt (1953), released by Universal-International, October 1953, uncut. Certificate No. 16562 confirmed 19 May 1953. Minor cuts required at script submission stage.

tom thumb (1958), released by M-G-M, December 1958, uncut. Certificate No. 18918 confirmed 4 November 1958. At script submission stage, PCA assumed fight scenes would be in a light vein.

Tomorrow We Live (1942), released as *At Dawn We Die* by Republic Pictures, Inc., March 1943, cut to 78 minutes. Certificate No. 9174 confirmed 26 March 1943, subject to deletion of sound of a 'razzberry' and German officer's exclamation, 'What the Hell!'

Top Secret (1952), released as *Mr. Potts Goes to Moscow* by Stratford Pictures, opening at Little Carnegie Theatre, New York, 2 September 1953. Certificate No. 16934 confirmed 1 April 1954.

Torment (1949), released as *Paper Gallows* by Eagle-Lion Classics, Inc., November 1950, uncut. Certificate No. 14851 confirmed 6 November 1950, subject to deletion of all 'improper words'.

Traitor Spy (1939), released as *Torso Murder Mystery* by Arthur Ziehmn, Inc., October 1940, cut to 70 minutes. Certificate No. 02918 confirmed 13 September 1940, subject to deletion of profanity and trimming of scene in which several characters entered a men's room.

Traveller's Joy (1951) was submitted to the PCA in script form January 1949 and many problems noted. There is no evidence of a contemporary US release. Tentative Certificate No. 14054 issued 5 August 1949.

The Triumph of Sherlock Holmes (1935), released by Olympic Pictures Corporation, opening at Criterion Theatre, New York, 24 May 1935, cut to 72 minutes. Certificate No. 0510 confirmed 18 June 1935, subject to various deletions, including a choking scene and the branding of Douglas.

Trottie True (1949), released as *The Gay Lady* by Eagle-Lion Films, Inc., October 1949, cut by five minutes. Certificate No. 13349 confirmed 22 September 1949. Cuts required at script submission stage, including substitution of a nightgown for 'frilly drawers'.

Trouble in Store (1953), released by Republic Pictures, Inc., January 1955, uncut. Certificate No. 17272 confirmed 26 November 1954. Cuts required at script submission stage.

Trouble in the Glen (1954), released by Republic Pictures, Inc., November 1954, uncut. Certificate No. 16813 confirmed 23 September 1954, subject to deletion of 'damn', 'hell' and a kick by the heavy in the fight scene.

Trunk Crime (1939), released as *Design for Murder* by World Pictures Corporation, opening at the Central Theatre, New York, 27 November 1940, cut to 60 minutes. Certificate No. 02972 confirmed 27 September 1940, after deletion of profanity and line, 'We're better without laws and without moralities'.

Tudor Rose (1936), released as *Nine Days a Queen* by Gaumont British Picture Corp. of America, opening at the Roxy Theatre, New York, 2 October 1936, uncut. Certificate No. 01078 confirmed 1 June 1936.

The Tunnel (1935), released as *Transatlantic Tunnel* by Gaumont British Picture Corp. of America, opening at the Roxy Theatre, New York, 25 October 1935, uncut. Certificate No. 0710 confirmed 11 October 1935.

Turned Out Nice Again (1941) received tentative Certificate No. 03185 17 July 1941. There is no evidence of a contemporary US release.

21 Days (1937), released as *21 Days Together* by Columbia Pictures, 16 May 1940, cut to 72 minutes. Certificate No. 6002 confirmed 29 December 1939, after deletion of two uses of 'hell'.

The Two-headed Spy (1958), released by Columbia Pictures, January 1959, uncut. Certificate No. 18995 confirmed 24 November 1958. Cuts required at script submission stage.

2,000 Women (1944) received Certificate No. 03976, 3 April 1945, after deletion of profanity and a number of scenes showing women disrobing and in a semi-nude state. There is no evidence of a contemporary US release.

The Ugly Duckling (1959) received tentative Certificate No. 19366 on 22 May 1959, but it was cancelled 30 June 1961. There is no evidence of a contemporary US release.

Under the Red Robe (1937), released by 20th Century-Fox, opening at the Little Carnegie Theatre, New York, 31 May 1937, cut by two minutes. Certificate No. 01598 confirmed 6 May 1937, after deletion of sex-suggestive line.

The Upturned Glass (1947), released by Universal-International, November 1947, uncut. Certificate No. 12285 confirmed 13 August 1947. Cuts required at script submission stage, including changing 'lover' to 'girlfriend'.

Waltz Time (1945), released by Four Continents Films, Inc., opening at the Little Carnegie Theatre, New York, 10 February 1946, uncut. Certificate No. 04138 confirmed 13 June 1946.

The Ware Case (1938), released by 20th Century-Fox, January 1940, cut to 70 minutes. Certificate No. 02529 confirmed 3 May 1939, after deletion of Clive Brook's confession that he committed the murder of which he was acquitted, leaving him to kill himself only because of despondency at finding his wife infatuated with his attorney.

Waterfront (1950), released as *Waterfront Women* by Bell Pictures, Inc., opening Rialto Theatre, New York, 8 March 1952, cut to 74 minutes. Certificate No. 14381 confirmed 19 January 1950. Cuts required at script submission stage.

Waterloo Road (1945), released by Eagle-Lion Films, Inc., January 1949. Certificate No. 13595 confirmed 23 December 1948, subject to deletion of two uses of 'hell' and Stewart Granger slapping a girl on the posterior.

The Way Ahead (1944), released by 20th Century-Fox, opening at the Victoria Theatre, New York, 9 June 1945, cut to 106 minutes. Certificate No. 03906 confirmed 26 February 1945, after deletion of fourteen uses of 'hell' and one 'damn'.

The Way to the Stars (1945), released as *Johnny in the Clouds* by United Artists, opening at the Winter Garden Theatre, New York, 15 November 1945, cut to 88 minutes. Certificate No. 04053 confirmed 28 November 1945, subject to deletion of profanity and toilet gag-line, 'Under the washbasin there finds itself a pot'.

We Dive at Dawn (1943) received Certificate No. 10907, 12 June 1945, subject to deletion of profanity. There is no evidence of a contemporary US release.

The Weaker Sex (1948), released by Eagle-Lion Films, Inc., opening at the Little Carnegie Theatre, New York, 9 July 1949, uncut. Certificate No. 13092 confirmed 10 May 1949. Cuts required at script submission stage.

Went the Day Well? (1942), released as *They Came in Khaki* on a states rights basis by A.F.E. Corp., 1944. The film opened as *48 Hours* at the Little

Carnegie Theatre, New York, 24 June 1944, cut to 88 minutes. Certificate No. 03395 confirmed 25 July 1944.

West of Kerry (1938), released as *Men of Ireland* by J. H. Hoffberg Co., Inc., opening at the Squire Theatre, New York, 29 September 1938, cut to 64 minutes. Certificate No. 02246 confirmed 8 September 1938.

West of Suez (1957), released as *The Fighting Wildcats* by Republic Pictures, Inc., 27 December 1957, uncut. Certificate No. 18667 confirmed 19 July 1957.

When Knights Were Bold (1936), released by Fine Arts Film & Studio Corporation, opening at the Little Carnegie Theatre, New York, 30 March 1942. Certificate No. 03353 confirmed 27 March 1942, subject to deletion of profanity and a 'pansy joke' involving a husky soldier singing in a soprano voice.

Where No Vultures Fly (1952), released as *Ivory Hunter* by Universal-International, June 1952, cut to 97 minutes. Certificate No. 15058 confirmed 3 January 1952. Cuts required at script submission stage.

Where There's a Will (1936), released by Gaumont British Picture Corp. of America, 1937. Certificate No. 01646 confirmed 13 July 1937.

Where's Charley? (1952), released by Warner Bros., 30 August 1952, uncut. Certificate No. 15428 confirmed 23 November 1951. Cuts required at script submission stage.

Whispering Smith Hits London (1952), released as *Whispering Smith vs Scotland Yard* by RKO, March 1952, cut to 77 minutes. Certificate No. 15370 confirmed 22 February 1952. Cuts required at script submission stage.

White Cradle Inn (1947), released as *High Fury* by United Artists, November 1948, cut to 71 minutes. Certificate No. 04612 confirmed 28 July 1948.

The White Unicorn (1947), released as *Bad Sister* by Universal-International, June 1948, cut to 90 minutes. Certificate No. 13090 confirmed 28 May 1949. Cuts required at script submission stage, relating to Margaret Lockwood's breast exposure, the actress on a massage table, hint by Joan Greenwood of an abortion, etc.

Who Goes There? (1952), released as *The Passionate Sentry* by Fine Arts Films, Inc., opening at the Beekman Theatre, New York, 11 November 1953. Certificate No. 16249 confirmed 14 January 1953, subject to deletion of two uses of 'cripes'.

Wife of General Ling (1937), released by Gaumont British Picture Corp. of America, opening at the Globe Theatre, New York, 19 February 1938, uncut. Certificate No. 01928 confirmed 21 February 1938, subject to deletion of profanity and a disparaging reference to Boy Scouts. As General Ling was a war lord rather than a gangster, his portrayal was permitted with a gun in his hands.

The Wind Cannot Read (1958), released by 20th Century-Fox, February 1960, uncut. Certificate No. 19543 confirmed 3 February 1960.

The Winslow Boy (1948), released by Eagle-Lion Films, Inc., March 1950, cut to 97 minutes. Certificate No. 14488 confirmed 21 March 1950.

A Woman Alone (1936), released as *Two Who Dared* by Grand National Pictures, Inc., 8 May 1937, cut to 73 minutes. Certificate No. 01587 confirmed 19 April 1937, subject to minor deletions.

The Woman in the Hall (1946), released by Eagle-Lion Films, Inc., May 1949, uncut. Certificate No. 12352 confirmed 1 April 1949. The PCA did not approve the original basic story of a woman who obtains money under false pretences, lies in court to save her daughter from a charge of forgery and is not punished.

Women of Twilight (1952), released as *Twilight Women* by Lippert Pictures, Inc., July 1953, uncut. Certificate No. 16399 confirmed 23 April 1953.

Yellow Canary (1943), released by RKO, April 1944, cut to 84 minutes. Certificate No. 03777 confirmed 31 March 1944, subject to deletion of profanity.

Yes, Mr Brown (1935) received Certificate No. 0615 on 21 August 1935. There is no evidence of a contemporary US release.

You Will Remember (1941), released by English Films, Inc., 1948. Certificate No. 04605 confirmed 4 June 1948.

Young and Innocent (1937), released as *The Girl Was Young* by Gaumont British Picture Corp. of America, opening at the Criterion Theatre, New York, 10 February 1938. Certificate No. 01729 confirmed 26 January 1938, subject to deletion of two references to God and one 'damn.'

Your Witness (1950), released as *Eye Witness* by Eagle-Lion Classics, Inc., opening at the Little Carnegie Theatre, New York, 27 August 1950, uncut. Certificate No. 14778 confirmed 6 November 1950.

Appendix 2

British Films Released in the USA without a Production Code Seal of Approval

The following titles, given here with their American distributors and American release dates, are known to have been screened without a Certificate, but the list should in no way be considered definitive. Also included here are films submitted at some point to the PCA for Code approval but on which there was no follow-up by the producer or distributor and for which there is no evidence of a contemporary US release.

Abdullah's Harem (1956), released by 20th Century-Fox, June 1956.

Across the Bridge (1957) – see p. 28.

The Agitator (1945), released by Four Continents Films, Inc., opening at the Trans-Lux 60th Street Theatre, New York, 18 August 1949.

Albert, RN (1953), released as *Break to Freedom* by United Artists, July 1955.

Alive and Kicking (1959), released by Seven Arts Associated Corp., opening at the Music Hall Theatre, Beverly Hills, 26 June 1964.

An Alligator Named Daisy (1955), released by Rank Film Distributors of America, Inc., October 1957.

The Angel Who Pawned Her Harp (1954) was submitted to the PCA in script form in April 1953 and met the requirements of the Production Code. No Certificate was issued and the film was released by Dominant Pictures, Inc., December 1956.

The Angel with the Trumpet (1950), released by Snader Productions, Inc., 20 December 1951.

Angels One Five (1952), released by Stratford Pictures, May 1954.

Animal Farm (1954), released by RKO, opening at the Paris Theatre, New York, 29 December 1954. In May 1955, producer Louis de Rochemont submitted a script and the PCA confirmed it met the requirements of the Production Code, but as the film had already been released, no further action was taken.

Another Shore (1948) − see p. 30.

Antarctic Crossing (1958), released by Schoenfeld Films, Inc., June 1959.

Appointment in London (1953), released by Famous Pictures Films Corporation, 1955.

Appointment with Crime (1946), released by Four Continents Films, Inc., opening at the Bryant Theatre, New York, 18 February 1951.

As Long as They're Happy (1955), released by Rank Film Distributors of America, Inc., opening at the Hawaii and State Theatres, Los Angeles, 9 October 1957.

Assassin for Hire (1951), released by Realart Pictures, December 1951.

At the Villa Rose (1939), released as *The House of Mystery* by Monogram Pictures, Inc., 7 May 1941.

The Baby and the Battleship (1956), released by Distributors Corp. of America, opening at the Four Star Theatre, Los Angeles, 30 May 1957.

Bachelor of Hearts (1958), released by Continental Distributing, Inc., May 1962.

The Bad Lord Byron (1949) − see p. 33.

The Battle (1934) was viewed by the PCA on 27 December 1934, and found to be in conformity with the Production Code. It opened, without a Certificate, at the Criterion Theatre, New York, on 22 November 1934, and was subsequently released by Ritchey International Corp. as *Thunder in the East*.

Before the Raid (1943), released by British Information Service, opening at the Stanley Theatre, New York, 25 February 1944. Classified as a newsreel and not subject to PCA approval.

The Belles of St Trinian's (1954), released by Associated Artists Productions, January 1955. Classified 'B' by the National Legion of Decency because of 'low moral tone'.

Big Fella (1937), released by Monogram Pictures, Inc., 1940.

The Big Money (1958), released by Lopert Films, Inc., March 1962.

Bitter Springs (1950), released by Bell Pictures, Inc., 1 October 1951. Tentative Certificate No. 13913 was issued on 6 June 1949, but never confirmed.

The Black Tent (1956), released by Rank Film Distributors of America, Inc., June 1957.

Blarney (1938), released by William Alexander as *Ireland's Border Line*, opening at the Belmont Theatre, New York, 12 October 1939. Reissued in 1943 as *It Happened in Ireland.*

Blind Spot (1958) was submitted to the PCA for approval on 8 September 1959 by Bernard L. Schubert, Inc., but had no contemporary US release.

Blue Murder at St Trinian's (1957), released by Continental Distributing, Inc., opening at the Baronet Theatre, New York, 26 May 1958.

A Boy, a Girl and a Bike (1949) was first submitted to the PCA in script form in July 1948 and met the requirements of the Production Code. No certificate was issued and there is no evidence of a contemporary US release.

Boys in Brown (1949) was submitted to the PCA in script form in March 1949 and met the requirements of the Production Code. No Certificate was issued and there is no evidence of a contemporary US release.

Brandy for the Parson (1952) was submitted to the PCA in script form in July 1951 and met the requirements of the Production Code. No Certificate was issued and the film was released by Arthur Mayer–Edward Kingsley, Inc., August 1952.

The Brave Don't Cry (1952), released by Arthur Mayer–Edward Kingsley, Inc., opening at Loew's State and the Hawaii Theatres, Los Angeles, 17 July 1953.

Brewster's Millions (1935) – see p. 41.

Brighton Rock (1947), released as *Young Scarface* by M.K.D. Distributors, Inc., 7 November 1951.

Brothers in Law (1957), released by Continental Distributing, Inc., opening at the Guild Theatre, New York, 19 August 1957.

Bulldog Jack (1935), released as *Alias Bulldog Jack* by Gaumont British Picture Corp. of America, 15 September 1935.

Campbell's Kingdom (1957), released by Rank Film Distributors of America, Inc., March 1958.

Cardboard Cavalier (1949) was submitted to the PCA in script form in May 1948 and met the requirements of the Production Code. No Certificate was issued and there is no evidence of a contemporary US release.

Carry On Teacher (1959), released by Governor Films, Inc., May 1962.

Carve Her Name with Pride (1958), released by Rank Film Distributors of America, Inc., 1958.

The Case of the Frightened Lady (1940), released as *The Frightened Lady* by J. H. Hoffberg Co., Inc., 7 November 1941.

Cast a Dark Shadow (1955), released by Distributors Corp. of America, 1957.

Castle in the Air (1952) was submitted to the PCA in script form in September 1950 and rejected because of a theme concerned with the comedic break-up of marriage, divorce and collusion in adultery. It was released by Allied Artists, Inc., 22 December 1952.

Champagne Charlie (1944), released by Bell Pictures, Inc., opening at the Park Avenue Theatre, New York, 6 August 1948.

Chance of a Lifetime (1950), released by Ballantine Pictures, Inc., February 1951.

The Colditz Story (1955), released by Distributors Corp. of America, opening at the Paramount and Egyptian Theatres, Los Angeles, 21 February 1957.

The Constant Husband (1955), released by Allied Artists, Inc., opening at the Plaza Theatre, New York, 25 July 1957. US première on NBC, 6 November 1955, as the first colour feature to be seen on American television.

Cosh Boy (1953) was viewed by the PCA on 8 December 1952 and rejected because 'There were no decent people in this saga of unrelieved evil'. The distributor was asked to discontinue its request for a Certificate and the film was released as *The Slasher* by Lippert Pictures, Inc., July 1953. It was banned outright in New York.

Cottage to Let (1941), released as *Bombsight Stolen* by Monogram Pictures, Inc., May 1943.

Counterspy (1953), released as *Undercover Agent* by Lippert Pictures, Inc., November 1953.

Crimes at the Dark House (1940), released by Times Pictures, Inc., January 1942.

Dance Hall (1950) – see p. 53.

Dancing with Crime (1947), released by Screencraft Pictures, Inc., January 1953.

Dangerous Exile (1957), released by Rank Film Distributors of America, Inc., October 1958.

Dangerous Fingers (1937), released as *Wanted by Scotland Yard* by Monogram Pictures, Inc., 1939.

Dear Mr Prohack (1949) was submitted to the PCA in script form in December 1948 and met the requirements of the Production Code. No Certificate was issued and the film was released by Pentagon Pictures Corp., opening at the Trans-Lux 72nd Street Theatre, New York, 14 July 1950.

Derby Day (1952), released on a states rights basis, 1955.

Devil Girl from Mars (1954), released by Distributors Corp. of America, opening at Loew's State, Los Angeles, 27 April 1955.

Devil's Plot (1953), released by Herbert Bregstein, opening at the Rialto Theatre, New York, 19 June 1953.

Diamond City (1949) – see p. 56.

The Diamond Wizard (1952), released by United Artists, July 1954.

Don't Ever Leave Me (1949) was submitted to the PCA in script form in December 1948 and met the requirements of the Production Code. The rules regarding depiction of a kidnapping did not apply here because the kidnapping was not completed and a child was not involved. No Certificate was issued and there is no evidence of a contemporary US release.

The Edge of the World (1937) – see p. 58.

Eight o'clock Walk (1954), released by Associated Artists, Inc., May 1955.

Elizabeth of Ladymead (1949). On 1 July 1949, the PCA confirmed to Theodore Smith, Herbert Wilcox's New York representative, that no Certificate had been issued. There is no evidence of a contemporary US release.

Emergency Call (1952), released as *Hundred Hour Hunt* by Abner J. Greshler, opening at the Normandie Theatre, Los Angeles, 16 June 1953.

The End of the Road (1959), released by Distributors Corp. of America, 1959.

Escapade (1955), released by Distributors Corp. of America, September 1957.

Eureka Stockade (1949) was submitted to the PCA in script form in December 1947 and met the requirements of the Production Code. In January 1948, the J. Arthur Rank Organization, Inc., submitted a final shooting script but then asked that the PCA not read or comment upon it. No Certificate was issued and there is no evidence of a contemporary US release.

Expresso Bongo (1959) was viewed by the PCA in January 1960 and rejected on a number on counts. In February 1960, the application for a Certificate was withdrawn and the film released by Continental Distributing, Inc., April 1960.

Face in the Night (1957), released as *Menace in the Night* by United Artists, October 1958.

Family Doctor (1958), released as *RX Murder* by 20th Century-Fox, August 1958.

Father's Doing Fine (1952), released by Allied Artists, Inc., 22 April 1953.

The Feminine Touch (1956), released as *The Gentle Touch* by Rank Film Distributors of America, Inc., 10 August 1957.

The Final Test (1953) was submitted to the PCA in script form in November 1952 and met the requirements of the Production Code. No Certificate was issued and the film was released by Continental Distributing, Inc., opening at the Baronet Theatre, New York, 25 January 1954.

The Flesh is Weak (1957), released by Distributors Corp. of America, opening at the Rialto Theatre, New York, 8 November 1957. In September 1959, it was banned in Kansas because of the prostitution theme.

The Flying Doctor (1936), released by Specialty Pictures, Inc., 1943.

Folly to be Wise (1952), released by Fine Arts Films, Inc., opening at the Art and Beekman Theatres, New York, 27 December 1953.

Fools Rush In (1949) was submitted to the PCA in script form in November 1948 and met the requirements of the Production Code. No Certificate was issued and there is no evidence of a contemporary US release.

For Better for Worse (1954), reportedly released by Allied Artists, Inc., but the film does not appear on its release schedule.

For Them That Trespass (1949), released by Stratford Pictures, opening at the Little Cinemet, New York, 26 September 1950.

Forbidden Cargo (1954) – see p. 66.

Four Dark Hours (1937), released as *The Green Cockatoo*, opening at the Rialto Theatre, New York, 18 July 1947.

The Four Just Men (1939) was viewed by the PCA on 13 July 1939 and met the requirements of the Production Code. No Certificate was issued and the film was released as *The Secret Four* by Monogram Pictures, Inc., 15 January 1940.

The Franchise Affair (1951), released by Monogram Pictures, Inc., 1952.

Front Page Story (1954), released by Associated Artists, Inc., April 1955.

Further up the Creek (1958) was submitted to the PCA in script form and met the requirements of the Production Code. No Certificate was issued and there is no evidence of a contemporary US release.

The Galloping Major (1951) was submitted to the PCA in script form in June 1950 and met the requirements of the Production Code. No Certificate was issued and the film was released by Souvaine Selective Pictures, Inc., opening at the Trans-Lux 60th Street Theatre, New York, on 15 December 1951.

The Gaunt Stranger (1938) was viewed by the PCA on 15 April 1939 but approval denied because the criminal, 'The Ringer', escaped punishment at the film's conclusion and a revenge killing was also featured. No Certificate was issued and the film released as *The Phantom Strikes* by Monogram Pictues, Inc., 15 November 1939.

Gift Horse (1952) was submitted to the PCA in script form in August 1951 and met the requirements of the Production Code. No Certificate was issued and the film released as *Glory at Sea* by Souvaine Selective Pictures, Inc., opening at the Beekman and Art Theatres, New York, 10 March 1953.

The Girl from Maxim's (1933) – see p. 70.

A Girl in a Million (1946), released by Oxford Films, Inc., opening at the Little Carnegie Theatre, New York, 22 July 1950.

Girls Will Be Boys (1934), released by Alliance Films, Inc., 1935.

Going Gay (1933), released as *Kiss Me Goodbye* by P. A. Powers Celebrity Pictures, Inc. (its first release), 1935.

The Golden Madonna (1949), released by Monogram Pictures, Inc., opening at the Beacon Theatre, New York, 3 September 1949.

The Great Mr Handel (1942), released by Midfilms, Inc., 1944.

The Green Man (1956), released by Distributors Corp. of America, opening at the Beverly Canon Theatre, Los Angeles, 10 September 1957.

Guilt Is My Shadow (1950), released by Stratford Pictures, 1951.

The Guv'nor (1935), released as *Mister Hobo* by Gaumont British Picture Corp. of America, opening at the Roxy Theatre, New York, 7 February 1936.

The Gypsy and the Gentleman (1958), released by Rank Film Distributors of America, Inc., November 1958.

The Halfway House (1944), released by A.F.E. Corp., 4 August 1945.

The Happiest Days of Your Life (1950) received tentative Certificate No. 15082 on 12 January 1951, but when the applicant Pacemaker Pictures, Inc., discovered the fee would be $150, it withdrew its application. The film was initially released by London Films, Inc., opening at the Little Carnegie Theatre, New York, 16 September 1950.

The Happy Family (1952), released as *Mr Lord Says No* by Souvaine Selective Pictures, Inc., opening at the Guild Theatre, New York, 13 February 1952.

Happy Is the Bride (1958), released by Kassler Films, Inc., April 1959.

Heart of a Child (1958), released by Rank Film Distributors of America, Inc., 1958.

Helter Skelter (1949) was first submitted to the PCA in script form in September 1948 and met the requirements of the Production Code. No Certificate was issued and there is no evidence of a contemporary US release.

High Tide at Noon (1957), released by Rank Film Distributors of America, Inc., 1957.

A Hill in Korea (1956), released as *Hell in Korea* by Distributors Corp. of America, October 1957.

The History of Mr Polly (1949) – p. 77.

Hobson's Choice (1954), released by United Artists, June 1954. The MPAA advised the distributor that the trailer contained the word 'ass', which could not be used 'in front of family and mixed audiences'.

Home at Seven (1952), released as *Murder on Monday* by Arthur Mayer–Edward Kingsley, Inc., November 1953.

House of Secrets (1956), released as *Triple Deception* by Rank Film Distributors of America, Inc., opening at the Paramount Theatre, Los Angeles, 6 November 1957.

Hue and Cry (1947), released by Fine Arts Films, Inc., opening at the Sunset Theatre, Los Angeles, 3 February 1951.

The Huggetts Abroad (1949) was first submitted to the PCA in script form in October 1948 and met the requirements of the Production Code. No Certificate was issued and there is no evidence of a contemporary US release.

I Am a Camera (1955) – see p. 80.

I Give My Heart (1935) – see p. 82.

I Killed the Count (1939), released as *Who is Guilty?* by Monogram Pictures, Inc., 2 September 1940.

Ill Met by Moonlight (1957), released by Rank Film Distributors of America, Inc., 1957.

Inside Britain (1942), released by British Ministry of Information, 1942. Classified as a newsreel and not subject to PCA approval.

The Intimate Stranger (1956), released as *Finger of Guilt* by RKO, October 1956.

The Invader (1936), released as *An Old Spanish Custom* by J. H. Hoffberg Co., Inc., 1936.

Invitation to the Waltz (1935), released by J. H. Hoffberg Co., Inc., July 1938.

It's Not Cricket (1949) was first submitted to the PCA in script form in January 1948 and met the requirements of the Production Code. No Certificate was issued and there is no evidence of a contemporary US release.

Jet Storm (1959), released by United Producers Releasing Organization, April 1962.

John and Julie (1956), released by Distributors Corp. of America, 1957.

John Wesley (1954), released by Radio and Film Commission of the Methodist Church, first screened in New York, 22 April 1954.

A Kid for Two Farthings (1955), released by Lopert Films, Inc., April 1956.

A King in New York (1957), released by Classic Entertainment, Inc., December 1973.

Lady Godiva Rides Again (1951) – see p. 93.

The Ladykillers (1955) was submitted to the PCA in script form in February 1955 and met the requirements of the Production Code. No Certificate was issued and there is no evidence of a contemporary US release.

Last Days of Dolwyn (1949), released as *The Women of Dolwyn* by Lopert Films, Inc., opening at the World Theatre, New York, 29 August 1949 as *Dolwyn*.

Last Holiday (1950), released by Stratford Pictures, opening at the Paris Theatre, New York, 13 November 1950.

Laughter in Paradise (1951), releeased by Stratford Pictures, opening at the Trans-Lux 60th Street Theatre, New York, 11 November 1951.

Life with the Lyons (1954), released as *Family Affair* by Lippert Pictures, Inc., 1954.

Lilacs in the Spring (1955), released as *Let's Make Up* by United Artists, opening at the Paramount Theatre, New York, 1 February 1956.

The Lisbon Story (1946), released by Four Continents Films, Inc., opening at the RKO 81st Street Theatre, New York, 5 September 1951.

The Long Memory (1952) – see p. 97.

Look Before You Love (1948) – see p. 98.

Love at Second Sight (1934), released on a states rights basis, opening at the Central Theatre, New York, 7 January 1938.

The Love Lottery (1954) was first submitted to the PCA in script form in December 1952 and met the requirements of the Production Code. No Certificate was issued and the film was released by Continental Distributing, Inc., opening at the Fox Theatre, Hollywood, 19 June 1957.

Love's a Luxury (1952), released as *The Caretaker's Daughter* by Beverly Pictures, Inc., opening at the Beacon Theatre, New York, 19 August 1953.

The Loves of Joanna Godden (1947) was submitted to the PCA in script form in July 1946 and met the requirements of the Production Code. No Certificate was issued and there is no evidence of a contemporary US release.

Lucky Jim (1957), released by Kingsley International Pictures Corp., opening at the Music Hall Theatre, Beverly Hills, 20 May 1960. As early as June 1958, the film played the Exeter Theatre, Boston.

Made In Heaven (1952) was first submitted to the PCA in script form in February 1952 and met the requirements of the Production Code. Joseph I. Breen refused to issue a Certificate because of an ongoing problem with Rank's failing to submit the final film for approval and there is no evidence of a contemporary US release.

Make Me an Offer (1954), released by Associated Artists, Inc.–Dominant Pictures, Inc., March 1956.

Make Mine a Million (1959), released on a states rights basis, March 1965.

The Man from Morocco (1945) was submitted to the PCA in script form in November 1946 and met the requirements of the Production Code. No Certificate was issued and the film was released by English Films, Inc., 23 November 1946.

Man of Africa (1956), released by Eden Picture Co., opening at the Embassy Theatre, New York, 10 October 1956.

Man on the Run (1949), released by Stratford Pictures, opening at the Trans-Lux 72nd Street Theatre, New York, 26 February 1952.

The Man Who Wouldn't Talk (1958), released by Show Corp. of America, January 1961.

The Marriage of Corbal (1936), released as *Prisoner of Corbal* by Unity, Inc., opening at the Central Theatre, New York, 25 August 1939.

Marry Me! (1949) was first submitted to the PCA in script form in November 1948 and met the requirements of the Production Code. No Certificate was issued and the film was released by Manhattan/Ellis Films, Inc., opening at the Pantages Theatre, Hollywood, 30 May 1952.

The Mask of Cain (1948) was submitted to the PCA in script form in April 1947 and met the requirements of the Production Code. No Certificate was issued and there is no evidence of a contemporary US release.

Maytime in Mayfair (1949), released by Realart, opening at the Trans-Lux 60th Street Theatre, New York, 22 April 1952.

Meet Maxwell Archer (1939), released as *Maxwell Archer, Detective* by Monogram Pictures, Inc., opening at the New York Theatre, New York, 28 April 1942.

Meet Mr Lucifer (1953) was submitted to the PCA in script form in November 1952 and met the requirements of the Production Code. No Certificate was released and there is no evidence of a contemporary US release.

Men of Two Worlds (1946) was submitted to the PCA in script form in March 1945 and met the requirements of the Production Code. No Certificate was issued and there is no evidence of a contemporary US release.

The Mind of Mr Reeder (1939), released as *The Mysterious Mr Reeder* by Monogram Pictures, Inc., opening at the Central Theatre, New York, 1 May 1940.

Miss Pilgrim's Progress (1950), released by Federal Films, 1950.

Mr Cohen Takes a Walk (1935), released by Warner Bros, opening at the Astor Theatre, New York, 12 February 1936.

Mr Perrin and Mr Traill (1948) was submitted to the PCA in script form in December 1947 and met the requirements of the Production Code. No Certificate was issued and the film was released by Eagle-Lion Films, Inc., December 1948.

Mrs Fitzherbert (1947), released by Stratford Pictures, opening at the Normandie Theatre, New York, 10 May 1950.

Mother Riley Meets the Vampire (1952) – see p. 107.

My Teenage Daughter (1956), released by Distributors Corp. of America, April 1957. Reissued as *Bad Girl* by Hal Roach, Inc., March 1959.

The Naked Truth (1957), released as *Your Past is Showing* by Rank Film Distributors of America, Inc., July 1958.

Never Take No For An Answer (1951), released by Souvaine Selective Pictures, Inc., August 1952.

Next To No Time (1958) was submitted to the PCA in script form in June 1957 and met the requirements of the Production Code. No Certificate was issued and the film was released by Show Corporation of America, opening at the Little Carnegie Theatre, New York, 27 May 1960.

The Night My Number Came Up (1955) was submitted to the PCA in script form in October 1954 and met the requirements of the Production Code. No Certificate was issued and the film was released by Continental Distributing, Inc., opening at the Hollywood Theatre, Hollywood, 15 February 1956.

A Night to Remember (1958), released by Rank Film Distributors of America, Inc., February 1958.

The Night We Dropped a Clanger (1959), released as *Make Mine a Double* by Ellis Films, Inc., February 1952.

No Orchids for Miss Blandish (1948), released by Renown Pictures of America, Inc., February 1951.

No Place for Jennifer (1950), released by Stratford Pictures, August 1951.

No Trees in the Street (1959), released by Seven Arts Associated, Inc., February 1964.

Nor the Moon by Night (1958), released as *Elephant Gun* by Lopert Films, Inc., July 1959.

Odette (1950), released initially by Lopert Films, Inc., January 1951, and subsequently by United Artists, June 1951.

The Old Curiosity Shop (1935), released by First Division, Inc., opening at the World Theatre, New York, 21 December 1935.

On Approval (1944) – see p. 114.

Once a Jolly Swagman (1948) was submitted to the PCA in script form in April 1948 and met the requirements of the Production Code. No Certificate was issued and as *Maniacs on Wheels*, the film was released by International Releasing Organization, 11 July 1951.

The One that Got Away (1957), released by Rank Film Distributors of America, Inc., March 1958.

The Oracle (1953), released as *The Horse's Mouth* by Arthur Mayer-Edward Kingsley, Inc., January 1954.

Orders to Kill (1958), released by United Motion Picture Organization, November 1958.

Out of the Clouds (1955) was submitted to the PCA in script form in June 1954 and met the requirements of the Production Code. No Certificate was issued and the film was released by Rank Film Distributors of America, Inc., July 1957.

Outcast of the Islands (1952) was viewed by the PCA on 20 February 1952 and contained unacceptable scenes, including a naked native boy and open-mouth kissing. It was 'written off' by the PCA in April 1952, and released by Lopert/United Artists, June 1952.

Passport to Shame (1959) was viewed by the PCA on 3 December 1958 and found in violation of Paragraph 5, Section III of the Code: 'The methods and techniques of prostitution and white slavery shall never be presented in detail' and 'Brothels in any clear identification as such may not be shown.' The film was released as *Room 43* by the newly-formed Cory Film Corp., May 1959.

Peeping Tom (1960), released by Astor Films, Inc., opening at the Fox Theatre, Brooklyn, 13 June 1962. The film did not open in Los Angeles until 1980.

Pink String and Sealing Wax (1945) was submitted to the PCA in script form in November 1947 and rejected because of its suicide ending and delineation of the details of a crime. No Certificate was issued and the film was released by Pentagon Pictures, Inc., opening at the Art Theatre, New York, 3 October 1950.

Portrait of Clare (1950), released by Stratford Pictures, opening at the Midtown Theatre, New York, 25 December 1951.

The Prince of Wales (1933), released by Gaumont British Picture Corp. of America, 1937. Classified as a newsreel and not subject to PCA approval.

The Private Secretary (1935) was viewed by the PCA on June 2, 1936 and the distributor advised of a problem with the comic characterization of a clergyman. No Certificate was issued and the film was released as *Behind Office Doors* by Atlantic Film Corporation, July 1936.

Pursuit of the Graf Spee (1957), released by Rank Film Distributors of America, Inc., November 1957.

The Quatermass Experiment (1955), released as *The Creeping Unknown* by United Artists, June 1956.

A Queen is Crowned (1953), released by Universal-International, June 1953. Classified as a newsreel and not subject to PCA approval.

The Queen of Spades (1949), released by Monogram Pictures, Inc., 1950.

A Question of Adultery (1958) – see p. 124.

Quiet Weekend (1946), released by Distinguished Films, Inc., 1948.

Richard III (1955), released by Lopert Films, Inc., March 1956.

The Ringer (1952) – see p. 127.

The Robber Symphony (1936), released by Al Friedlander and Fortune Film Corp., opening at the Venice Theatre, New York, 25 January 1937.

Rockets Galore (1958), released as *Island Fling* by Rank Film Distributors of America, Inc., February 1959.

Room at the Top (1959), released by Continental Distributing, Inc., May 1959.

Room in the House (1955), released by Gibraltar Motion Picture Distributors, Inc., opening at the State Theatre, Los Angeles, 14 September 1964.

Rooney (1958), released by Rank Film Distributors of America, Inc., June 1958.

The Root of All Evil (1947) was submitted to the PCA in script form in February 1946 and rejected because of an illicit sex affair between the central characters. No Certificate was issued and there is no evidence of a contemporary US release.

Rose of Tralee (1937), released by the Dublin Film Co., 15 October 1938, opening at the Irish Theatre (formerly the Miami), New York, 21 October 1938.

The Runaway Bus (1954), released by Kramer-Hyams, Inc., opening at the Trans-Lux Normandie Theatre, New York, 23 October 1954.

Sailor Beware (1956), released as *Panic in the Parlor* by Distributors Corp. of America, December 1957.

Saints and Sinners (1949), released by London Films, Inc., opening at the Little Carnegie Theatre, New York, 17 September 1949.

School for Danger (1947), released by English Films, Inc., opening at the Gotham Theatre, New York, 8 November 1947.

School of Secrets (1940), released as *Secret Flight* by Herbert Bregstein, opening at the Beacon and Midtown Theatres, New York, 2 July 1952.

Sea of Sand (1958), released as *Desert Patrol* by Universal-International, March 1962.

The Secret (1955), released by Distributors Corp. of America, 1957.

The Secret Place (1957), released by Rank Film Distributors of America, Inc., February 1958.

Seven Days to Noon (1950), released by Arthur Mayer–Edward Kingsley, Inc., February 1951.

Seven Thunders (1957), released by Rank Film Distributors of America, Inc., 1957. Reissued as *The Beasts of Marseilles* by Lopert Films, Inc.

She Didn't Say No! (1958), released by Seven Arts Associated, Inc., May 1962.

The Ship that Died of Shame (1955) was first submitted to the PCA in script form in September 1954 and met the requirements of the Production Code. No Certificate was issued and the film was released by Continental Distributing, Inc., August 1956.

Silent Dust (1949), released by Stratford Pictures, opening at the Embassy Theatre, New York, 29 December 1949.

The Sleeping Tiger (1954), released by Astor Films, Inc., opening at the Orpheum Theatre, Los Angeles, 4 May 1955.

The Small Back Room (1949), released by Snader Productions, Inc., 4 February 1952.

The Smallest Show on Earth (1957), released by Times Film Corp., November 1957. Reissued as *Big Time Operators* in 1964.

So Little Time (1952), released by McDonald Pictures, Inc., opening at the Little Carnegie Theatre, New York, 14 August 1953.

Spellbound (1941), released as *The Spell of Amy Nugent* by PRC, 10 February 1945.

Stop Press Girl (1949) was submitted to the PCA in script form in December 1948 and met the requirements of the Production Code. No Certificate was issued and there is no evidence of a contemporary US release.

The Strange World of Planet X (1958), released as *Cosmic Monsters* by Distributors Corp. of America, January 1959.

The Stranger's Hand (1954), released by Distributors Corp. of America, March 1955.

Street Of Shadows (1953), released as *Shadow Man* by Lippert Pictures, Inc., 16 October 1953.

The Student's Romance (1936), released as *Student Romance* by Alliance Films Corp., opening at the 55th Street Playhouse, New York, 10 October 1936.

A Tale of Two Cities (1958), released by Rank Film Distributors of America, Inc., opening at the Sutton Theatre, New York, 4 August 1958.

Talk of a Million (1951), released as *You Can't Beat the Irish* by Stratford Pictures, opening at the Park Avenue Theatre, New York, 1 May 1952.

The Teckman Mystery (1954), released by Associated Artists, Inc., August 1955.

The Tell-Tale Heart (1934), released as *Bucket of Blood* on a states rights basis, 1942 (except Ohio, where release was required utilizing the original title).

Ten Minute Alibi (1935) – see p. 133.

These Dangerous Years (1957), released as *Dangerous Youth* by Warner Bros, May 1958.

They Came to a City (1944), released by A.F.E. Corporation, opening at the Little Carnegie Theatre, New York, 18 February 1945. The original US release appears to have been a limited one, and the film was reviewed in *The Hollywood Reporter* in 1947 as if it was new to the USA.

They Drive by Night (1938) – see p. 134.

Three Cases Of Murder (1954), released by Associated Artists, Inc., March 1955.

3 Steps to the Gallows (1953), released as *White Fire* by Lippert Pictures, Inc., 10 February 1954.

Thunder in the City (1937), released by Atlantic Film Corporation, 25 April 1937.

Tiger by the Tail (1955), released as *Cross-Up* by United Artists, January 1958.

Time Gentlemen Please! (1952) was submitted to the PCA in script form in September 1951 and met the requirements of the Production Code. No Certificate was issued and the film was released by Arthur Mayer–Edward Kingsley, Inc., 1953.

Time Without Pity (1957), released by Astor Films, Inc., January 1958.

Timeslip (1955), released as The *Atomic Man* by Allied Artists, Inc., February 1956.

To Paris with Love (1955), released by Continental Distributing, Inc., April 1955.

Tony Draws a Horse (1950) – see p. 139.

A Town Like Alice (1956), released by Rank Film Distributors of America, Inc., July 1957.

Train Of Events (1949) was first submitted to the PCA in script form in December 1948 and met the requirements of the Production Code. No Certificate was issued and the film was released by Fine Arts Films, Inc., opening at the Esquire Theatre, Los Angeles, 21 September 1951.

Treasure Hunt (1952), released by Souvaine Selective Pictures, Inc., July 1953.

The Trials of Oscar Wilde (1960) – see p. 139.

The Trollenberg Terror (1958), released as The *Crawling Eye* by Distributors Corp. of America, December 1958.

The Truth about Women (1958) was submitted to the PCA in script form in January 1957 and met the requirements of the Production Code. No Certificate was issued and the film was released by Continental Distributing, Inc., opening at the Warner Theatre, Hollywood, 4 November 1959.

Turn the Key Softly (1953) – see p. 140.

29 Acacia Avenue (1945) – see p. 142.

Twist of Fate (1954), released by United Artists, November 1954.

Two's Company (1936) was viewed by the PCA on 30 November 1939 and met the requirements of the Production Code. No Certificate was issued and the film was released by Times Pictures, Inc., December 1939.

Uncle Silas (1947) was first submitted to the PCA in script form in July 1946 and failed to meet the requirements of the Production Code in that the central character committed suicide. No Certificate was issued and the film was released as *The Inheritance* by Fine Arts Films, Inc., opening at the Symphony Theatre, New York, 10 February 1951.

Undercover (1943), released as *Underground Guerrillas* by Columbia Pictures, opening at the Hawaii Theatre, Los Angeles, November 7, 1944.

Value for Money (1955), released by Rank Film Distributors of America, Inc., July 1957.

Vice Versa (1948) was submitted to the PCA in script form in March 1947 and met the requirements of the Production Code. No Certificate was issued and there is no evidence of a contemporary US release.

The Voice of Merrill (1952), released as *Murder Will Out* by Kramer-Hyams Films, Inc., opening at the Normandie Theatre, New York, 4 April 1953.

Vote for Huggett (1949) was submitted to the PCA in script form in July 1948 and met the requirements of the Production Code. No Certificate was issued and there is no evidence of a contemporary US release.

Waltzes from Vienna (1934), released as *Strauss' Great Waltz* by Tom Arnold, opening at the Westminster Theatre, New York, 6 April 1935.

Welcome the Queen (1954), released by the British Information Service, September 1954. Classified as a newsreel and not subject to PCA approval.

Western Approaches (1944) – see p. 145.

What Every Woman Wants! (1954) was submitted to the PCA in script form in May 1954 and the producer was advised the story was a technical violation of the Production Code in that it involved the kidnapping of a child. No Certificate was issued and there is no evidence of a contemporary US release.

When the Bough Breaks (1947) was submitted to the PCA in script form in February 1947 and met the requirements of the Production Code. No Certificate was issued and there is no evidence of a contemporary US release.

While the Sun Shines (1947), released by Stratford Pictures, May 1950.

Who Done It? (1956) was submitted to the PCA in script form in August 1955 and met the requirements of the Production Code. No Certificate was issued and there is no evidence of a contemporary US release.

Whom the Gods Love (1936), released as *Mozart* by Mozart Films, Inc., 3 October 1940.

Wide Boy (1952), released by Realart, April 1953.

Will Any Gentleman? (1953), released by Stratford Pictures, September 1955.

The Woman with No Name (1950), released as *Her Panelled Door* by Souvaine Selective Pictures, Inc., 27 August 1951.

Women Without Men (1956), released as *Blonde Bait* by Associated Film Distributing Corp., October 1956.

The Wooden Horse (1950) – see p. 147.

World of Plenty (1943), released by the British Information Service, July 1943. Classified as a newsreel and not subject to PCA approval.

Yangtse Incident (1957), released as *Battle Hell* by Distributors Corp. of America, opening at the Egyptian Theatre, Hollywood, 8 May 1957.

Yield to the Night (1956), released as *Blonde Sinner* by Allied Artists, Inc., December 1956.

You Know what Sailors Are (1954), released by United Artists, May 1955.

Select Bibliography

Carmen, Ira H. *Movies, Censorship and the Law* (Ann Arbor, MI: University of Michigan Press, 1966).

de Grazia, Edward and Roger K. Newman. *Banned Films: Movies, Censors and the First Amendment* (New York: R. R. Bowker, 1982).

Farber, Stephen. *The Movie Rating Game* (Washington, DC: Public Affairs Press, 1972).

The Film Daily Year Book of Motion Pictures, 1933–1960 (New York: Film Daily, 1934–61).

Gardiner, Harold C. *Catholic Viewpoint on Censorship* (Garden City, NY: Hanover House, 1958).

Gardner, Gerald. *The Censorship Papers: Movie Censorship Letters from the Hays Office, 1934 to 1968* (New York: Dodd, Mead, 1987).

Gifford, Denis. *The British Film Cataloque, 1895–1985* (Newton Abbot: David & Charles, 1986).

Hall, Barbara. *Oral History with Albert E. Van Schmus* (Beverly Hills, CA: Academy of Motion Picture Arts and Sciences, 1990/1992).

Harrison's Report Film Reviews, 1919–1962 (Hollywood, CA: Hollywood Film Archive, 1995).

Inglis, Ruth A. *Freedom of the Movies: A Report of Self-Regulation from the Commission on Freedom of the Press* (Chicago, IL: University of Chicago Press, 1947).

Jacobs, Lea. *The Wages of Sin: Censorship and the Fallen Woman Film, 1928–1942* (Madison, WI: University of Wisconsin Press, 1991).

Leff, Leonard J. and Jerold L. Simmons. *The Dame in the Kimono: Hollywood, Censorship and the Production Code from the 1920s to the 1960s* (New York: Grove Weidenfeld, 1990).

Martin, Olga J. *Hollywood's Movie Commandments: A Handbook for Motion Picture Writers and Reviewers* (New York: H. W. Wilson Co., 1937).

Motion Picture Exhibitor Reviews of Features and Shorts, 1931–1960 (Hollywood, CA: Hollywood Film Archive, undated).

The New York Times Film Reviews, 1913–1968 (New York: New York Times & Arno Press, 1970).

Schumach, Murray. *The Face on the Cutting Room Floor* (New York: William Morrow, 1964).

Variety Film Reviews, 1907–1980 (New York: Garland Publishing, 1985).

Vasey, Ruth. *The World According to Hollywood: 1918–1939* (Madison, WI: University of Wisconsin Press, 1997).

Vizzard, Jack. *See No Evil: Life Inside a Hollywood Censor* (New York: Simon and Schuster, 1970).

Walsh, Frank. *Sin and Censorship: The Catholic Church and the Motion Picture Industry* (New Haven, CT: Yale University Press, 1996).

Index of Films

General Index